Culture and Customs of Syria

Map of Syria. Cartography by Bookcomp, Inc.

Culture and Customs
of Syria

JOHN A. SHOUP

Culture and Customs of the Middle East

GREENWOOD PRESS
Westport, Connecticut • London

Library of Congress Cataloging-in-Publication Data

Shoup, John A.
   Culture and customs of Syria / John A. Shoup.
      p. cm. — (Culture and customs of the Middle East, ISSN 1550–1310)
   Includes bibliographical references and index.
   ISBN-13: 978–0–313–34456–5 (alk. paper)
   1. Ethnology—Syria.   2. Syria—Social life and customs.
3. Civilization, Islamic. I. Title.
  GN635.S97S56   2008
   306.095691—dc22   2007049786

British Library Cataloguing in Publication Data is available.

Library of Congress Catalog Card Number: 2007049786
ISBN: 978–0–313–34456–5
ISSN: 1550–1310

First published in 2008

Greenwood Press, 88 Post Road West, Westport, CT 06881
An imprint of Greenwood Publishing Group, Inc.
www.greenwood.com

Printed in the United States of America

The paper used in this book complies with the
Permanent Paper Standard issued by the National
Information Standards Organization (Z39.48–1984).

10 9 8 7 6 5 4 3 2 1

Every reasonable effort has been made to trace the owners of copyrighted materials in this book, but in
some instances this has proven impossible. The author and publisher will be glad to receive information
leading to more complete acknowledgments in subsequent printings of the book and in the meantime
extend their apologies for any omissions.

Contents

CONTENTS

Series Foreword

AT LAST! Culture and Customs of the Middle East fills a deep void in reference literature by providing substantial individual volumes on crucial countries in the explosive region. The series is available at a critical juncture, with, among other events, the recent war on Iraq, the continued wrangling by U.S. interests for control of regional oil resources, the quest for Palestinian independence, and the spread of religious fundamentalist violence and repression. The authoritative, objective, and engaging cultural overviews complement and balance the volley of news bites.

As with the other Culture and Customs series, the narrative focus is on contemporary culture and life, in a historical context. Each volume is written for students and general readers by a country expert. Contents include:

Chronology
Context, including land, people, and brief historical overview
Religion and world view
Literature
Media
Cinema
Art and architecture/housing
Cuisine and dress
Gender, marriage, and family
Social customs and lifestyle

Preface

FOLLOWING THE END of the First World War Syrians expected to be independent and manage their own affairs. The Allied powers, however, had a different plan and had already divided up the map of the Ottoman Empire into their own spheres even before the fighting concluded. Syrian hopes were briefly sustained by the American King–Crane Commission that after a visit to the region recommended full and immediate independence for most of the former Ottoman provinces including Syria. However, the British and French overruled the recommendations by the Americans and set up a number of mandates, promising independence "when the people are ready." It is hard to say what would have happened if Syria, Lebanon, Palestine, and Jordan had become the Kingdom of Syria under King Faysal ibn Husayn al-Hashimi, but the result of what did occur is continued unrest, wars, and the political radicalization of the Middle East. Syria, which began the twentieth century as a potential friend and ally of the United States began the twenty-first century as part of American President George Bush's "axis of evil"; how much things have changed.

Syria is a key state in any final peace in the Middle East, and it is essential to understand it and its people. Syrians are proud of their past and of being Arabs. They are the cultural heirs of the oldest civilizations in the world as well as that of Greece, Rome, and Classical Islam. Damascus and Aleppo contend for the being the oldest continually inhabited cities in the world. Yet Syrians are not stuck in the dreams of a glorious past but are a vibrant people with a modern culture that is part of both the Arab/Islamic world and the Mediterranean.

Acknowledgments

When I finished the first book I did for Greenwood Press, *Culture and Customs of Jordan,* I was asked if I would be interested in doing any others for the series. Syria came to mind instantly. Syria is a fascinating country, and it is hard to write about Jordan, Lebanon, and Palestine without constant reference to Syria. I would like to thank Wendi Schnaufer and especially Kaitlin Ciarmiello of Greenwood Press for the opportunity to contribute this volume on Syria to the Culture and Customs series. I would also like to thank everyone who made my visits to Syria starting in 1976 to be among my fondest memories. I would like to mention Faris 'Izz al-Din, Murhaf Jouejeti, Lou'ai Serrafi and his parents, Mr. and Mrs. Faysal Serrafi, Nasser Kurdi, George Wisneiwski, and Muhammad al-Bukhari for their help and discussions about Syria while I was a student many years ago. They have been a great influence on me even if they didn't know it. I would also like to thank Dr. Michael Fuller and his wife Neathery Batsell-Fuller who directed the archeological excavations at Tall Tunaynir in northern Syria for their help and encouragement. I would also like to thank my parents, Mr. and Mrs. John Shoup, who have always been fully supportive of my decisions.

Chronology

NEOLITHIC

8000–4000 B.C.   Neolithic period is characterized by the domestication of plants (wheat, barely, and legumes) and livestock (pigs, sheep, goats, cattle, and donkeys). People begin to live in permanent settlements, many of which form the basis for large urban centers such as Damascus and Aleppo.

EARLY ANTIQUITY

3100–2150 B.C.   Early Bronze Age.

2900   Founding of Mari on the middle Euphrates and Ebla on the northern Syrian plains.

2500   Expansion of Mari as a major trade center between Iraq and Syria.

2400–2250   Ebla becomes a major urban center based on agriculture and trade.

2250   Both Mari and Ebla sacked and razed by Sargon of Akkad (2340–2284).

2150–1600   Middle Bronze Age.

2100   Arrival of the Amorites (western Semites) establish control over much of Syria including Damascus and Aleppo.

2000   Ebla rebuilt under the Yamkhad dynasty of Aleppo.

1900–1757	Mari recovers under Amorite dynasty, one of a number of small Amorite states in northern Syria.
1759–1757	Hammurabi of Babylon conquers Mari and destroys it but the other Amorite states are able to remain outside direct Babylonian rule.
1674–1567	Hyksos period—much of coastal Syria devastated by the Hyksos.
1600	Hittites from Anatolia destroy Ebla.
1600–1200	Late Bronze Age.
1660–1500	Rise of Hittite power in Anatolia and conquest of Mesopotamia; rise of New Kingdom in Egypt; rise of Mitanni in northeastern Syria. All three vie for control of Syria.
1400–1365	Ugarit on the Mediterranean coast flourishes—major center for international trade and develops the first alphabet, which its merchants spread throughout the eastern Mediterranean.
1400–1300	Egypt tries to include Syria in its sphere of influence and comes into conflict with the Hittites.
1350	Hittites eliminate Mitanni as a serious rival.
1286	Battle of Qadesh between Pharaoh Ramses II and the Hittite ruler Muwatallis; Egyptian and Hittite spheres of influence established by formal treaty two years later.
1200–539	Iron Age.
1200	Sea Peoples invade Syria and devastate much of the Mediterranean coast; Ugarit destroyed by the Sea Peoples.
1200–1150	Arameans, another wave of Semitic peoples, arrive in Syria and establish control over much of the interior.
900–800	Rise of Aramean Neo-Hittite states in the North; Aramean Kingdom of Aram-Damascus in the south blocks expansion of Israel under David and Solomon.
856–612	Assyria dominates Syria.
853	Battle of Qarqar Assyrians defeat coalition of Aramean states.
732	Assyrians conquer Damascus and destroy Aram-Damascus.
605–562	Neo-Babylonian control of Syria.

MIDDLE ANTIQUITY

| 539–333 B.C. | Persian Period; Persian rule is marked by a degree of local control under Persian governors; Jews taken to Babylon allowed to return to Palestine and rebuild the temple in Jerusalem. |

333–323   Alexander the Great conquers Persian Empire.

323   Alexander dies in Babylon and his empire is divided among his generals.

311   Seleucus I Nicator establishes the Seleucid rule; 301 B.C. Seleucus I Nicator settles 50,000 Greek soldiers in what will come to be knows as the Decapolis or Ten Cities to spread Hellenistic culture; Syria contested between Seleucids and Ptolemies of Egypt.

198   Seleucid Antiochus III, known as the Great, seizes southern Syria from the Ptolemies.

164–138   Civil wars weakens Seleucid control; Maccabee Revolt in Palestine results in new Jewish state; Nabatean Arabs push north from base in Jordan; rise of new Persian state under the Parthians threaten the eastern borders.

Late Antiquity

64 B.C.   Pompey formally abolishes the Seleucid state and creates Syria a Roman province ruled by a Roman Legate in Antioch; the Arab Nabateans of Petra (in today's Jordan) control Damascus.

43–36   Mark Anthony governor of Syria; conspires with Cleopatra VII Philopater Ptolemy of Egypt.

31   Battle of Actium; Augustus defeats combined forces of Mark Anthony and Cleopatra.

20   Rome and Parthia treaty sets boundary between the two empires.

98–117 A.D. Trajan, Emperor of Rome, annexes Nabatean kingdom as Provincia Arabia; pushes Parthians back from the Euphrates; and briefly occupies Mesopotamia.

117–138   Hadrian Emperor of Rome; Parthians push border back to the Euphrates; Hadrian visits Syria.

193–211   Septimius Severus Emperor of Rome and begins short-lived Syrian dynasty; reorganizes Syria into five provinces.

224   Ardashir takes power in Persia; first of the Sasanian rulers who pursue an aggressive policy towards the Romans.

244–249   A native of Syria, Philip "The Arab" Emperor of Rome.

256   Sasanians take Dura Europus on the Euphrates.

260   Sasanians push west as far as Antioch; Roman Emperor Valerian captured and executed by Shah Shapur I; the new Emperor Gallienus

	seeks help from the Arab king of Palmyra (Tadmur) Odenathus who pushes the Sasanians back across the Euphrates.
267–272	Odenathus killed, and his wife, Zenobia, takes the throne; Zenobia challenges Roman control of Syria and Egypt.
272	Emperor Aurelian takes Palmyra and captures Zenobia; the city rises in rebellion put down by Aurelian one year later.
Fourth century	Bani Ghassan Arabs arrive in Syria and become clients of the Byzantines, while the Arab Lakhamids play a similar role for the Sasanians. They serve as an important buffer between the Byzantines and the Persians until the coming of Islam.
306–337	Constantine I Emperor; 330 Constantine I dedicates Constantinople as the new capital of the empire.
395–636	Byzantine Period; numerous ecumenical councils fail to end the split between factions within the Christian church resulting in persecution of those who do not follow the official line as endorsed by the Emperors; Syria becomes a place of refuge for dissident factions; tensions remain between Byzantium and Persia despite treaties of peace.
395	Roman Empire formally splits into Western (Rome) and Eastern (Constantinople) Empires.
527–565	Justinian Emperor.
573	Khosraw I raids Syria as far west as Antioch.
590–627	Khosraw II made Shah of Persia with the help of Byzantine Emperor Maurice; when Maurice is murdered by Phocas in 602, Khosraw breaks the treaty of peace with Byzantium and raids Syria.
610–641	Heraclius Emperor.
611–614	Persians campaign in Syria and conquer most of it.
622–628	Byzantine counter-offensive pushes Persians back into Iraq.
635	Arab Muslim army captures Damascus for the first time.
636	Battle of the Yarmuk results in defeat of the Byzantines and their withdrawal from all of Syria; Damascus taken for the second time.
637	Aleppo taken by the Arab Muslims; Persians defeated at the Battle of Qadisiyah in Iraq by the Arab Muslims ending the Sasanian Empire.

Islamic Period to World War I

Rise of Islam to the Umayyads

632–661   Period of the Rightly Guided *Khalifah*s following the death of the Prophet Muhammad in 632; initial period of Muslim expansion into Syria, Iraq, Iran, and Egypt.

640–661   Mu'awiyah governor of Syria; 656–661 struggle between Mu'awiyah and 'Ali ibn Abi Talib over who should be the Khalifah, ends in 661 when 'Ali is assassinated by one of his former followers.

661–681   Mu'awiyah first Umayyad Khalifah; moves capital to Damascus; 672 first Muslim siege of Constantinople.

705–714   al-Walid Khalifah; Muslim conquest of North Africa secured and Byzantine enclaves taken; Muslim conquest of Spain; construction on the Umayyad Mosque (formerly Church of John the Baptist) in Damascus.

744–750   Marwan II, last Umayyad Khalifah.

The 'Abbasids to the Saljuqs

750–754   Abu al-'Abbas al-Safah defeats Marwan II and declares himself the new Khalifah; orders the massacre of the Umayyad family, only one young prince, 'Abd al-Rahman, able to escape and eventually founds the Umayyads of Spain; capital is moved from Damascus to Kufah in Iraq.

754–775   Al-Mansur the Khalifah builds Baghdad as the new capital; builds al-Raqqah on the Euphrates and places his son Harun al-Rashid as its governor.

813   Syria revolts against the 'Abbasids.

842   Revolts in Syria; begins period of general unrest and the spread of Shi'ism especially in the rural regions.

868–969   Syria generally ruled by 'Abbasid governors in Egypt, first the Tulunids then the Ikhshidids; neither are able to effectively control Syria, most of southern Syria controlled by the radical Qaramitah Shi'ites.

944–1003   Hamdanid dynasty based in Aleppo rules northern Syria.

969   Fatimids establish themselves as a rival *Khalifat* to the 'Abbasids; spread east from Tunisia and conquer Egypt; Cairo built as their new capital.

969–997   Byzantines take advantage of the unstable conditions in Syria and attempt to regain parts of northern and coastal Syria; in the end Byzantines are forced out by the Fatimids.

978–1076   Fatimids take control of southern Syria.

1023–1079   Bedouin Mirdasids control Aleppo and the nearby region.

1037   Saljuq Turks (Sunnis) take control of the 'Abbasid Khalifah in Baghdad ending Buwayhid (Shi'ite) dominance.

1055   Saljuqs able to take northern Syria in the name of the 'Abbasid Khalifah.

1071   Battle of Manzikert Saljuqs defeat the Byzantines and open Anatolia to Turkish expansion as well as secure Saljuq control over all of Syria including Palestine.

1070–1092   Malik Shah I Saljuq Sultan; Saljuq power lost after his death.

1095   Pope Urban II preaches the First Crusade.

1098   First Crusade takes Edessa and Antioch.

1099   First Crusade takes Jerusalem with great slaughter; establishes the Latin Kingdom of Jerusalem.

1108   Crusaders able to take the Syrian coastal city of Latakia (al-Ladhaqiyah).

1109   Crusaders able to take coastal city of Tripoli (Turabulus al-Sham).

1116–1154   *Atabek* Tughtagin establishes short-lived dynasty in Damascus and rules on behalf of the Fatimids.

1119   Battle of Sarmadah or Ager Sanguinis (Latin for Field of Blood) first major defeat for the Crusaders by the Saljuqs of Aleppo.

1124–1125   Crusader attempt to conquer Aleppo fails.

The Zangids to the Ayyubids

1128–1146   *Atabek* 'Imad al-Din Zangi established in Aleppo; asked to help repel Crusader attempt to take Damascus; 'Imad al-Din begins Sunni resurgence in Syria and forces the Isma'ili Shi'ites into the Jabal al-Ansariyah; retakes Edessa, first Crusader state to fall to the Muslims in 1144.

1146–1174   Nur al-Din Zangi consolidates all of Syria under his rule.

1147–1149   Second Crusade defeated by Nur al-Din outside of Damascus.

1171   Nur al-Din's general Salah al-Din al-Ayyubi restores Egypt to nominal 'Abbasid rule ending the Fatimid dynasty.

1176–1193	Salah al-Din unites Syria, Egypt, and Iraq under his rule in 1186; 1187 defeats the King of Jerusalem at the Battle of the Horns of Hattin in Palestine; Jerusalem falls.
1187–1192	Third Crusade ends in keeping a small part of the Mediterranean coast, and Christians allowed to visit Jerusalem,
1193	Following Salah al-Din's death, his kingdom is divided among his brothers and sons, who feud over territory.
Thirteenth century	Period of brilliant urban architecture in Syria under Ayyubid patronage.
1217–1221	Fifth Crusades tries to regain Jerusalem by conquering Egypt, the major center of Ayyubid power, but fails; Ayyubid Sultan al-Kamil gives Jerusalem back to the Christians through negotiations with German Emperor Frederick.
1244	Jerusalem recovered by the Muslims.
1248–1250	Sixth Crusader once more tries to take Egypt but are defeated; last Ayyubid Sultan dies, and the power vacuum is filled first by his wife Shajarat al-Durr and then by his Mamluks.
1258	Mongols under Hülegü Khan take Baghdad and kill the 'Abbasid Khalifah.

MAMLUK PERIOD

Bahri Mamluks 1260–1382

1260	Mamluks defeat the Mongols at the Battle of 'Ayn Jalut in Palestine.
1260–1277	Al-Zahir Baybars Sultan; installs a distant relative of the dead 'Abbasid Khalifah as the new 'Abbasid Khalifah in Cairo; campaigns against the remaining Crusader castles takes Antioch and Krak des Chevailers.
1280–1290	Mamluk Sultan Qalawun defeats second Mongol invasion in 1281 and takes the Crusader castles of Marqab, Latakia, and Tripoli.
1291	Mamluk Sultan al-Ashraf Khalil takes Acre forcing the King of the Latin Kingdom of Jerusalem to seek refuge on Cyprus.
1300–1303	Third Mongol invasion and Damascus occupied.
1302	The last Crusader fortress in Syria, located on the island of Arawd off the coast of Tartus, falls to the Mamluk Sultan al-Nasir Muhammad.

Burji Mamluks 1382–1516

1400–1401   Timur Lang invades Syria and takes Damascus; forces skilled Syrian craftsmen to move to his capital Samarqand in Central Asia.

1453   Constantinople falls to the Ottoman Turks under Fethi Mehmed or Muhammad the Conqueror, ending the Byzantine Empire.

1500–1516   Sultan Qansuh al-Ghawri last of the Mamluk Sultans.

OTTOMAN PERIOD

1516   Ottomans defeat the Mamluks at the Battle of Marj Dabiq outside of Aleppo; quickly consolidate control of Syria.

1517   Ottomans inflict final defeat on the Mamluks on the outskirts of Cairo and take Egypt.

1520–1566   Sulayman known in the west as "The Magnificent" and in the east as "The Lawgiver"; period of the great architect Sinan and major building projects; new pilgrimage road from Damascus to Makkah constructed.

1590–1635   Rise of Fakhr al-Din Ma'ani, Druze prince able to rule much of Syria, Lebanon, Palestine, and Jordan as a nearly autonomous region.

1831–1840   Muhammad 'Ali, Ottoman governor of Egypt, able to challenge Ottoman control of much of the Middle East; European powers force him to return to Egypt.

1840–1870   Ottomans slowly reassert their authority over Syrian provinces by establishing new administrative districts; Egyptian withdrawal provokes tensions between Druze and Christians in Lebanon which in 1860 finally erupt into massacres that spread to Damascus.

1876   First Ottoman Constitution issued as part of greater attempt to reform the empire fuels Arab hopes for greater share in political power.

1876–1909   'Abd al-Hamid II Sultan tried to thwart the reform movement; 1900–1908 Hijaz Railway built linking Damascus with Madinah; 1908 the Young Turks take control of the government and in 1909 defeat 'Abd al-Hamid's attempt to regain real control the state; 'Abd al-Hamid II replaced as Sultan by Muhammad V al-Rashad.

1914–1918   World War I Turkey sides with Germany and Austria; 1916–1918 Arab Revolt against the Turks led by *Sharif* Hussein ibn 'Ali, *Sharif* of Makkah.

1918   Damascus liberated by the Arab army led by T. E. Lawrence and tribal *shaykh*s and Turkish army retreats north into Anatolia.

Mandate Period

1918–1919   Faysal ibn Hussein, son of the *Sharif* of Makkah, named King of Syria with Damascus the capital; Syrian hopes for independence dashed at the Versailles Peace Conference, and Britain and France set themselves up as mandate powers in the Arab provinces of the Ottoman Empire.

1920   French defeat the Syrians at the Battle of Maysalun outside of Damascus and impose the mandate; San Remo Conference confirms British and French mandates; French High Commissioner detaches parts of Syria and creates Greater Lebanon (modern borders of the country).

1925–1926   Syrian Revolt begins in the Hawran in southern Syria and spreads quickly to Jabal Druze and eventually Damascus; the revolt is crushed by the French.

1936   France agrees to Syrian independence in principle.

1939   France cedes Antioch and Alexandretta to Turkey; never recognized by independent Syria.

1941   British and Free French occupy Syria; Free French promise end to the mandate.

INDEPENDENCE TO PRESENT

1945   Syria granted its independence; joins the United Nations and founding member of the Arab League.

1946   Last French troops leave Syria.

1948   First Arab-Israeli War.

1949   Adib al-Shishakli seizes power in the third coup of the year.

1954   Shishakli deposed by military coup; return to civilian government.

1955   Skukri al-Quwatli elected president.

1958   Unity between Syria and Egypt as United Arab Republic; Egyptian President Gamal Abdul Nasser (Jamal 'Abd al-Nasir) head of the new state.

1961   Military coup seizes power and dissolves the union between Egypt and Syria.

1963	Military coup; Ba'athist cabinet formed under President Amin al-Hafiz.
1966	Salah Jadid heads military coup and overthrows Amin al-Hafiz; Hafiz al-Asad appointed Minister of Defense.
1967	Six Day War; Syria loses Golan (Jawlan) Heights to Israel.
1970	Hafiz al-Asad seizes power from Salah Jadid and President Nur al-Din Atasi.
1973	October War with Israel.
1976	Syria interferes in Lebanese civil war to support the Maronite Christians and maintain the political status quo.
1980	The Iranian revolution inspires Muslim groups in Syria who stage riots in Aleppo, Homs, and Hama; attempted assassination of al-Asad by a member of the Muslim Brotherhood; Iran-Iraq War begins and Syria sides with Iran.
1982	Muslim Brotherhood uprising in Hama, Homs, and Aleppo crushed by the Syrian army; Israel invades Lebanon to drive out the Palestine Liberation Organization.
1987	More Syrian troops sent to Lebanon to enforce a ceasefire in Beirut.
1990–1991	Iraqi invasion of Kuwait and Syria joins United States–led coalition.
1991	Syria participates in the Middle East peace conference in Madrid, Spain.
1994	Basil al-Asad, al-Asad's eldest son and chosen heir dies in a car accident.
2000	Hafiz al-Asad dies and is replaced by his son Bashar al-Asad; the new president begins a new era with greater openness.
2001	Muslim Brotherhood allowed political participation after 20 years of oppression; Pope John Paul II visits Syria and is the first Pope to visit a mosque; Syrian troops pull out of Beirut; arrests of reformists dash hopes for a more politically open Syria; visit by British Prime Minister Tony Blair.
2002	U.S. President George Bush includes Syria in his "Axis of Evil."
2003	United States invades Iraq and overthrows Saddam Hussein's regime.
2004	President al-Asad first post-independence Syrian leader to visit Turkey.

2005   Syrian troops forced to leave Lebanon after assassination of former
        Lebanese Prime Minister Rafiq al-Hariri; Syria blamed for the assas-
        sination.

2006   Israel invades southern Lebanon and thousands of Lebanese seek ref-
        uge in Syria from the bombing, joining thousands of Iraqis fleeing
        the chaos in Iraq; Syria and Iraq restore diplomatic relations after
        nearly 25 years of hostility; the Iraq Study Group recommends direct
        talks between the United States, Syria, and, Iran.

2007   U.S. President George Bush rejects Iraq Study Group Report; De-
        spite official objections to speak directly to Syria, both Syria and the
        United States attend a conference in Iraq on Iraq's continued secu-
        rity problems.

        March: Three U.S. Congressmen visit Syria followed shortly by
        Speaker of the House Nancy Pelosi who is the highest ranking U.S.
        official to visit Syria in years; in a complete turn around of stated
        U.S. policy, U.S. Secretary of State Condoleezza Rice meets with
        Syrian Foreign Minister Walid Moallem during a summit at Sharm
        al-Shaykh, Egypt.

        September: Israel bombs a Syrian military base claiming it was a sus-
        pected nuclear facility raising tensions in the region to a new high.

        November: Syria sends its Deputy Foreign Minister Fayssal Mekdad
        to the Middle East Peace Summit organized by the United States in
        Annapolis.

1

Land, People, and History

SYRIA HAS SERVED as a major artery linking Mesopotamia and the Iranian Plateau with the Mediterranean and Anatolia with Egypt since before recorded history. As a result, Syrian history has been turbulent; Syria is open to invasions (both peaceful and armed) by peoples pushing in from the north, east, south, and west. Syria's people reflect this diversity both in the wide range of ethnicities found in the country as well as in the equally wide range of religions that have found refuge in its more distant and isolated regions. Syrians have always been open to outside influences making the Syria of today rich in culture. Syria is heir to ancient Mesopotamia, Egypt, Greece, and Rome, as well as the brilliance of classical Islam. Syrians are well aware of their long history and their own role in shaping their culture. They are proud of both their pre-Islamic and Islamic heritage and of being who they are, whether Arab or Kurd, Muslim or Christian.

GEOGRAPHY

Syria's geography has been a major factor in its historical and cultural development. Open plains, major river courses, mountains, and a narrow coastal plain have helped the movement of peoples into the country as well as served as important places where minority populations could flourish well away from interference by central authorities. It isn't easy to define exactly what and where Syria is because the term *Syria* has several applications. According to the classical Arab geographers today's Syria is but a part of a larger region called *Bilad al-Sham,* or the lands of the left hand (*Yaman* or Yemen being the lands of the right hand). The lands include today's Jordan, Palestine-Israel, Lebanon, and Syria. The term Syria as used by the Greeks and Romans included the same large region, sometimes today referred to in Arabic as *Suriya al-Kubra,* or Greater Syria, which has taken on important political meaning in the twentieth century due to the writings of Syrian nationalists. The region as a whole has experienced much the same history and has developed a more or less common culture and even dialect of Arabic generally referred to as *Shami,* or Levantine.

Syria has a Mediterranean climate, meaning hot, dry summers and cold, wet winters. The desert regions get cold enough in the winter for water to freeze and on occasions it can even snow. The modern country of Syria can be divided into several major geographical areas: the Levant or Mediterranean coast, which includes several mountain ranges rising up behind the narrow strip (only 20 miles or 32 kilometers at its widest part) of coastal plains; the Rift Valley, a deep depression running from southern Turkey into East Africa and back out into the Indian Ocean; wide, fertile but semiarid and arid steppes that eventually become the Syrian Desert or *Badiyat al-Sham;* the upper Jazirah or Mesopotamia, a broad fertile plain between the Euphrates and Tigris Rivers in the northeast of the country; southern regions of Hawran, Jawlan, and al-Lajja' of volcanic cones and basalt-strewn plains separated from the country of Jordan by the Yarmuk River. Only 10% of Syria receives 10 inches (250 millimeters) or more of annual precipitation sufficient to support agriculture, while the vast part of the country is desert.

The Mediterranean coast is shared with Turkey's Hatay Province (split from Syria and given to Turkey by the French during the Mandate period), Lebanon, and Palestine-Israel. The strip under Syrian control is relatively short, being just under 120 miles (193 kilometers) long. It includes two of Syria's major cities, Tartus and Latakia (al-Ladhakiyah), of which Latakia is the most important sea port today. Both are heavily used by Syrians as vacation spots and again Latakia is the better developed with more hotels, restaurants, and vacation colonies belonging to large companies. Rising immediately behind the narrow coastal plain are a series of mountain ranges most of which run parallel to the sea. In Syria proper there are the Jabal al-Ansariyah and the Jabal 'Akkar of which the later is part of the more known Jabal Lubnan, or Mount Lebanon. The highest peak of the Jabal al-Ansariyah is Nabi Yunis at 5,194 feet (1,583 meters), while the highest peak in the Jabal 'Akkar—Jabal Lubnan range is Qarnat al-Sawda' at 10,131 feet (3,086 meters), which lies just inside the northern borders of today's Lebanon. These peaks are high enough for precipitation to fall as snow in the winter. The coastal mountains act as a block to moisture and while they have high yearly averages of around 40 inches (1,000 millimeters) of precipitation, regions behind them are semi-arid to arid receiving 10 inches (250 millimeters) or less per year.

The second major feature is the Great Rift Valley that begins in southern Turkey near Mara'ash. It then forms the 'Amq (meaning deep in Arabic) Depression and creates the Amuk Gölü Lake in the Hatay near Antioch. It continues into Syria where it forms the Orontes River valley, the Ghab, and Lake Qattinah near the city of Homs. South of Homs the Rift Valley forms the Biqa' Valley of Lebanon separating Jabal Lubnan from the Jabal al-Sharqi or Anti-Lebanon ranges. The Rift Valley briefly touches Syria again along the Golan or Jawlan Heights, which overlook the Sea of Galilee and where the Yarmuk River empties into the Jordan River. The Rift system forms a narrow strip of land which receives about 15 inches (400 millimeters) of annual precipitation.

The Orontes River is called al-'Asi, or the Rebel in Arabic, as it is the only river in Syria that flows north. It empties into the Mediterranean near the Turkish town of Samandagi. The Orontes flows through the Ghab, a narrow, well-watered, fertile region heavily exploited for agriculture since early antiquity. Two of Syria's major historical cities lie along the river, Homs and Hama. While neither has been able to challenge Damascus or Aleppo in importance, both Homs and Hama date back to the origins of cities in the Neolithic period. Homs has long been a major market center for many of Syria's Bedouin and today still boasts the largest sheep market in the Middle East. Numerous villages and towns dot the course of the Orontes as it flows north into Turkey, and there are strong cultural and family ties between the villagers on both sides of the border.

To the east of the Rift Valley system lie the broad open steppe lands that eventually merge into the Syrian Desert. The steppe is broadest in the north, between Hama and Aleppo, where it is some 60 miles (100 kilometers) wide. The steppe narrows as it goes south and vanishes into true desert just south of 'Amman in Jordan. The steppe receives an average of around 10 inches (250 millimeters) of annual rainfall, and in good years it can support wheat and barley crops. In general it has been best used by pastoral nomads and villagers to graze their flocks and herds. It has also been a frontier between areas under direct government control and marginal areas where Bedouin tribes have often dominated.

The steppes merge into the Syrian Desert where annual rainfall is below 6 inches (150 millimeters) making dry land farming impossible. The Syrian Desert is called a *badiyah* in Arabic meaning that it is able to support nomadic pastoralism or *badawah* of the *Badw,* or Bedouin. All three words come from the same root and indicate how closely the terms are related not only in the language but in the culture of the Bedouin. Areas closer to the Orontes and Euphrates are exploited by Bedouin who raise mainly sheep while the deep desert is the home to those tribes who traditionally have raised camels.

The Baradah and the 'Awaj Rivers drain eastward into the desert and both are heavily exploited for the rich, fertile Ghutah Oasis that surrounds Damascus. The rivers flow rapidly down the eastern slopes of the Anti Lebanon range and eventually fan out and die in the desert. Both are so heavily used for irrigated agriculture they no longer reach beyond the limits of the oasis. The Ghutah and the Hawran are dominated by Jabal al-Shaykh in the Anti Lebanon range which towers above them at the height of 9,232 feet (2,814 meters). The mountain gets its Arabic name, Jabal al-Shaykh or the Old Man Mountain, from the fact its peak is snow covered most of the year; thus being white-headed like an old man. There are several other oases in the Syrian Desert, Tadmur (ancient Palmyra) and al-Sukhnah being the most important. They are fed by the rains that fall on the Abu Rujmayn range (4,921 feet or 1,000 meters) the rises up in the middle of the desert and by underground water sources. Tadmur became a major caravan city in later antiquity being located about half way between Damascus and Iraq.

The Euphrates River forms the northern border of the Syrian Desert. Between the Euphrates and Tigris Rivers lies the Jazirah (meaning island in Arabic) region. This is also mainly wide semiarid plains watered by two major tributaries of the Euphrates, the Balikh, and the Khabur. In the past the area was heavily used by pastoralists, but in recent decades dams and irrigation schemes have brought more of the region under the plow producing large commercial crops of wheat, sunflowers (for cooking oil), and cotton. The Jazirah is dotted with tells or man-made hills; remains of numerous cities that once covered the region in ancient times. Two large mountains rise up from the plains; Jabal 'Abd al-'Aziz and Jabal Sinjar. Jabal 'Abd al-'Aziz is fully within Syria and rises to a height of 1,640 feet (500 meters) and separates the Balikh and Khabur drainages. Jabal Sinjar is mainly within the present day borders of Iraq and separates the Khabur basin from that of the Tigris.

The Hawran, between Damascus and the Yarmuk River, is its own area, even seen by some as its own cultural area. It includes the volcanic regions of Jabal Druze, al-Lajja', and the rich farming area of the Jawlan. Jabal Druze rises to 4,921 feet (1,500 meters); high enough to catch some of the moisture that has been able to clear the coastal mountain ranges. Here hardy agriculturalists have competed with pastoral Bedouin for control over the meager resources of water and arable land. Historically villagers made use of the volcanic basalt to build fortified villages as protection against Bedouin raiders. Over time Christians, Druze, and Muslims for various reasons sought refuge away from the central authorities in the mountain and developed their own social and political institutions to deal with both the harsh conditions and their Bedouin neighbors.

PEOPLE

Syria is an Arab country, and its people are very proud of their Arab identity and of Syria's role in Arab history. Syrians call their country "the Citadel or Bastion of Arabism" (*Qala'at al-'Arubah*) and certainly Syrians played a major role in the Arab Awakening of the nineteenth and early twentieth centuries that contributed to the rise of Arab nationalism. Despite the strong Arab identity of the people, the country is also home to significant numbers of both ethnic and religious minorities. In fact, as proud of the Arab nature of their country, Syrians are equally proud of the fact so many different peoples through out history have found refuge in Syria.

Arabs

Arabs make up the vast majority of Syrians—around 90% of its 18,881,361 people (according to United Nations 2006 estimate). Syria was already greatly Arabized in late antiquity; Arab peoples moved into the Syrian Desert from Arabia and eventually penetrated into the more fertile agricultural regions further west. Arabs dominated much of the trade during the Roman period and established important states in Petra and later Tadmur. Starting the fifth century A.D. local Arab leaders assumed the responsibility of protecting the eastern frontiers not only against the arrival of other Arabs but also against the Persians. One such leader from southern Syria, Philip the Arab, rose to become the Emperor of Rome in 244 A.D. By the Islamic conquest in the seventh century, much of Syria's population was either Arab or Arabized; that is, Arabic speaking and identifying themselves as Arabs.

Syria's Arab peoples belong to the wide range of religions found in the country. They form a majority of Syrian Christians, as well as are the overwhelming majority of Isma'ili Shi'ites, Druze, 'Alawis, and Jews. Many of these religious communities live in more remote areas where they were able to practice their religions in relative peace. Thus they are concentrated more in certain regions such as the Jabal al-Ansariyah, the northeastern Jazirah, and Jabal Druze. Most of Syria's Arabs are Sunni Muslims whether they are urban dwellers, villagers, or Bedouin.

The classical Arab concept of society divides people into two major categories: *hadar,* or those who are settled living in cities, towns, and villages; and *badw,* or the Bedouin who live by nomadic pastoralism in the deserts and steppes. Each of these categories is further broken into more specific divisions based on type of economic activities. The camel-breeding Bedouin tribes who live in the desert occupy the highest social level being engaged in the most "noble" of economic pursuits. These people "know their ancestors" being tribally organized and for whom tribal identity remains important social makers. They are able to recite their lineage back to before the time of the Prophet Muhammad, and some as far back as the Biblical Adam. The lowest positions in the social scheme are occupied by those who "dig in the ground" (farmers) or "labor with their hands" (urban craftsmen and laborers) and who often were not tribally organized, thus lacking "knowledge" of their ancestors. Not only were their jobs less "noble," they also lacked the same proven "nobility" of descent, unable to recite their lineage beyond several generations. While such concepts have been greatly replaced by the economic realities of contemporary daily life, nonetheless, they are still important aspects of personal identity and pride for the Bedouin.

Many of Syria's urban upper class is of Turkish or Circassian origins that have Arabized over the centuries of living in the country. During the long period of Mamluk and Ottoman rule those sent to govern the region intermarried with local urban notable families. They came to own large rural estates in addition to controlling much of the urban commerce. While the majority of these notables were Sunni Muslim, certain Christian and Druze families were able to gain large rural estates often worked by peasants of their same faith. These families have played, and continue to play, important roles in the history of Syria and Lebanon.

Syria is also the home for a two large populations of Arab refugees: Palestinians who mainly arrived after the 1948 War with Israel; and most recently Iraqis escaping the violence in their country after the 2003 American-led invasion. Most of the Palestinians in Syria are concentrated in Damascus where their so-called camps have blended into the cities growing working-class neighborhoods. Damascus received Palestinian refugees in the past as well and several of its historical areas were founded by refugees from the First Crusade, for example. Iraqis began arriving shortly after the 2003 invasion and since January 2007 between 30,000 and 40,000 new refugees arrive per month. It is estimated that by February 2007 over 800,000 Iraqis were in Syria while other estimates puts the number closer to one and a half million.

Non Arabs

Syria is also home to a number of non-Arab peoples including Kurds, Turks, Turkomen, Circassians, Shishans, Armenians, and Aramaic-speaking Christians. Of them the Kurds are the single largest ethnic minority comprising about 5% of the total population of the country. Some of these peoples, such as the Kurds, have lived in Syria since antiquity, while others, such as the Circassians, have arrived more recently. Syria's long history of population movements is such that some ethnicities, such as the Armenians, have long-established communities in major Syrian cities.

Kurds are Indo-Europeans, and their language is closely related to Persian. The northeastern part of Syria is part of historical Kurdistan, which covers much of eastern Turkey, northern Iraq, and northwestern Iran. Kurds are perhaps the modern descendants of the ancient Medes, who with the Persians conquered the eastern Mediterranean under Cyrus the Great in 539 B.C. Kurds, like many Arabs, were traditionally organized into tribes (at least in the rural areas) and are both pastoralists and settled farmers, though most Kurds in Syria are settled in villages and cities. Kurds and Arabs in Syria have lived together even before the arrival of Islam—the Arab Bani Rabi'a, Bani Mudar, and Bani Bakr tribes established themselves in northern Syria/Iraq and southern Turkey during the sixth century. Arabs and Kurds competed for much the same resources of pasture and water and there are occasional problems between tribes yet today. Syrian Kurds are Sunni Muslims and have been major players in Islamic history; the great Muslim leader Salah al-Din al-Ayyubi, or Saladin, was a Kurd born in Syria. In Syria, Kurds have benefited from the more positive government policies towards minorities and Kurdish holidays, such as *Naw Ruz,* or Persian New Years, are openly celebrated. Kurdish language, music, dance, foods are all allowed (unlike policies in some other nearby states), and Kurds hold important positions in government, state security, and the military.

Turks and Turkomen are Sunni Muslims and also have long histories in Syria. Tribes of pastoral Turkomen arrived in northern Syria near Aleppo in the eleventh century, precursors to the arrival of the Saljuq Turks who established control over much of Syria for the 'Abbasids of Baghdad in 1055. There are close relations between the towns and cities of southern Turkey such as Gaziantep, Birecik, Urfa, and Diyarbakir with those in Syria such as Aleppo, Jarablus, Ras al-'Ayn, and al-Hasakah. Many of these Syrian towns and cities have neighborhoods where Turkish and Turkomen families have lived for centuries. Foods from Aleppo have a strong Turkish influence, such as the use of red pepper in yogurt sauces. Turkish music is widely heard and available for sale in much of northern Syria.

Circassians and Shishans (Chechens) are Sunni Muslims from the Caucasus Mountains who began arriving just before the defeat of their great leader Shaykh Shamil by the Russians in 1859. Numbers of Circassian and Shishan families sought refuge with the Ottomans, who settled them in Syria and Jordan. The Ottomans gave them land in areas that until recently had been under Bedouin tribal control. The Circassians and Shishans were able to fend off Bedouin raids and established flourishing villages and towns in Syria, Jordan, and Palestine. Today most of them have greatly Arabized, losing much of their own languages and maintaining only a few distinctive cultural features. In recent years there has been a cultural revival among the Circassians and Shishans in Jordan where they are a larger and more important minority than they are in Syria.

Armenians are the second largest ethnic minority in Syria and belong to their own unique language group. They may be the modern descendants of the ancient Hurrians. Historical Armenia is in eastern Turkey and the Caucasus Mountains and was part of both the Persian and Roman empires. They were among the very first converts to Christianity and stood in opposition to a number of the decisions made by the religious councils held by the Byzantine emperors. Armenian religious authorities separated from the Greek Orthodox Church and the Roman Catholics remained in communion with the Egyptian and Ethiopian Copts. Armenians have long been part of Syria's urban communities, and cities such as Damascus and Aleppo have well-established Armenian quarters that pre-date the arrival of the last wave of Armenian refugees in 1915. Accused of assisting the Russians against Turkey in World War I, Armenians were subjected to mob actions that resulted in the murders of large numbers of men, women, and children as well as more dying of exposure and starvation as they fled into Syria. Many found refuge in Syria, but more sought escape in Egypt and beyond. Armenians are both an ethnic and religious minority and as such have their own school systems where Armenian and Arabic are used as languages of instruction.

Perhaps the smallest minority in Syria is one of the oldest and perhaps the one in the greatest danger of being absorbed into the broader, Arabic-speaking society. This minority lives in the once isolated cluster of Christian villages along the eastern slopes of the Anti-Lebanon Mountains north of Damascus. The people still speak Aramaic—the language of Jesus and his disciples. Aramaic is a Semitic language (closely related to Arabic) that was at one time widely spoken through out the eastern Mediterranean. It has remained the liturgical language for many eastern Christians while Arabic has become the language for everyday use. The relative isolation of the Ma'alula, Yaburd, and a few other nearby villages helped preserve Aramaic as the language of everyday use. Since independence in 1945, national integration has brought these villages into greater contact with Arabic speakers. In addition, the village of Ma'alula in particular has become a major tourist destination because the people have preserved the Aramaic language. However, the greater exposure to the outside also is a danger for the language's survival. Both the local people and the Syrian state would like to preserve the unique linguistic character of the villages, but television, education, jobs, and tourism threaten its future.

FROM THE RISE OF CITIES TO THE END OF THE ROMAN EMPIRE

Syria, like many countries of the Middle East, has a long, complicated history stretching back into the earliest of times. Many of Syria's cities claim to be the oldest continually inhabited cities in the world. Damascus, Dimashq in Arabic, takes its name from two words common in Semitic languages; *dam* meaning blood and *shaq* meaning to spill. Popular legend supported by Jewish, Christian, and Muslim texts says the city took its name from the murder of Abel (Habil in Arabic) by his brother Cain (Qabil in Arabic), and the place venerated as Abel's tomb is located just to the west of city. Aleppo, *Halab* in Arabic, takes its name from the Semitic root *halab* or *halap,* meaning milk due to the white color of the soil. These are ancient names recorded in some of the oldest texts known to man.

Syria is part of the Fertile Crescent stretching from southern Iraq, arching along the Euphrates River, and following the Mediterranean coast and the Rift Valley south to the Sinai Peninsula and the Gulf of 'Aqabah. Domestication of wheat and other plants as well as the domestication of livestock such as pigs, sheep, and goats prompted the rise of settlements. By the fourth millennium B.C. these settlements were large enough to become urban centers supported by rural areas producing agricultural surpluses. Northern Syria has a large number of tells, or ancient mounds made up of layers of settlements, especially in the Jazirah where early developments in irrigation allowed even more land to be cultivated. Urban elite specializing in religion, government, and trade built massive structures modeled on those of the Sumerian cities in southern Iraq. Sumer exercised a good deal of cultural influence as its great city states set the standards in learning and the arts. Cuneiform system of writing was adapted to the local languages.

Syria's first major city-states, Ebla and Mari, emerged in the third millennium B.C. Mari was, perhaps, the richest of the two located in the middle Euphrates River Valley not far from today's border between Syria and Iraq. By 2500 B.C. Mari had become a major trade center exchanging goods between the Mediterranean and Mesopotamia. The city was conquered by Akkadian king Sargon around 2550 B.C. but Mari was able to rise again; and, with the arrival of the Semitic Amorites around 2000 B.C., Mari reemerged as an important trading city.

Ebla, located south of Aleppo in the semiarid steppe lands, seems to have been founded by western Semites around the same time as Mari. Ebla gained control over much of northwestern Syria, developing the regions agricultural potential. Between 2400 and 2250 B.C. Ebla experienced the height of its power economically and politically. The city developed trade and diplomatic links with Mari as well as with other states in the region. In 1975 a large cache of clay tablets were discovered written in Eblite as the Semitic language of the city has come to be called. The tablets contain names familiar from the Bible such as Abram and Abraham, which when first discovered thrilled biblical scholars. Among the most interesting of the finds is a map giving names of other cities and states including Aleppo and Damascus. Like Mari, Ebla fell to Sargon of Akkad around 2250 B.C. While Mari was able to recover its importance, Ebla did not and became instead a dependent of the Yamkhad dynasty based in Aleppo.

Mari recovered under the Amorites and flourished as an economic and cultural center. Most of the ruins now visible at the site date from this period and include the palace of Zimri-Lim who ruled from 1775 to 1760 B.C. His palace was a wonder of the times with a courtyard paved in bitumen (blacktop) and numerous frescos decorating the walls. The palace, and the city, was destroyed in 1759 B.C. when Hammurabi of Babylon conquered it. Hammurabi deliberately and methodically destroyed the city and though it would be occupied again, like Elba before it, the city never recovered its importance.

Though Mari was conquered by the Babylonians, they were not able to subdue the other Amorite states in Syria. Many of Syria's coastal cities, safe from the Babylonians, were devastated by another invasion this time from the north. The Hyksos, more famous for their conquest of Egypt, moved along the Mediterranean coast taking city after city until they conquered Lower Egypt. Northern Syria was also invaded by other Indo-Europeans, the Hittites, the Hurrians, and the Mitannis who dominated the Amorite states.

During much of the Late Bronze period, from 1600 to 1200 B.C., Syria was contested between the Hittites, the Mitannis, and the Egyptians. By the end of the period Mitanni, located in the northeast of Syria, was eliminated by the Hittites leaving only Egypt as the main rival. In 1286 B.C. the Egyptian Pharaoh Ramses II met the Hittite ruler Muwatallis at the Battle of Qadesh (today's Tal Nabi Mand near Homs) and though Ramses would claim victory, the battle marked the furthest limit of Egyptian hegemony. Two years later the two leaders signed a formal treaty establishing their spheres of influence.

While the Egyptians and Hittites fought to dominate Syria, local dynasties survived by recognizing the supremacy of one of the two main powers. Along Syria's coast, cities recovered from the devastation caused by the Hyksos and Ugarit (today Ras Shamra just north of Latakia) flourished between 1400 and 1365 B.C. Ugarit developed important trade links with Cyprus, Crete, and the Greek mainland. Ugarit's merchants took the cumbersome cuneiform system of writing and developed the first true alphabet of 30 letters, cuneiform symbols that stood for one symbol for one sound. Use of this alphabet made recording—and learning to read—much easier, and the ruins of city yielded a massive number of documents; commercial accounts, political and diplomatic records, and religious texts in a Semitic language. Ugarit was destroyed around 1200 B.C. by another wave of invaders, the Sea Peoples, who came from the north and eventually attempted to conquer Egypt, much like the Hyksos before them.

The Sea Peoples caused a great deal of devastation as they progressed down the Mediterranean coast and eventually were defeated by the Egyptians who pushed them back into Palestine where they settled. Around the same time the interior of Syria was invaded by new wave of Semitic peoples, the Arameans, who established a number of small kingdoms. They copied the architecture and art of the Hittites but never were able to match the high level attained by the Hittites. The strongest of the Aramean kingdoms was Aram-Damascus, which blocked the expansion of Israel under its kings David and Solomon.

The Assyrians pushed into Syria from northern Iraq and dominated the numerous Aramean kingdoms and defeated their coalition at the Battle of Qarqar in 853 B.C. Among the names of the leaders mentioned by the victorious Assyrians are several Arab tribal shaykhs. In 732 B.C. the Assyrians conquered Aram-Damascus and destroyed it ending attempts to throw off Assyrian domination. The Assyrians themselves were conquered by the Babylonians in 605 B.C., who pushed onward and exerted their control over Syria, Lebanon, and challenged Egyptian domination of Palestine and Jordan.

The Babylonians were in turn conquered by the Persians and Medes under their ruler Cyrus the Great in 562 B.C. The Persians went on to bring the whole eastern Mediterranean under their rule by conquering Egypt, Palestine, Syria, and Anatolia. The Persians divided their new empire into provinces ruled by a Persian governor appointed by the king, but they also allowed local dynasties a degree of freedom including freedom of worship. Their rather enlightened policy towards the diverse peoples of the empire allowed the remaining Jews to return to Palestine and rebuild their temple in Jerusalem. The Persian period was brought to an end by the conquest of Alexander the Great in 333 B.C.

Alexander lived only a short time and died in Babylon in 323 B.C. Immediately upon his death, his generals argued and fought over the empire he had built and eventually Seleucus I Nicator was able to secure most of Syria by 311 B.C. Taking the example of Alexander, Seleucus settled 50,000 Greek soldiers in ten existing and newly built cities that came to be known as the Decapolis in order to spread the Greek language and Hellenistic culture to the local peoples. Antioch was the capital and it became a major center for

Greek sciences and learning until the rise of Christianity in the third century A.D. The Seleucids were challenged by the Ptolemies of Egypt, descendants of another of Alexander's generals. During the height of Seleucid power under Antiochus III, all of Syria, Lebanon, and most of Palestine fell under his control. However, Seleucid power began to fade and in the second century B.C. the state was fraying at the edges. Local rebellions such as by the Maccabees in Palestine were successful; in southern Jordan the Nabatean Arabs grew in strength; and in the east, the newly established Parthians in Persia challenged the Seleucids. In addition, new vigor was found among the Ptolemies of Egypt who supported many of the rebellious local princes in Palestine, Jordan, and Syria.

The squabbles between local princes, instability in Syria, and the growing threats from both Egypt and Parthia brought Roman intervention in 64 B.C. The Roman general Pompey annexed most of Syria as a new province for the Republic in the same year ending the Seleucid dynasty. Rome recognized the autonomy of Judea under first the Hasmoneans and then the Herodians. The Nabateans remained independent and were able to gain control of Damascus twice before they too were absorbed by the Romans in 104 A.D.

The Roman period brought peace and stability to much of the region, but the eastern frontier with the Parthians was a source of trouble. The Romans under Trajan not only absorbed the Nabateans but pushed the border with the Parthians far to the east, briefly occupying Mesopotamia. However, the Parthians were able to recover and pushed the frontier back to the Euphrates River not far from the present Syrian-Iraqi border.

In 193 Septimius Severus became Emperor of Rome. He was an able general born in North Africa and married a Syrian woman, who was a priestess of one of the many eastern cults popular among Rome's elite. Severus and his wife founded a so-called Syrian dynasty of emperors who ruled until 222 when Marcus Antoninus Elagabalus was replaced because of his extreme eccentricities. In 224 Ardashir seized power in Persia and founded the Sasanian dynasty, which took an aggressive policy towards Rome and the borders of the two empires. In 224 another Syrian was made Emperor of Rome, Philip known as "The Arab." Philip was from a small town in southern Syria near Jabal Druze, which he endowed with his name Philippopolis as well as with a number of major buildings. Philip ruled until 249.

By 256 Roman–Sasanian relations had deteriorated into war, and the Persians pushed west taking the city of Dura Europus, which had been originally founded by the Seleucids to control the middle Euphrates. Since the rise of the Parthians it had come to serve as the major border post for the Romans. Under the Romans the city had flourished producing an interesting blend of Hellenistic and Semitic cultures. Its synagogue, dating from the first century A.D., is unique in having frescos showing people painted in a definite Hellenistic style. The city also has the oldest recognizable Christian chapel. The Sasanians were able to push on into Roman Syria and by 260 had sacked Antioch. The Roman Emperor Valerian was captured in the field, and the Persian Shah, Shapur I, had Valerian executed. The new emperor, Gallienus, sought help from local Arab leaders and Udhaynah ibn Hayran ibn Wahb Allat or Odenathus II, ruler of the trading city-state of Palmyra (Tadmur), defeated the Persians and pushed them back across the Euphrates frontier.

Udhyanah was assassinated at Rome's instigation and his widow, the famous Queen Zenobia or Zaynab took her husband's throne and ruled along with her son Vaballathus or Wahb Allat. Between 267 and 272 Zenobia was able to conquer all of Syria, Palestine, and even Egypt, before the Romans eventually defeated her. The Emperor Aurelian captured Palmyra but when the city rose in rebellion one year later he had it destroyed. Zenobia lives on today in popular Syrian myth as a national heroine and is the subject of plays and television dramas and her image is on contemporary Syrian currency.

Arab tribes had been able to penetrate the eastern borders of the empire for sometime and by the fourth century much of the eastern desert areas were controlled by tribal leaders. Both the Romans and the Persians used Arab clients as buffers against the other. During the fourth century the Bani Ghassan established themselves in Roman territory and by the fifth century had taken over the responsibility for manning the frontier posts. The Lakhamids had done the same in Iraq where they served the Sasanians.

The Emperor Constantine I moved the capital from Rome to his newly built city of Constantinople in 330 and began imperial patronage of Christianity— there is some debate if he himself actually converted though it is generally held that he did. The Roman Empire officially split into two parts, the Latin Western and the Greek Eastern Empires in 395, which begins the Byzantine period in the east. The rise of the Christian church in both parts of empire was marked with a number of populist movements, which caused imperial intervention. A number of ecumenical councils were called to debate and decide on official doctrines, some of the councils meeting to reverse previous decisions. The decisions were sanctioned by the emperor and those who did not follow the instructions from the councils were seen as heretics. Many of those seen to be out of step with official Christian doctrine sought refuge in the more distant and difficult to reach parts of Syria, or even with the Sasanians. Syria is still the home for a number of these Christian movements that survived Byzantine persecution.

The last decades of Roman–Byzantine rule in Syria was marked by the conflict with Persia. In 573 the Sasanian Shah Khosraw I raided Syria and reached as far west as Antioch demonstrating the weakness of the Byzantines. Khosraw II was made Shah with the assistance of the Byzantine Emperor Maurice in 590 but Maurice was assassinated by Phocas in 602, which provoked a long, devastating war with Persia. The Persians and their Arab allies invaded Syria conquering Palestine and Jordan, as well as Lebanon and Syria between 611 and 614. The Byzantines were slow in their response, but in 622 they and their Arab allies, the Bani Ghassanids and the Arab tribes attached to them, began a counter offensive. By 628 the Persians had been pushed back again beyond the Euphrates frontier, but both Persia and Byzantium were exhausted by the prolonged conflict and both were about to be challenged by the rising new power of Islam.

RISE OF ISLAM TO THE OTTOMAN PERIOD

The Prophet Muhammad was born in Makkah around 570. He received his first revelation in 610 when the angel Gabriel demanded that he "Read in the name of thy Lord who creates—creates man from a clot of blood" (*Surah 96 al-ʿAlaq*). Despite being scorned and persecuted by the ruling Quraysh tribe, of which Muhammad belonged, the number of converts grew. In 622 Muhammad was asked to come to Yathrib, an oasis town north of Makkah, to help settle the on-going disputes between its tribes, and a new era began. Muhammad and his followers left Makkah in what has been called the *Hijrah,* or migration, and met up again in Yathrib, now called *al-Madinah* or the City. By Muhammad's death in 632 most of the tribes in the Arabian Peninsula had converted to Islam, and he had personally led the first expedition into Byzantine-held territory, where the Jewish and Christian Arabs of southern Jordan made a treaty with him.

The Islamic expansion into Byzantine territory began in earnest after the death of the Prophet Muhammad and his first successor or *Khalifah,* Abu Bakr. ʿUmar ibn al-Khattab became the Khalifah in 634, and Muslim expansion into Byzantine and Persian territory began with well-planned military campaigns led by proven commanders. The Byzantines suffered defeats at Ajnadayn in Palestine in 634 (a month before the death of Abu Bakr) and Yarmuk in Syria in 636, and Byzantine troops were withdrawn back into Anatolia by 638. In 637 the Persians were also defeated at al-Qadisiyah in Iraq, and though the Sasanians would hang on until 651 in the far east of their former empire, Persia became fully part of the new Islamic state based in Arabia.

Muʿawiyah ibn Abi Sufyan was appointed governor of Syria in 640 and when the Khalifah ʿUthman ibn ʿAffan, a relative of Muʿawiyah, was assassinated in 656, Muʿawiyah refused to accept the election of ʿAli ibn Abi Talib as the next Khalifah accusing 'Ali of being complicit in the murder. Supported by the people of Syria, Mu'awiyah was able to challenge 'Ali's succession as Khalifah and forced mediation. The mediation led to early split in the Muslim community and upon 'Ali's death in 661, Mu'awiyah was able to emerge as the next Khalifah and the first of the Umayyad dynasty. With the general acceptance of Mu'awiyah as the Khalifah the old Quraysh aristocracy of Makkah gained control of the emerging Muslim empire. He moved the capital to Damascus close to his main support among the Bani Kalb Bedouin in the Syrian Desert as well as had his son Yazid declared his successor.

The Umayyad period continued the Islamic expansions in North Africa, Spain, and further into Asia. Mu'awiyah even sent an expedition into Anatolia that besieged Constantinople in 672. The wealth of the empire flowed back to Syria, and the Umayyads built the first major Islamic monuments in Jerusalem, Damascus, and Aleppo. They also built a number of desert pleasure palaces where leaders of their allies, the Bedouin Bani Kalb, could have easy access to them. The palaces were also far healthier than the cities such as Damascus that frequently suffered outbreaks of contagious diseases.

The Umayyad dynasty fell to the 'Abbasids in 750. The 'Abbasids were from another branch of the Quraysh and had built their support among those who had backed 'Ali against Mu'awiyah (although the 'Abbasids themselves were Sunni) and among the discontented converted non-Arabs of the empire, especially in Iraq and Iran. The 'Abbasids exploited the ancient rivalry between northern and southern Arab tribes and capitalized on Umayyad reliance on the Bani Kalb. The 'Abbasids were ruthless in their destruction of rivals and not only killed nearly every member of the Umayyad family—one young prince escaped and eventually found refuge in Spain—but also the descendents of 'Ali ibn Abi Talib, many of whom also escaped death and fled to distant parts of the empire or were kept under close guard. The 'Abbasids moved the capital away from Syria to Iraq, first to Kufah and then to their newly built capital Baghdad.

Pro-Umayyad sentiment remained strong in Syria, and the province was held in deep suspicion by the 'Abbasids during the reigns of the first Khalifahs Abu al-'Abbas al-Saffah and Abu Ja'far al-Mansur. Al-Mansur built a new administrative city on the Euphrates, al-Raqqah, from which his son and heir Harun al-Rashid governed Syria. Relations between the Syrians and the 'Abbasids remained poor, and Syrians rose in pro-Umayyad rebellions in 813 and again in 842. The general unrest in Syria increased following the last of these rebellions, and a number of rural people joined radical Shi'ite groups such as the Qaramitah. The 'Abbasids placed Syria under the control of Turkish military strong men based in Egypt (first the Tulunids, who governed from 868 to 905, and then the Ikshidids, who governed from

935 to 969), but they proved unable to deal with the rural unrest. During the tenth century the Qaramitah were not only able to defeat the Ikhshidids but took control of much of southern Syria.

The strength of the central government in Baghdad was greatly weakened starting with the second half of the ninth century, and many of the more distant provinces of the empire established local dynasties that governed in the name of the 'Abbasid Khalifah. By the middle of the tenth century the Arab Hamdanid dynasty (944–1003) was able to establish a nearly independent state based in Aleppo and Mosul. The Hamdanid princes copied the opulence of 'Abbasid Baghdad and were patrons of the arts. One prince, Sayf al-Dawlah (945–967) was himself a celebrated poet, and his court in Aleppo rivaled the major capitals of the then known world.

The 'Abbasids lost Tunisia and then Egypt to a rival caliphate, that of the Shi'ite Fatimids, who rose to power in 909. The Fatimids first established firm control over Tunisia and then moved east to take Egypt in 969. They transferred their seat of power as well to Egypt with the founding of al-Qahirah (the Victorious) or Cairo in same year. The Fatimids were Isma'ili Shi'ites who followed the line of the Imams from 'Ali ibn Abi Talib to the seventh Imam, where a split occurred over who should be considered the next in line, Isma'il or his brother Musa al-Kadhim. For the Isma'ilis the next was Isma'il while the mainstream Shi'ites followed Musa al-Kadhim and his descendants. The Isma'ilis found fertile ground for their movement among the Berbers of North Africa just as the Qaramitah had found support among Syria's rural population.

The Fatimids pushed eastward into Syria and were able to take control of most of the southern part while the Hamdanids were able to retain control over the northern part. The Byzantines took advantage of the struggles between rival Muslim states and the great social unrest caused by the political instability and tried to re-conquer at least the coastal strip of Syria between 969 and 997. However, in the end the Fatimids defeated them, forcing them to retreat into Anatolia. The Byzantine incursion greatly weakened the Hamdanids, who were replaced by the Mirdasids, who were of Bedouin origin. The Mirdasids were able to rule from Aleppo but were challenged first by the arrival pastoral nomadic Turkomen tribes. Eventually they succumbed to the Saljuq Turks in 1079.

The rise of the Fatimids in North Africa and Egypt and the Byzantine incursion had demonstrated the weakness not only of the 'Abbasids but of the Shi'ite Buwayhids, who gained control the 'Abbasid Khalifahs, as well as much of the old Persian heartland since the middle of the tenth century. The Saljuqs were Turkish tribes from Central Asia who had recently converted to Sunni Islam. Organized into a strong fighting force they invaded

Iran and by 1037 had pushed into Iraq defeating the last of the Buwayhids and establishing Sunni protection for the 'Abbasid Khalifahs. The Saljuqs saw themselves as the defenders of Sunni orthodoxy against what at the time seemed like a wave of Shi'ism. The Saljuqs pushed westward and brought northern Syria under their control in 1055. In 1071 the Saljuqs defeated the Byzantines at the Battle of Manzikert, which opened Anatolia to Turkish and Muslim penetration. They were also able to defeat the Fatimids and pushed them back into Egypt bringing all of Syria back under Sunni leadership. The Saljuqs were less tolerant of European Christian pilgrims to Palestine than the Fatimids had been, which resulted in a number of complaints to the Pope in Rome. Responding to both the complaints of pilgrims and more importantly to the pleas from the Byzantines who were still losing large areas of Anatolia to the Turks, Pope Urban II declared the First Crusade in 1095.

The First Crusade reached the borders of Syria in 1098 taking the city of Antioch. The Europeans proceeded on to Jerusalem, which by the time they arrived had been retaken by the Fatimids. Not distinguishing between Muslim states and the possible friendly stance of the Egyptians, the Crusaders took Jerusalem by storm, slaughtering Muslims, Jews, and Christians alike. Over the next decade Syrian and Lebanese coastal cities fell to the Crusaders, and by 1109 the entire coast was under the Europeans. A number of Crusader states emerged running from the County of Edessa in the north to the Kingdom of Jerusalem in the south.

Muslim response was slow due to the lack of unity among Muslim princes. While the Saljuqs under their great leaders Alp Arslan (1063–1072) and Malik Shah (1072–1092) had been able to end Shi'ite domination and re-turn the primacy of Sunni orthodoxy, the Saljuq system of dividing power and land among princes caused a quick breakdown of power. Princes were given their own areas to rule under the guidance of *atabeks,* or guardians loyal to the princes' fathers. The system had been a successful part of the Saljuq's nomadic pastoral past in Central Asia and had proven successful as well with the penetration of Muslims into Anatolia as princes were encouraged to colo-nize new lands; however, the lack of strong central power made it difficult to respond to outside attack. The Turkish military commander of Damascus deserted the Saljuqs and gave his loyalty to the Fatimids in Cairo, while the Turkish princes of Aleppo and Mosul were as willing to fight each other as the Crusaders. The first major defeat inflicted upon the Europeans in 1119 at the Battle of Sarmadah close to Aleppo was not followed up by any vigor-ous campaign.

In a number of the small Saljuq principalities the atabeks were able to take full control by marginalizing the princes and eventually replacing them. The Muslim response to the Crusader states began with one such atabek, 'Imad al-Din Zangi, the atabek of Mosul. 'Imad al-Din first brought Aleppo under his control, and as a staunch Sunni launched a vigorous campaign against the Shi'ites forcing many Isma'ilis to seek refuge in the rugged Jabal al-Ansariyah. He then turned his attentions north to the County of Edessa, which he conquered in 1144. 'Imad al-Din was succeeded by his son, Nur al-Din, whose ambition was to unify Syria with Iraq. When the Second Crusade attacked Damascus despite the friendly relations its rulers had cultivated with the Kingdom of Jerusalem, Nur al-Din came to the city's rescue and soundly defeated the Crusaders in 1149. One by one the petty principalities of Syria fell under Nur al-Din's control, and when the Fatimids invited outside assistance to deal with crisis between rival *wazirs*, or ministers of state, Nur al-Din sent his trusted Kurdish lieutenant Shirkuh and Shirkuh's equally competent nephew, Salah al-Din al-Ayyubi, to Egypt. Outmaneuvering the King of Jerusalem, Salah al-Din eventually became the de facto ruler of Egypt, and upon Nur al-Din's death, the ruler of the combined area that encompassed Egypt, Syria, and upper Iraq.

Salah al-Din used both Cairo and Damascus as his capitals traveling back and forth between them. His lines of communication were threatened by the Crusader castles in Jordan, particularly Karak. The reckless actions of Renauld de Chatlion, who held Karak for the King of Jerusalem, sparked war in 1187. Salah al-Din defeated the King of Jerusalem at the Battle of the Horns of Hattin in Palestine. He marched on to take Jerusalem as well as many of the Crusader forts including all of them east of the Jordan River. The fall of Jerusalem caused the Third Crusade led by the kings of England and France and the German Holy Roman Emperor. The contest between Richard the Lion Heart, King of England, and Salah al-Din has been the source of numerous novels and legends, but the fact is that Salah al-Din fought the Europeans to a standstill. The Crusade could not retake the lands and castles lost to the Muslims, but the Muslims could not press on and eliminate the last remaining Crusader enclaves. The Kingdom of Jerusalem was limited to a small area along the coast with Acre ('Akka) the new capital.

Salah al-Din died in 1193 in Damascus. His kingdom was divided between his brothers, and his sons who soon feuded over territory. The internal squabbles between rival Ayyubid princes allowed the Crusader states a respite. It also gave rise to a brilliant period in architecture as each prince vied to out build the others. They built mosques, schools, hospitals, and other splendid public buildings incorporating forms from Central Asia, Iran, and Iraq with local Syrian styles. Damascus, Aleppo, and Cairo were rival capitals though eventually Cairo emerged as the strongest of the Ayyubid states.

Noting the strength of Egypt, the Fifth and Sixth Crusades aimed at the conquest of Palestine via Egypt. Both attempts were defeated at the hands of the Ayyubids and their professional slave army or Mamluks. The Sixth Crusade coincided with the death of the last of the Egyptian Ayyubids, al-Malik al-Salih Najm al-Din, in 1249. Though two more Ayyubids would sit on the throne, they were merely figureheads in the hands of Najm al-Din's capable wife, Shajarat al-Durr. She would rule even after she was forced to marry again 1250. She chose as her new husband one of Najm al-Din's Mamluks, Aybak. Shajarat al-Durr was eventually assassinated by another woman and with her death the Mamluk period begins.

The Mamluks were slaves bought as boys and educated in both Islamic sciences and the arts of war. The system was begun under the 'Abbasids who preferred to have a professional army than rely on tribal levies for their palace guards. The system was generalized under the Ayyubids who did not trust Arab and Turkish tribal troops. The Ayyubids, being Kurds, first tried to rely on mainly Kurdish soldiers, but the need for a strong standing army forced them to begin buying boys from Central Asia and Mongolia, places with a ready supply of young boys. The first Mamluks, the Bahri line, were made up mainly of Central Asian Turks and Mongols. The system brought firm loyalty to their commanders even after they were freed upon reaching adulthood. It also bred rivalry between contesting military amirs or commanders, and palace coups were frequent.

The Mamluks proved their military value both against the European Crusaders and again in 1260 when they defeated the Mongols at the Battle of 'Ayn Jalut in Palestine. The Mongol leader Hülegü Khan, a son of Genghis Khan, invaded Iran and Iraq capturing Baghdad and executing the 'Abbasid Khalifah al-Musta'sim in 1258. He then invaded Syria sending part of his army south to Damascus and Palestine spreading terror and destruction as they went. The Mamluks under their Sultan Qutuz, met and defeated the Mongols at 'Ayn Jalut. Qutuz was replaced as Sultan by Baybars I al-Bunduqdari, who ushered in a brief age of stability. Baybars used Cairo, Karak, and Damascus as his three capitals and ruled as much from horseback as from the throne. He pursued an aggressive policy against the Crusader states, conquering the Principality of Antioch and the major castle of Krak des Chevailers that guarded the pass between Homs and Tartus. In addition, Baybars brought a relative of the last 'Abbasid Khalifah to Cairo and installed him as the new Khalifah al-Mustansir. The Cairo 'Abbasids would serve as the head of state until the Ottoman conquest of Egypt in 1517.

The Sultans who followed Baybars also pursued an active policy against the ever shrinking Crusader holdings as well as holding off attempts by the Mongols to press westward from Iran. In 1291 Sultan al-Ashraf Khalil took Acre forcing the Kingdom of Jerusalem to relocate to the island of Cyprus. Taking advantage of political unrest among the Mamluk amirs in Cairo, the

Mongols attempted another invasion of Syria and were able to reach Damascus which they occupied from 1300 to 1303. However, the Mamluks once again regained the advantage and were able to push back the Mongols as well as take the last Crusader castle in Syria, when in 1302 the Island of Arwad was taken by the Sultan al-Nasir Muhammad.

The Bahri Mamluks were unable to continue to purchase boys from Central Asia and Mongolia as a result of the Mongol occupation of Iran; however, they found another source among the Circassians and Shishans from the Caucasus Mountains. The new Mamluks became the second dynasty, the Burji. The Burji Mamluks inherited a much improved international situation yet, like the Bahri before them, suffered from numerous palace coups staged by rival amirs. The rivalry included trying to outdo one another in building magnificent public buildings such as mosques, schools, hospitals, caravansaries, baths, and hostels for *Sufi* mystics. While Cairo as the capital of the state and the seat of both the Khalifah and the Sultan received much of the attention, Damascus as the regional capital of Syria also enjoyed the attention of those amirs sent to govern the province.

Mamluk control of Syria was threatened one final time by Timur Lang who was able to reach Damascus in 1401. Timur was unable to keep Syria but when he left he took with him hundreds of Syria's most skilled craftsmen whom he employed in the beautification of his capital, Samarqand in Central Asia. Timur also invaded Turkey defeating the Ottoman Sultan Bayezid I, but, like his conquest of Syria, he did not remain there for long. Both the Mamluks and the Ottomans rebuilt, but the Mamluks dependency on outside sources for future manpower was threatened by the resurgent Ottomans in Anatolia and the first stirrings of the Shi'ite Safavids in Azerbaijan. Palace intrigue continued to plague the Mamluks, and the massive building projects kept the state in a near bankrupt condition. Weakened central authority allowed Bedouin tribes to push the limits of the eastern frontier in Syria, and in the early sixteenth century Bedouin were able to threaten Mamluk control of both Jordan and Palestine. Eventually the Sultan Qansuh al-Ghawri was able to rouse the amirs in both Egypt and Syria and once again established Mamluk control over most of Syria, but the end of the Mamluk period was close at hand.

OTTOMAN PERIOD TO THE BEGINNING OF THE FRENCH MANDATE

The Ottoman Turks established themselves in western Anatolia and by 1345 had begun conquests in Europe. The Ottomans conquered Constantinople, which they renamed Islambul or the City of Isalm (which eventually became Istanbul), in 1453 ending the Byzantine Empire. They fought an inconclusive war with the Mamluks between 1466 and 1470 but continued to expand their territory in Europe as well as eastward towards Azerbaijan. In 1514 Sultan Salim I Yavuz (meaning "the Grim" in Turkish) defeated the new Safavid Shah of Iran, Isma'il I at the Battle of Chalidran. He then turned his attention south to the Mamluks whom he suspected had been in correspondence and perhaps collusion with the Shah. In 1516 Salim launched his campaign against the Mamluks and soundly defeated them at the Battle of Marj Dabiq near Aleppo. Among the Mamluks killed was the Sultan Qansuh al-Ghawri. Salim proceeded south encountering little opposition as the Mamluk army withdrew to Egypt. Mamluk amirs governing parts of Syria surrendered to him and some swore allegiance to him as the new Sultan. By 1517 all of the former Mamluk territory was in Ottoman hands including Egypt and the Hijaz. Salim had the 'Abbasid Khalifah al-Mutawakkil III removed to Istanbul where he signed his position as Khalifah over to Salim and retired into private obscurity.

Salim's successor Sulayman I (1520–1566), known in the West as "The Magnificent" and in the East as "The Lawgiver," ordered a number of major building projects in Syria, many of which were designed by his famous architect Sinan. Sulayman had a new, easier *Haj* or pilgrim road built from Damascus to Madinah, which was protected by a series of forts located along the road manned by Turkish garrisons. The more marginal regions of Syria were left to local elite to govern with little to no Ottoman intervention. One of the local elite who rose to power was Fakhr al-Din al-Ma'ani, a Druze prince from Lebanon. The Sultan Murad IV recognized Fakhr al-Din as governor of much of Syria including Lebanon, Palestine, and Jordan. Fakhr al-Din used his position to begin negotiations with European powers as though he was independent of the Ottomans. The Sultan at first tolerated Fakhr al-Din's autonomy but alarmed at the growth of his power, the Sultan defeated and killed Fakhr al-Din in 1635. Today, he is seen as a Lebanese national hero and is the subject of numerous plays and books.

Following the defeat of Fakhr al-Din, Lebanon came under the control of another Druze family, the Shihabs, who served as the governors until 1832. While the Shihabs and their Druze and Maronite Christian allies governed Lebanon like feudal fiefdoms, much of Ottoman Syria was fortunate to have a period of peace and prosperity under the 'Azm family who served as the governors of Damascus as well as of other major Syrian cities starting in 1725. The 'Azms not only brought a period of "good governance," but also one of taste and refinement in architecture and other fine arts. Their legacy today includes a number of elegant palaces, places of commerce or *khan*s, and caravansaries in Damascus, Homs, and Hama. As'ad al-'Azm Pasha was deposed as governor of Damascus in 1757 by Sultan Mustafa III, who confiscated

'Azm Pasha's personal wealth which included a magnificent collection of fine Chinese porcelains; a collection so large that the Sultan had the Chinese Pavilion at the Top Kapi Serai in Istanbul built to house them.

During the first centuries of Ottoman rule in Syria, only Aleppo had been directly ruled by them. No local elite were able to gain control and those who tried, such as the Junbalat family, were forced to flee, in their case to Lebanon. Aleppo was a major trading center and was the largest city in Syria. Its size and importance in international trade, being on the major western terminus on the Euphrates route from Iraq and the East to the Mediterranean, was such that a number of European countries such as England and France established consulates there. Damascus fell to the rank of Syria's second city governed by a *wali* often chosen from among local elite. Damascus regained its place as Syria's first city in the late eighteenth and early nineteenth centuries.

Syria became more important to the Ottomans as a result of the Egyptian invasion and occupation that lasted from 1831 to 1840. Egypt had embarked on a policy of radical reform under the dynamic Muhammad 'Ali Pasha. Though he governed Egypt as a province of the Ottomans, he was able to gain a good deal of autonomy. His reforms were mainly focused on the military, but also included education and engineering. He had come to the rescue of the Sultan in Arabia and then in Greece where his more modern military reversed the situation. His son, Ibrahim Pasha, successfully invaded the Sudan and brought huge new territories under Egyptian control. Seeing the weakness of the Ottomans, Muhammad 'Ali launched an invasion of Syria in 1831 and 1832 under the leadership of his able military commander and son Ibrahim Pasha. All of Syria quickly fell to the Egyptians who set about reforming the region's administration, improving collection of taxes, and making all citizens, regardless of religion, equal before the law. Some local elite were co-opted to assist the Egyptians such as Bashir II Shihab while others kept their distance. The Egyptian army continued its advance and reached Konya deep inside Anatolia in 1832 forcing the Ottoman Sultan Mahmud II to grant Muhammad 'Ali the governorship of all of Syria for his lifetime.

Muhammad 'Ali's success alarmed the major European powers who did not want a strong, new state in the eastern Mediterranean. At the Convention of London in 1840 Britain, Russia, and Austria (only France remained a strong ally of the Egyptians and opposed the agreement) forced the Sultan 'Abd al-Majid I and Muhammad 'Ali to agree to the withdrawal of Egyptians from Syria in exchange for Muhammad 'Ali and his descendants being granted Egypt as a near independent state, but still nominally under the Sultan. The Egyptian withdrawal brought the downfall of the Shihabs in Lebanon, and the Ottomans began the process of bringing more of Syria under stronger central authority.

In 1839 'Abd al-Majid I became Sultan and the success of the Egyptians gave him needed support to instigate real reform to the Ottoman military and government. Previous attempts at reform by Ottoman Sultans had been unsuccessful due mainly to the opposition by the Janissary military corps, who saw any change as a threat to their special privileged position at court. The first step towards reform was the *Khatt-i Sharif* or Noble Decree issued in 1839 that set out a number administrative changes. This began the *Tanzimat* or Reform period, where many of the innovations introduced during the Egyptian occupation of Syria became universal in the empire. Not all of the reforms were well received by local people, and there were Muslim riots in 1850 in Aleppo and in 1860 in Lebanon and Damascus against the civil laws making Christians and Jews equal with Muslims. The 1860 disturbances not only set Muslims and Christians against each other but the disturbances also set Christians and Druze against one another in Lebanon. Britain and France became involved, each major power being seen locally to support one of the confessional groups. The riots spread to Damascus before the authorities were able to suppress them. The Druze community in what is today called Jabal Druze in the south of Syria moved there as a result of their clashes with their Maronite Christian neighbors in Lebanon.

Land reform laws passed in 1858 were designed to help the large number of landless peasants in the empire, but in Syria they helped landlords expand the area under cultivation as they began to reclaim marginal areas that had been controlled by Bedouin tribes. The Ottoman state began to receive Muslims from the Caucasus as a result of Russia's war of conquest and many of the Circassian and Shishan refugees were given lands in these marginal areas in Syria and in Jordan. Fierce fighters the Circassians and Shishans were a match for the Bedouin and quickly brought these areas under Ottoman central authority. The reform measures culminated in the 1876 Constitution, the first such document for the empire as a whole; Tunisia, technically an Ottoman province, issued its own constitution in 1861.

Education was another part of the *Tanzimat* movement and a number of foreign, often Christian, mission schools were allowed to open in Palestine, Lebanon, and Syria. The missions first targeted the sons of Christian families and introduced a western curriculum that included experimental sciences as well as English and French languages. By the end of the nineteenth century many sons of Muslim families were also attending such schools, and, in some instances, their daughters were also studying there. Education played a major role in what has been called the Arab Awakening; a realization of the Arab role in history and a rebirth of Arab pride in their cultural achievements. Those educated in such schools formed the first Arab nationalist organizations.

The *Tanzimat* movement died with the Sultan 'Abd al-Majid in 1876, the same year as the historic first constitution. 'Abd al-Majid was eventually (two Sultans would be installed in 1876 before 'Abd al-Hamid) succeeded by 'Abd al-Hamid II who was deeply suspicious of reformers. At first he allowed the reform to continue, and it was under him that the constitution was announced. A parliament was opened in 1877 but 'Abd al-Hamid suspended the constitution and closed the parliament in 1878. Nonetheless, he continued the drive towards re-imposing direct Ottoman control over all of Syria including tribally organized marginal areas such as Jordan. In 1900 he initiated the Hijaz Railway that would be able to safely move large numbers of Muslim pilgrims from Damascus to Makkah. The first reaction of many of the Arabs in Jordan and the Hijaz was very hostile to the idea—they had been able to demand large amounts of money to supply transportation and security for the pilgrim caravans and they noted troops could be moved just as easily as pilgrims—and forced the government to back down to a degree. The railroad would end in Madinah, not Makkah, thereby pacifying some of the Bedouin in the Hijaz who would still be needed to supply transportation to Makkah. By 1908 the railway was completed and opened with a grand ceremony.

'Abd al-Hamid's reactionary policies were unpopular not only with the Arabs of the empire but with many of those in the Turkish officer corps. In 1908 the Young Turks or more properly the Committee for Union and Progress, a group of young army officers, took control of the government and marginalized the Sultan, making him a figurehead rather than actual ruler. 'Abd al-Hamid plotted to regain control and in 1909 attempted a counter-coup which failed. As a result, he was removed once and for all as Sultan and replaced by his relative Muhammad V al-Rashad, who served as a figurehead until his death in 1918.

The new government was originally supported by many Arab nationalists in Syria, and there was great hope that they would once again push the reforms of 'Abd al-Majid. The government released the Sharif of Makkah, Hussein ibn 'Ali, whom 'Abd al-Hamid had placed under house arrest in Istanbul. Hussein's release was seen as an indication of the new openness expected of the Young Turks. Hussein and his sons Faysal, 'Abdallah, and 'Ali had been in touch with many of the Arab nationalists during their time in Istanbul and kept up the contact once they were back in Makkah. The new Turkish rulers were aware of these contacts and kept the Sharif, his sons, and the other Arab nationalist under close watch. The Arab nationalists were seen as a threat to the state because their aspirations clashed with the growth of

Turkish nationalism among the governing Young Turks. Proposals to impose Turkish language and Turkish identity in the Arab provinces were not well received.

While the Young Turks cemented their relationship with Germany, Arab nationalists looked to other great powers of the day for possible assistance. Hussein opened up a line of communications with the British in Egypt exploring British support for an independent Arab state with Damascus as its capital. When World War I broke out, Turkey sided with Germany. Hussein maintained his communications with the British in Egypt and when in 1916 he thought he had British support for an independent Arab state, he declared the Arab Revolt. The execution of a number of Syrian Arab nationalists in Damascus by the Turks in 1916 only served to strengthen Arab nationalists' resolve against the state. Many Arab officers serving in the Turkish army defected to the Arab Revolt once it was declared.

The Arab Revolt brought Hussein's son Faysal to the fore as the main military commander. Faysal used his connections with the Arab nationalists in Syria, many of whom he knew personally, to secure political support for the cause among the more sophisticated urban Arabs. He used his political abilities with the Bedouin *shaykh*s to gain not only their support but to help supply men for the army. With material assistance provided by the British, Faysal was able to bring the Bedouin of the Hijaz and Jordan to his side. Legendary T. E. Lawrence, Lawrence of Arabia, fought with the Arab Army as it moved north from the Hijaz and took the port at al-'Aqabah in southern Jordan in 1917. As the Arab Army advanced northward, many Arab tribes joined the revolt, and in 1918 the Arab Army liberated Damascus. The Turkish troops were pursued by Arab and British forces, and in the same year all of Syria was in allied hands.

MANDATE TO INDEPENDENCE

World War I ended in 1918 with the defeat of Germany, Austria, and Turkey. The Turkish army had withdrawn from the Arab provinces of Syria and Iraq leaving Arab and British forces in control. In Damascus Faysal ibn Hussein was declared King of the newly independent Kingdom of Syria with Damascus its capital. While none of the European powers recognized the new state, Faysal moved to Damascus and a provisional government was formed. The Arabs expected to be participate in the Versailles Peace Conference as partners in victory, not as subject peoples. British promises to the Kurds for an independent state and to the European Zionists for a Jewish homeland in Palestine complicated the question of what to do with the former Turkish Empire. In addition, representatives of Britain and France had met in 1916 and signed the Sykes-Picot Agreement to divide post-war Turkey between them, including the Arab provinces.

The British and French had already made up their minds to not grant the Arabs their independence, and Britain had recognized Faysal's father, Sharif Hussein, only as King of the Hijaz in 1916. The Americans under President Wilson proposed the right of self determination as a major principle of what to do with the peoples of the former Austrian Empire, and the Arabs at the Peace Conference pressed for the same principles to apply to the former Ottoman Empire. The Americans were willing to listen and sent the King–Crane Commission to Syria to investigate Arab ability to govern themselves. The Commission was not endorsed by the European powers and though the Commission recommended full and immediate independence for Syria, its conclusions were ignored. Angered over this, the Arabs then stated that if they were to be under a mandate power until they were deemed ready to rule themselves, they requested the mandate be given to the United States. The Americans were unwilling to take on such a responsibility and retreated behind a policy of isolationism leaving the Arabs to the British and French. The Conference decision was to place Palestine (which included at that time much of the Transjordan) and Iraq under the British and Lebanon and Syria under the French.

The Syrians refused to accept the decision of the Conference and in full defiance the Syrian National Congress proclaimed Faysal King of Syria and Palestine in 1920 knowing full well the French already had troops in Lebanon. The British and French mandates were ratified at San Remo Conference giving the French High Commissioner for Syria, General Gouraud, the green light to invade Syria. The Syrians fought the French at Maysalun outside of Damascus but were defeated. The French moved in and occupied Damascus forcing King Faysal to flee. Faysal's brother 'Abdallah gathered an army of tribesmen and moved north into Jordan causing a serious diplomatic crisis for the British. In order to solve the problem, the British proposed to recognize 'Abdallah as Amir or Prince of the Transjordan. Transjordan was detached from Palestine, and Faysal was placated by placing him on the throne of Iraq.

'Abdallah allowed a number of dissident Syrian nationalists to find refuge in Jordan. Some of them became members of his new government in 'Amman while others still made raids across the border into Syria. The French pressured the British to force 'Abdallah to stop the attacks on French positions inside Syria, which he reluctantly did. Resentment of the French in Syria smoldered from 1921 to 1925. In 1925, the Syrian Revolt broke out first in Jabal Druze where Arab nationalists had fled in 1916 to escape arrests by the Turks. The leadership of the region had been in contact with Faysal and his agents following the declaration of the Arab Revolt in 1916 and when the

Arab Army approached, the leadership rose to join their ranks. The tribal forces from the Hawran and Jabal Druze areas were among those who liberated Damascus in 1918. When the French defeated the Syrians at Maysalun some of their leaders sought refuge again among the tribal Druze leaders of the region such as Sultan al-Atrash. French control was more nominal than real in the region, and local people had aided the nationalists' attacks on the French. The French had sought to end problems by making peace with the local leaders, including Sultan al-Atrash, seeing them as feudal lords and not really coming to an understanding of local society. The Syrian Revolt began as a result of several years of drought and lower grain production, but the French authorities continued to demand payment of high rates of tax despite the conditions. As a result the revolt first erupted as a rural movement that encompassed all segments of the society. The revolt spread quickly beyond Jabal Druze into the Hawran and into Damascus. The French had thought that by 1925 they had been successful in dominating the major cities where they believed any possible nationalist trouble would emerge. The French underestimated the economic, social, and political integration of the Syrian countryside with the cities and initially considered they were dealing with a group of bandits. The revolt was hard to put down as both urban and rural populations rose against the French. Eventually the revolt was contained and smashed but a number of its leaders fled across the border into Jordan in 1926. 'Abdallah refused to arrest them and for awhile Azraq in northeastern Jordan served as refuge for Syrian rebels.

The Syrian Revolt was not successful in forcing the French to leave but it did force them to rethink their treatment of the Syrian nationalists. Attempts to divide the country along what the French had mistakenly thought were geographical and cultural divisions were proven false. The French authorities realized that they would have to deal with the Syrian nationalists if they were to prevent another revolt from happening. Despite their great reluctance to deal with the nationalists, the French agreed in 1936 in principle to Syrian independence. A national assembly, elections, political parties were allowed. The move towards independence was cut short by the outbreak of World War II and the fall of France to Nazi Germany.

The British could not allow a Vichy French government to exist in Lebanon and Syria so close to vital British interests, the Suez Canal and oil fields in Iraq. In 1941 the British and Free French occupied Lebanon and Syria. In order to gain the support of local political leaders, the Free French promised to end the mandate and grant Syria full independence. However, the French were very unwilling to make good their promise and did not grant independence until in 1945 when the British had to use the threat of force. Still reluctant to leave, the last French troops did not leave Syria until 1946.

INDEPENDENCE TO PRESENT

Syria became independent in 1945 and declared itself to be a republic with a representative government. Within months of its independence Syria joined both the United Nations and was a founding member of the Arab League. The country was weak and poor with an economy based primarily on agriculture yet its government was committed to assist other Arab countries still under colonial authority, especially in Palestine. The period under French control had allowed more radical elements among the nationalists to gain a strong say, and those who had supported more conservative agendas, such as support for the Hashemite family, faded into the background.

Syria supported the Palestinians in their conflict with the Jewish settlers starting early in the mandate period. Private citizens provided material assistance during the Palestinian Revolt of 1936, and some Syrians volunteered as fighters. Palestinian nationalism had begun as part of Arab/Syrian nationalism in the late nineteenth century, but with the imposition of the mandate system and the separation of region into three mandates, they focused more on Palestine rather than on the pan-Syrian agenda. They were encouraged by the resistance shown by Syrians in 1925 and by the eventual independence Syria achieved in 1945. When in 1948 Israel declared its existence within the borders of Palestine, Syria came to the assistance of the Palestinians. The Arab armies greatly underestimated the Israelis, which resulted in a number of defeats that clearly demonstrated not only the capabilities of the Israelis but the incompetence of the Arab military commanders and civilian authorities. Only the Jordanians did fairly well and were able to hold any significant part of Palestine; the West Bank including East Jerusalem. The Egyptians held on to the Gaza Strip while the Syrians were forced back across the border into the Golan Heights.

Syria was gripped by political instability as a result of the 1948 War. In 1949 there were three military coups and the third brought to power Adib Shishakli. Shishakli was himself removed by another coup in 1954, and there was an attempt to return to a civilian government. In 1955 Shukri Quwatli was elected President of Syria. In the meantime King Faruq of Egypt was deposed by a military coup in 1952 that brought Jamal 'Abd al-Nasir (Gamal Abdul Nasser) to power. Nasser quickly became the voice and the symbol of Arab nationalism throughout the Arab world. Initially Nasser had no specific political ideology, but eventually he embraced Arab Socialism, which he saw as different from the European forms. Nasser's speeches broadcast over the powerful radio station *Sawt al-'Arab,* or Voice of the Arabs, appealed to the vast majority of ordinary Arabs. Under pressure from the Syrian people, President Quwatli approached Nasser about unifying Syria and Egypt as one country.

Syria and Egypt joined as the first step in a unified Arab world and took the name United Arab Republic. Nasser was elected the president and Cairo was the capital leaving Syria as a province of Egypt. Almost immediately the unity began to run into problems. In an attempt to impose the same legal system, Egyptian laws took precedence over Syrian laws. For example, land reform enacted to redistribute land to Egypt's peasants were put in place in Syria with no regard to the difference in land types (irrigated or dry land) or other important differences, which caused serious problems for the majority of Syria's farmers. Egyptian military officers were senior to Syrians and by 1961 the Syrian military had enough. In a coup staged by Syrian officers the union with Egypt was broken and a new military government was put in place in Damascus.

Syria was again subject to a military coup in 1963, which brought in Amin al-Hafiz as president. Al-Hafiz included a number of Ba'athists in his cabinet turning Syria politically to the left. The Ba'ath party was founded in 1943 by two Syrians, Michel Aflaq and Salah al-Din Bitar; one Christian and the other Muslim. The party ideology drew heavily on the symbols of Arab history emphasizing the common cultural heritage of all Arabs despite religious affiliation. They stated that the socialist nature of their ideology was part of the shared cultural heritage and social organization common to all Arabs and they de-emphasized any connection with European concepts of socialism. The word *ba'ath* means Renaissance in Arabic and the word was a symbol of the connection between the party's ideologies with the writings of the Arab nationalists of the Arab Awakening before World War I. The Ba'ath party appealed to the educated among especially the lower middle class, such as school teachers and other lower level government employees. The party had little political influence during the numerous previous governments and only came to the fore with the 1963 coup.

Amin al-Hafiz was overthrown in another military coup staged by Salah Jadid in 1966. Jadid was a more confirmed Ba'athist and from his government onwards Syria would be governed by the Ba'ath party. Jadid placed trusted officers from the army in important government posts, and Hafiz al-Asad, an air force officer, was made Minster of Defense. Syria's recent history of political instability was further compounded by economic problems. In 1958 a severe drought devastated the country causing major problems for the economy heavily dependent on agriculture and for the rural population. It took some time to recover from the effects of the drought and rebuild the county's agricultural sector.

Syria, Egypt, and Jordan entered into a mutual defense pact in order to deal with what the Arab states saw as the increasing military threat from Israel. The 1948 war with Israel had created a large number of Palestinian refugees in Lebanon, Syria, Egypt, and Jordan. Slowly the Palestinians began their own resistance movements, which launched raids across the borders into Israel. Israeli responses were far in excess of what the Palestinian raids were able to do causing the Arab states to continue to build their militaries to defend their territories. Though the leaders of Syria, Egypt, and Jordan did not trust nor like each other that much, they felt they had no other option than to seek mutual aid in case of attack.

In 1967 the Egyptians felt strong enough to close access to the Suez Canal by the Israelis in response to what they called Israeli aggression against the Arabs. This provoked the Six Day War of June 1967. Within six days the three Arab armies suffered severe defeat losing large areas of territory: Gaza Strip, Sinai Peninsula, West Bank, and the Golan Heights. Jordan absorbed even more Palestinian refugees, some made refugees for the second time. For Syria the loss of the Golan was a major blow to national pride though the actual land area seized by the Israelis was not large. Nonetheless, Syrians were made refugee as the majority of the civilian population of the region left; only the Druze refused to leave and have continued to remain despite all pressures put on them by Isreal. The recovery of Golan remains the number one priority of any possible Syrian negotiations with Israel.

Raids launched from Jordan by increasing militant Palestinian groups and their relative autonomy inside Jordan eventually caused a conflict with the Jordanian army, which erupted into a civil war in 1970. Syria's leaders put their army on alert and sent troops to the Jordanian border initially to support the Palestinians; however, the Syrians only stopped any cross-border incursions into Syrian held lands. The Jordanian army was able to swiftly defeat the Palestinian fighters forcing the militant wings of Palestinian organizations to relocate to Lebanon. Inside the Syrian military Hafiz al-Asad consolidated his support and replaced both Salah Jadid and the civilian president, Nur al-Din Atasi, in what became called the Corrective Movement—portrayed as a "correction" of policies within the Ba'ath Party—rather than a coup.

Hafiz al-Asad came from a modest rural background and was a member of one of Syria's heterodox Shi'ite groups, the 'Alawi, also called the Nusayris. Historically the 'Alawis have been regarded as on the very fringe of Islam, and many Sunnis considered them to be heretics beyond the fringe. Seeking refuge from persecution by the dominant Sunnis, the 'Alawis built their communities in the rough and difficult Jabal al-Ansariyah range. They remained socially, politically, and economically deprived for generations. With independence 'Alawi youth found a viable outlet in the army where many from Syria's minorities were able to break the boundaries set by the old Sunni elite. Hafiz al-Asad was able to gather a number of 'Alawi and other minority officers around him, many with similar rural or small town backgrounds. They embarked on a new economic policy that emphasized improving the general conditions in the rural regions. They felt that too much attention had been given to Syria's urban centers at the expense of the rural population. Taking a practical approach to developing the rural regions, they were willing to set aside party ideology if necessary but expanded government services (and direct government presence) throughout the country.

In 1973 Syria and Egypt launched the October or Ramadan War, which shattered the belief in Israeli invulnerability. Though in the end the Syrians were not able to hold the ground they initially took back in the Golan, the Arabs were given a new pride in their militaries. Syria began opening up to the West in a way it had not done for decades. It reopened its diplomatic representation in the United States, which had been broken in the 1967 war, and in the early 1980s began to open its economy to the outside as well.

Syria began its interference in Lebanon in 1976 when it entered into the Civil War (1975–1990) initially on the side of the Maronite Christians in order to prevent them from being defeated by the leftist coalition composed mainly of the Druze and Palestinians. For the Syrians, and for most of the Arab governments, it was vital to maintain Lebanon's status quo—a political arrangement that had more or less worked since independence in 1943. Lebanese politics is a shifting balance of political parties representing the interests of specific religious communities with the Maronite Christians occupying the top post in the government. Syria's military presence in Lebanon became an aspect of daily life in the country, which did not end until international pressure forced them to leave in 2005. Knowledge of Lebanese politics and personal acquaintances with a good number of Lebanese politicians allowed Syria's leaders to make the numerous shifts in power and support needed to keep their troops on the ground for so long. For Syrian nationalists, and for many in the Syrian government, Syria was not occupying Lebanon in that the entire country is a part of Greater Syria and certain parts; the Biqa' Valley and Tripoli (Tarabulus al-Sham) were split from Syria by the French during the first decade of the mandate. Syria participated in the Taif Agreement, which eventually brought an end to the Lebanese Civil War. The agreement was an initiative by Saudi Arabia and supported by the majority of Arab governments. The agreement was signed by all parties in 1989 as the National Reconciliation Charter. It took until 1990 for the last of the die hard opponents of the agreement (mainly a fringe Maronite group) to be defeated by the Syrians, and in 1991 Syria and Lebanon signed the Treaty of Brotherhood and Cooperation, which outlined conditions for Syrian interests in Lebanon.

In 1980 Iraq's President Saddam Hussein attacked Iran claiming violation by Iran of the treaty regarding use of the vital Shatt al-'Arab waterway. Unlike the rest of the Arab world, the Syrians supported Iran. Not only was Syria supporting a non-Arab state against a fellow Arab country but Syria was also supporting an Islamic republic against a secular, and fellow Ba'athist, republic. The cause for Syria's support had less to do with ideology and more to do with the problems between Saddam Hussein and Hafiz al-Asad. Despite al-Asad's support for Iran he was able to keep good relations with Saudi Arabia, which had become one of Syria's main financial backers since the 1973 war.

The success of the Islamic revolution in Iran in 1979 encouraged Islamic groups in Syria as well. Riots erupted in the Sunni strongholds of Aleppo, Homs, and Hama. The *Ikhwan al-Muslimin,* or Muslim Brotherhood, had been banned for decades but had been able to function as an underground opposition to the secular government. Following the success of Ayatollah Khomeini in Iran, Muslim groups in the Arab countries became emboldened and from 1980 to 1982 the Muslim Brotherhood in Syria engaged the government in a low-level urban conflict even attempting in 1980 to assassinate al-Asad. In 1982 the Muslim Brotherhood felt strong enough to more openly challenge the state and organized an uprising in Homs, Hama, and Aleppo. The uprising was crushed with great loss of life especially in Homs where the Ikhwan had a good deal of popular support.

In the same year, 1982, Israel invaded Lebanon in an attempt to once and for all destroy the military capability of the Palestinians. The Syrians were not eager to confront the Israelis, and the Israelis made an effort to stay clear of Syrian controlled parts of Lebanon. No Arab country came to the aid of the Palestinians or the Lebanese, and the Israeli army was able to occupy Beirut, forcing the Palestinian fighters to evacuate to Tunisia, one of the few places willing to take them. The Israelis, like everyone else who has become involved in Lebanon, were seen as allies of certain Maronite Christian leaders, and they were initially welcomed by Shi'ite villagers in the south as well; however, the Shi'ites quickly turned against them. Shi'ites, once the weakest of Lebanese confessional groups, had emerged as one of the better organized and powerful militias as a result of the Lebanese Civil War. The more secular Shi'ite party *Amal* lost ground to the more militant and religious *Hizb Allah,* or Party of God, formed in 1982 to confront the Israelis. The Israeli occupation of Lebanon helped Hizb Allah gain popularity among the ordinary Lebanese Shi'ites. Hizb Allah was able to get a good deal of support from Iran and their armed opposition to the Israelis forced the Israelis to first withdraw to a southern buffer zone, which they eventually withdrew from in 2000.

Syria's opposition to Saddam Hussein made them strange bedfellows with the Americans when Iraq invaded Kuwait in 1990. Syria along with Egypt, Saudi Arabia, and the United Arab Emirates joined the United States–led coalition that forced Saddam Hussein out of Kuwait in 1991. Both Syria and Egypt supplied combat troops in the effort. Syria hoped to use its assistance in the war as an important card in the promised Middle East peace conference, which was to be held after the conclusion of hostilities. Syria wanted to maintain a solid front of all the Arab states in any negotiations with Israel, and Egypt's willingness to go it alone following the 1973 War had greatly angered Hafiz al-Asad. Syria had felt it been forced into a weaker position when Egyptian President Anwar Sadat signed the Camp David Agreement in 1979 and did not want a repeat of this with the new negotiations that would open up after the end of the Gulf War. Syria also hoped, and expected, more even-handed treatment by the Americans after helping defeat Saddam Hussein.

The Madrid Conference was held in 1991 and attended by the Arab confrontation states and Israel. The Arabs were split over the Gulf War; the Palestinian leader Yasir 'Arafat had given his support to Saddam Hussein after the Iraqi leader had promised to give his full military support to the Palestinians, and Jordan's King Hussein had not been supportive enough of the U.S. coalition against Iraq. Gulf countries and Saudi Arabia took severe measures against Palestinians and Jordanians working in their countries, and many were forced to leave and return to Jordan. Syria wanted to have a hard line in the negotiations with Israel but felt it was undercut by Egypt and Jordan, who were willing to make concessions to the Israelis, lured by American assurances of major economic support. Syria once more felt it was isolated in the negotiation process and held to its hard line. Nonetheless, Syria continued to slowly open up its economy to the outside and began a strategic withdrawal of dependency on the Soviet Union.

Syria's internal politics during the period of President Hafiz al-Asad was described as "Byzantine," full of "court" intrigues and possible plots. Among the problems was Hafiz al-Asad's younger brother, Rifa'at al-Asad. Rifa'at wanted to succeed his brother and used his position in state security to try to consolidate his power base. Rifa'at, however, was far too abusive of his position to be tolerated by President al-Asad. Rifa'at was warned on several occasions and at one point exiled to Europe. The final straw came when Hafiz al-Asad suffered a heart attack in 1983 and in anticipation of his possible death several army generals including Rifa'at brought troops into Damascus in order to secure the presidency for themselves. President al-Asad recovered, and those who had tried to seize power were disgraced. Rifa'at was able to survive and was even promoted to Vice President in 1984; however, Hafiz al-Asad eventually "relieved" him of his post in 1998 forcing Rifa'at out of Syrian politics.

Hafiz al-Asad had been grooming his son Basil for the presidency—not unlike the Umayyad Khalifah Mu'awiyah and his son Yazid. Basil al-Asad was truly popular with the Syrian youth, who saw in him a symbol of hope for their future. Basil was charismatic and handsome; a darling of not only his father but of many young Syrians. He was totally unlike the two hated sons of Saddam Hussein, Uday and Qusay, who terrorized and murdered their own people. When Basil died in a car accident in 1994, the entire country went into deep mourning that lasted for months. The death of Basil also began the true decline of Hafiz al-Asad's health. Basil was replaced in the succession by a younger son, Bashar al-Asad, a mild, sensitive young man who was trained in medicine. Bashar was reluctant to take his brother's place and had a short time to familiarize himself with the ins and outs of Syrian politics.

Hafiz al-Asad died in 2000 and the transition to his son Bashar as the new president went smoothly. Many people hoped that Bashar al-Asad would be more open to change and political reform. He had studied medicine in the West and had more first hand knowledge of both Western political systems and culture. Initially, the country experienced a greater openness. In 2001 the Muslim Brotherhood was allowed political participation for the first time in 20 years. In the same year Pope John Paul II visited Syria and became the first Pope to ever visit a functioning mosque. In addition, British Prime Minister Tony Blair made an official visit to the country. However, the honey moon came to an end in 2001 when a number of political reformers were arrested. Hopes for a more open and democratic Syria seemed dashed.

Bashar al-Asad was not able to push for the hoped for political reforms and had to deal instead with the power structure that had developed under his father. Syria's hard line with Israel and alleged support for groups the United States and Israel consider to be terrorist organizations dimmed prospects for greater openness. Syria was included in American President George Bush's "Axis of Evil" in his 2002 State of the Union Address. When the United States invaded Iraq in 2003, Syria did not come to the support of either side; though it could be argued the Syrians were not unhappy to see the end of Saddam Hussein's regime. However, the U.S. action against a sovereign state to replace the regime combined with hostile rhetoric by the U.S. government only strengthened Syrian suspicions of the American intentions vis-à-vis Syria.

The Syrians have proceeded to declare themselves open to negotiations with the Israelis and with the Iraqis. President al-Asad visited Turkey in 2004, the first Syrian president to make such a visit since independence in 1945. Syria has affirmed it will participate in any conference to deal with the internal civil strife in Iraq on a number of occasions. The Bush administration has repeatedly rebuffed Syria's offer, citing Syria's continued support for international terror organizations as the reason.

In 2005 former Lebanese Prime Minister Rafiq al-Hariri was assassinated in what was believed to be a plot supported by Syria's security police. Rafiq al-Hariri had supported the Syrian presence in Lebanon while he held the post of Prime Minister but had subsequently become very critical of the continued presence of Syrian troops in the country and the role played by Syrian security in Lebanese politics. His assassination became the focal point for popular Lebanese protests against the presence of Syrian troops, and, under pressure from the international community, Syria withdrew totally. A number of high-ranking Syrian officials were investigated by a United Nations international panel. Syria was accused of hiding the evidence and obstructing the investigation as well as staging the suicide of Syrian Interior Minister Ghazi Kanaʿan. As a result no final conclusions could be reached about Syria's involvement leaving only a nagging sense of doubt.

In July 2006, Israel invaded Lebanon as the result of a cross-border raid by Hizb Allah fighters in which a number of Israeli soldiers were killed and others taken prisoner. Israel accused Syria and Iran of supporting Hizb Allah either directly or indirectly by allowing military equipment to pass through Syria en route to Lebanon. While Syria did not come to the military aid of Hizb Allah, it did take in thousands of Lebanese refugees seeking escape from Israeli bombardments. Hizb Allah proved to be a difficult foe to defeat for the Israelis, and eventually they had to withdraw from Lebanon without achieving the stated goal of forcing the return of the soldiers Hizb Allah captured in the raid that began the whole affair.

In September 2006 the American embassy in Damascus was attacked by four gunmen. The gunmen opened fire on the embassy and threw hand grenades as well. Later it was discovered they had also tried to detonate a car bomb, but the devise failed. The embassy was protected by the Syrian security guards, who returned fire killing three of the four. The fourth gunman was apprehended by the Syrians and awaits trial. While the attack failed and no one at the U.S. embassy was hurt, it did underline the tensions in the region and the urgent need to settle the Palestinian-Israeli problem as well as bring an end to the civil strife in Iraq.

Since the American led invasion of Iraq in 2003, Syria has received Iraqi refugees fleeing the conflict. At first the numbers were few and included members of Saddam Hussein's government. The Syrians were uncomfortable hosts for them, and several leading figures were turned over to the Americans. The United States continues to accuse Syria of allowing foreign fighters (meaning non-Iraqis) to cross the border into Iraq and cites this as the major reason for refusing to speak directly to the Syrian government (in addition to supporting Palestinian and Lebanese terrorist groups). Syria's international credibility was greatly tarnished over the assassination of Rafiq al-Hariri thus any denials of allowing fighters to cross the border are not given much weight. Syria has been and continues to be one of the two main destinations for Iraqi refugees (the other is Jordan). Since the start of 2007 Syria receives on a monthly basis some 30,000 to 40,000 Iraqis. During the summer of 2006 Syria provided refuge for thousands of Lebanese fleeing the Israeli bombings in addition to thousands of Iraqis. While most of the Lebanese have returned home, the number of Iraqis in the country continues to grow. In March, 2007 the total number is estimated to be nearly one and a half million though the official number registered with the Syrian Ministry of the Interior is 800,000. Iraqi children have flooded many Syrian schools stretching the resources. In some schools it is reported that up to 60 students are crammed into classrooms meant for less than half that number. The semi-official newspaper *al-Ba'ath* has reported that prices in Syria have risen on the average 17% since the arrival of the large numbers of Iraqi refugees. In order to stem the flow, Syria has recently imposed harsher measures and restricted the length of stay to no more than a total of six and a half months. However, the same persons can return to Syria for another stay after being gone for a total of 30 days.

Syria and Iraq restored diplomatic relations in 2006 after 25 years of hostility. The move was not welcomed by the Bush administration, who at the time tried to isolate Syria and Iran. When the Iraq Study Group published their report, they clearly stated that Syria needs to be involved and the American government needs to begin direct talks with them. Initially President Bush announced in early 2007 that he did not agree with the recommendations put forth by the Study Group and rejected direct talks with both Syria and Iran. However, during the regional meeting held in Baghdad on restoring security to Iraq in March, 2007, the Americans seemed to back down and did engage in direct talks with the Syrian representatives. A few days after the Baghdad conference Ellen Sauerbrey, U.S. Assistant Secretary of State for Population, Refugees, and Migration, made the first official American visit to Syria since 2005 crisis over the assassination of Rafiq al-Hariri. The Syrians expressed their willingness to engage the United States in dialogue on all Middle Eastern issues including Iraq and Palestine.

In March three U.S. Congressmen visited Syria. Their visit was quickly followed by that of Speaker of the House, Nancy Pelosi, which proceeded over the objections of the White House. Ms. Pelosi held talks with a number of important figures in the Syrian government including President al-Asad. She told the Syrians that their support for organizations such as Hizb Allah and Hamas remain major problems in future negations, but she also brought with her a message from the Israelis stating that Israel is willing to re-start peace talks. The Syrians on their part stated their willingness to open dialogue with both the United States and Israel, but they also stated that they do not consider either Hizb Allah or Hamas to be terrorist organizations.

In a turn about in policy, the U.S. Secretary of State Condoleezza Rice met with Syrian Foreign Minister Walid Moallem during a summit held in the

Egyptian resort of Sharm al-Shaykh. It is clear that if the United States wants to bring stability to Iraq and to the Middle East as a whole, Syria needs to be engaged. Syria was invited to the Middle East Peace Conference hosted by the United States in the city of Annapolis in November 2007. The Syrians were not confident the conference would produce any real results but eventually did send the Deputy Foreign Minister Fayssal Mekdad to represent their position. While the Bush administration may not want to talk to Syria, it is clear that in the end they must.

CONCLUSION

Syria's position as a crossroads has shaped its long and complex history. Syria is a country proud of its past, its Arab heritage, and of being a place where ethnic and religious minorities have been able to find refuge. Syrians see themselves as among the least understood of all Arab peoples by the West. They see continued efforts to isolate them politically and economically as a manifestation of this misunderstanding, especially by the United States. Western rhetoric such as including Syria in the "Axis of Evil" only serves to harden Syrian resolve to be the "Citadel of Arabness"; the Arab state that constantly "defends the rights of all Arab people."

These opposing views—Syria as supporter of terror by the West and Syria as the defender of the Arab people by the Syrians (at least by those in the government)—helps explain the current situation in the region; however, nearly everyone agrees that for there to be a comprehensive peace in the Middle East, Syria must be included. Syria is a major player in the region and has been so through much of history. Syria is linked religiously, culturally, historically, and economically to Lebanon, Jordan, Iraq, Palestine-Israel, and Turkey. While Greater Syria does not exist as a political entity, it nonetheless remains an important cultural factor. Syrians as a people are linked by family and religious ties to all the countries that surround it and the future of one is linked to that of the others. Syrians are reminded on a daily basis of the strong ties between them and other Arabs in the motto of the Syrian Ba'ath Party: "The Arab nation is one, from the Atlantic to the Arab Gulf; and that is an eternal truth." While few in the Arab world still hold to the pan-Arab ideologies of Nasser or the Ba'ath Party, it remains an essential part of the official Syrian stance in their negotiations with Israel or with the United States.

2

Religions and World Views

SYRIA IS A country with numerous religious minorities, though the majority of its people are Sunni Muslims. Syria has been a place where both Christian and Muslim minorities have been able to survive in out of the way places. The mountains along the Mediterranean coast have protected communities of heterodox Christian and Muslims, while the desert fringes and upper Jazirah have sheltered numerous other such communities. A number of these communities owe their continued existence to the fact that they were able to find safe havens in Syria away from persecution by the authorities.

SUNNI ISLAM

The vast majority of Syrians are Sunni Muslims, between 70% to 80% of the total population including ethnic Arabs, Kurds, Turks, Circassians, and Shishans. Sunni Islam follows the order of succession from the Prophet Muhammad through the elections of the four Rightly Guided Khalifahs: Abu Bakr al-Saddiq (632–634), ʻUmar ibn al-Khattab (634–644), ʻUthman ibn ʻAffan (644–656), and ʻAli ibn Abi Talib (656–661). They accept as valid the subsequent succession of Muʻawiyah and consider both the Umayyads and the ʻAbbasids as legitimate political heirs to the Prophet. The term *sunni* means to follow the practices as set by the Prophet himself, and Sunnis form the majority of Arabs, and of Muslims, today.

There are four major *madhhab*s, or schools of thought and legal procedures, in Sunni Islam that the first arose in the eighth century. During the first few centuries of Islam the legal scholars worked more or less independent of each other, and there was no move, nor was it seen necessary to make a move, towards a more centralized, codified approach to Islamic jurisprudence. However, life in the major urban centers of Syria and more especially of Iraq encountered numerous problems not specifically covered by the Qur'an or by the sayings (*hadith*) or known and imitated actions (*sunnah*) of the Prophet. Islam encountered other cultures, Hellenistic–Roman and Persian, with well-established codes of law dealing with land, marriage, inheritance, and the like. Muslim religious scholars began the process of incorporating these with the practices from Arabia within the framework of Islam, and the strong central authority of the 'Abbasid state encouraged a more standardized legal practice. The first of these scholars to establish particular methods for legal rulings was Abu Hanifah (699–767), who lived and died in the Iraqi city of Kufah. Abu Hanifah included two other principles in Islamic jurisprudence in addition to the Qur'an, hadith, and sunnah, which are *qiyas* (analogy) and *ijma'* (scholarly consensus). He also placed emphasis on individual reasoning. Abu Hanifah's writings form the foundation of the first distinct madhhab, the Hanafi, which is named for him. Considered by many to be the most liberal of the schools, Hanafi madhhab was the official legal school of the Ottomans and is still favored among Turkish-speaking areas of Islam (Turkey and Central Asia), as well as in many of the non-Arab parts of the eastern Islamic world. Because of its association with the Ottomans, the Hanafi School is found wherever the Ottoman empire ruled, though not often that of the majority of people.

Most Syrians, like most other Sunni Arabs in the Arab east, follow the Shafi'i School founded by the scholar Muhammad ibn Idris al-Shafi'i (767–820), who died in Egypt. Like Abu Hanifah before him, al-Shafi'i included qiyas and ijma' as major sources for Islamic law along with the Qur'an, hadith, and sunnah. The difference between the two schools of thought has to do with where the actions or sayings of the Prophet seem to contradict the revealed word of God in the Qur'an. For al-Shafi'i the actions and sayings of the Prophet have to be seen in their specific contexts and where there is something that seems to contradict the Qur'an, there must also be another one that supports the Qur'an. Both the actions and sayings of the Prophet are to be considered as ways to understand the meaning of the Qur'an. Like the Qur'an, for al-Shafi'i, the sunnah of the Prophet was infallible. Al-Shafi'i also established a systematic use of analogy, giving subsequent scholars a better method of implementing analogy in legal cases. He stated that once the whole community had come to a decision (that is consensus), it was binding;

however, subsequent Shafi'i jurists would rule that only the educated scholars were capable of exercising consensus. Al-Shafi'i also stated that in order to be a good Muslim, one must know Arabic in that the religion functions in Arabic (prayers, Qur'an, etc.).

Most of North and West Africa follows the Maliki School founded by Malik ibn Anas (715–795), who died in Madinah. Malik was greatly influenced by the development of Islamic jurisprudence in Arabia rather than the more cosmopolitan Syria, Iraq, and Egypt. Malik felt that the use of reasoning should be done in light of the common good for the community as a whole. The Maliki madhhab does not have a large number of adherents in Syria, though his writings are studied along with those of Abu Hanifah and al-Shafi'i by all Syrian Islamic jurists.

The final and fourth school is that of Ahmad ibn Hanbal (780–855), which was strong in urban Syria starting in the twelfth century, and today is the main school of thought in much of the Arabian Peninsula. Ibn Hanbal rejected any consensus except those of the Companions of the Prophet, and the Hanbali School is considered to be among the most conservative of Sunni schools. The Hanbali madhhab was strengthened by the eighteenth-century reformer Muhammad ibn 'Abd al-Wahhab (1703–1792), and his form, popularly called Wahhabism, spread among many of the Bedouin tribes in the Arabian Peninsula and the Syrian Desert. It is the official form of Islam supported by the Saudi state as well as by a number of Arab Gulf states, though in a milder form than is practiced in Saudi Arabia. Some Syrian Bedouin tribes with close contact with Saudi Arabia follow the Hanbali madhhab.

While the majority of Syria's Sunni are Shafi'i, all four schools are taught in the faculties of religious sciences. This is a long-standing practice in Islamic institutions of learning, starting with the early *madrasah*s established by the Saljuqs and Ayyubids as a means to reestablish the primacy of Sunni Islam over Shi'ism starting in the late eleventh century. Traditional Islamic education began with the *kuttab* where both boys and girls were taught the basics of reading, writing, arithmetic, and memorized the Qur'an. Those boys who were seen to be especially bright were recommended to attend the next level, or the *madrasah,* where they would learn the basics of jurisprudence as well as study Arabic language, literature, astronomy, and what are called Islamic sciences. Those who demonstrated even more ability were sent to the highest level, the *jami'ah,* often associated with a major Friday mosque. In Syria the Umayyad Mosque in Damascus served as the most important of the Islamic institutions where all four schools of jurisprudence were taught. The Islamic system remained the main form of education in the Islamic world until the introduction of Western systems in the nineteenth century. The Umayyad Mosque remains an important source of Islamic training for religious scholars, but Syria's universities also provide courses in Islamic sciences. In addition, many Syrians who wish to pursue Islamic studies attend the famous al-Azhar Mosque and University in Cairo, which is the principle Islamic university for Sunnis.

Sunni scholars recognized the split between religious authority embodied in the person of the Khalifah, or successor to the Prophet Muhammad, and the person who wielded actual political authority, the Sultan (a term derived from the Arabic word *sultah* meaning political authority). When the 'Abbasids began to lose real political power to local governors and military strong men, Sunni scholars helped legitimize the change. Sunnis hold that it is better to have social and political order than to fall into chaos; thus, if a strongman can provide a stable life then he should have the support of the people, as long as he does not abuse them. While the institution of the Caliphate was supported until 1922 when Kamal Ataturk abolished the title, the person of the Khalifah had long lost any real authority. The abolition of the Caliphate had little impact on most Muslims in the world and none really in Syria.

One of the major institutions that differ between Sunni and Shi'i Islam is the position of *mufti*, or an official of the state responsible for issuing *fatwas*, or legal decisions. The mufti is chosen from among the ranks of the educated religious scholars and must be an expert in jurisprudence. Today muftis are employees of the Ministry of Religious Affairs and thus are responsible as much to the state as they are to the general Muslim population of their respective countries. While Syria is officially a secular, socialist state, the Syrian government still needs the sanction of religion. When Hafiz al-Asad became president in 1970 the mufti of the state had to issue a fatwa declaring that al-Asad, as a member of the 'Alawi minority, was a Muslim (a requirement of the Syrian constitution to be president).

SHI'ITE ISLAM

Syria has a number of different forms of Shi'ism practiced by a minority of its people. The most important in Syria is the Isma'ilis or 7ers, and its subsequent splinter group the Druze. The mainline Ithna 'Ashari, or 12er Shi'ism, does not constitute the majority of Shi'ites in Syria as it does in Lebanon and Iraq, though the 'Alawis or Nusayris claim to belong the 12er branch of Shi'ism and make up an important group in Syria. Shi'ism takes its name from the Arabic *Shi'atu 'Ali* (the Partisans of 'Ali); those who supported the succession of 'Ali ibn Abi Talib to the Khalifah, or Caliphate, against the claims by Mu'awiyah ibn Abi Sufyan, the first of the Umayyads. The Shi'ites continued to support the family of 'Ali as the only legitimate heirs to the Prophet and quickly attracted those who felt marginalized in the new

Islamic empire such as the Berbers in North Africa and the Persians in Iran. For a brief time in the tenth and early eleventh century, Shi'ism, particularly Isma'ili Shi'ism, gained popularity in Syria mainly as a means of expressing anti-'Abbasid sentiment.

Important in the discussion of Shi'ism is the role of the *Imam*. In Sunni Islam the term *imam* is used for anyone who leads prayer; being the person who stands in front, or *imam,* of the congregation. For Shi'ites, the term *Imam* has far more significance as being used only to designate the head of the Muslim community as a whole. They believe that only the descendants of 'Ali ibn Abi Talib and his wife Fatima Zahra (daughter of the Prophet Muhammad) are the legitimate leaders of the Muslim community. They do not accept the Umayyads or the 'Abbasids as legitimate and instead follow the line of Imams starting with Imam 'Ali through his sons Hasan and Hussein. Hussein died in battle in Iraq at Karbala' in 680 when he tried to challenge the Umayyads. His death is commemorated every year as a major Shi'ite ceremony of grief. Following Hussein's death, his descendants were seen as the true leaders of the Muslims in a line that ended in 878 when the twelfth and last Imam, Muhammad al-Muntazar, disappeared, most likely killed by agents of the 'Abbasids. The Ithna 'Ashari or 12ers constitute the mainstream of Shi'ites, but there are other groups who disputed the line of succession and have stopped at earlier Imams.

The Isma'ilis developed as a separate branch of Shi'ism in the eighth century when they disputed the succession to the Imamate following the death of the sixth Imam Ja'afar al-Sadiq in 765. The majority Shi'ites consider Ja'afar al-Sadiq's son Musa al-Kadhim to be the legitimate next Imam, while some feel Ja'afar's son Isma'il who died in 760 to be the legitimate successor despite the fact that he died five years before his father. Key to understanding the split is the concept of the hidden Imam; the Isma'ilis believe that Isma'il did not die and will return one day as the *Mahdi* or Expected Guide, not unlike a messiah. For mainstream 12er Shi'ites, the *Mahdi* is Muhammad al-Muntazar, whose name *al-Muntazar* means the expected one.

Little is known about the rise of the Isma'ili doctrine or about their early spread through the Islamic world. The Isma'ilis first came to attention as the Qaramitah movement that appealed to the rural population of Syria starting in the ninth century. The Isma'ilis made significant headway among the Berbers in North Africa who supported the person of 'Ubayd Allah al-Mahdi, who founded the Fatimid dynasty in Tunisia. With the rise of the Fatimids as a rival Shi'ite Caliphate to challenge the Sunni 'Abbasids in Baghdad and the Sunni Umayyads in Spain, the Isma'ilis became one of the major political movements in Islam. The Fatimids were able to conquer Egypt from the 'Abbasids and moved their capital to the newly built Cairo, or *al-Qahirah* (the Victorious), in 973. They were militarily successful as well against the 'Abbasids and the Byzantines in Syria. They controlled the greater part of Syria until the arrival of the European Crusaders at the end of the eleventh century.

The Isma'ilis had very active missionary organizations that spread their form of Shi'ism into India and present-day Pakistan. The Fatimids were successful in establishing several vassal states in the eastern Islamic world, the legacy of which lasts today with the community following the Agha Khan. A more radical branch of the Isma'ilis developed into the *Assassins,* followers of Hasan-i Sabbah, who began his activities in Iran around 1090. Hasan-i Sabbah was a mysterious figure who used *hashish* (the word *assassin* derives from the Arabic *Hashishiyin,* or users of *hashish*) as one of the means of controlling his followers. He believed in the need for political violence to protect the Isma'ili community, which was under pressure from the revival of Sunni power. His main base was at the mountain fortress at Alamut in Iran, but he established other fortresses in the Syrian mountains from which were dispatched assassins to eliminate powerful political figures of the day. In Syria the fort at Masyaf was the most important assassin stronghold presided over by Rashid al-Din Sinan (1162–1192). In a dispute with the Iranian leadership, Rashid al-Din established his independence and operated independently from Alamut. The Syrian branch was eventually destroyed by the Mamluk Sultan Baybars I, who took all of their forts by 1273.

The Isma'ilis initial success later largely collapsed with the conquest of much of North Africa by the Berber Sunni al-Murabatin and with the conquest of Iran, Iraq, and Syria by the Turkish Sunni Saljuqs in the first half of the eleventh century. The Fatimids themselves were replaced in Egypt by the Sunni Ayyubids from Syria in 1071. Despite the political collapse of the Fatimids and the reestablishment of Sunni Islam among most Syrians, some Isma'ili communities were able to survive finding refuge in the Jabal al-Ansariyah or along the western fringe of the Syrian Desert.

DRUZE

The Druze began as followers of a movement within Isma'ili Shi'ism. Now they are Syria's third largest religious minority. The Druze follow the succession of Fatimid Khalifahs to the sixth, al-Hakim (996–1021). Al-Hakim was eventually replaced as the Khalifah by an internal family coup; some say the coup was led by one of his sisters who was tired of his erratic and greatly troubling behavior. During his life time, al-Hakim had encouraged the growth of a personality cult that bordered on religious heresy, allowing himself to be proclaimed divine. His missionaries spread this newly developing doctrine in Lebanon and Syria, and the religion eventually took its name not for al-Hakim but from the name of his principle missionary, al-Darazi. Another of the missionaries, Hamza ibn 'Ali, gave the movement its final form. The Druze believe that al-Hakim was not murdered at the instigation of his family but like Isma'il before him has gone into hiding to return at some point in the future.

While the Isma'ilis hold to many of the same basic practices as other Muslims, the Druze have developed a number of major differences. The main day of worship is not Friday but Thursday. Instead of going to a mosque, worship is held in an indistinct, stark building. Most Druze are not well-versed in their religion (they are called the *juhhal,* meaning ignorant) because only initiated religious scholars (who are called the *'uqqal,* or sages) have the right to know the full scope of their belief. Due to the fact the Druze were persecuted even by the Fatimids, they have developed a number of means to survive and hide themselves among other Muslims including keeping the inner knowledge among a small, select few. What little is known about them comes from those who attack them and from a few of their sacred texts that were stolen during the religious disturbances between the Druze and Maronite Christians in 1860. Druze do not participate in the pilgrimage to Makkah nor do they fast during the month of Ramadan, but they do visit Muslim shrines, such as those to the figure Khidr. They believe there are a fixed number of souls, and one can be reincarnated in a number of ways. Those who believed in the teachings of Hamza during his lifetime are reborn as Druze—and they believe there is also a Druze community in China of such reborn souls. Druze are allowed to lie about their faith and to pose as Muslims; when they do, they usually claim to be Hanafi since Hanafi law is closest to their own beliefs about divorce and inheritance rights. The Druze have, historically been considered by both Sunnis and Shi'ites to be heretics, beyond the limits of Islam.

While the Isma'ilis lost any real political power after the fall of their forts to the Mamluks in the thirteenth century, the Druze have been able to build a relatively strong community initially centered around powerful landowning families, who are similar to feudal lords. Some of their leaders fought on the side of the Mamluks while others sided with the Ottomans at the Battle of Marj Dabiq in 1516. The leader of the Ma'ani family Amir Fakhr al-Din I sided with the Ottomans and was rewarded with the governorship of Lebanon. His descendants ruled in the name of the Ottomans until the fall of Amir Fakhr al-Din II in 1634. The Shihabi amirs were also Druze and governed much of Lebanon starting in the mid-seventeenth century until their fall with the withdrawal of the Egyptian forces in 1841. Druze leaders in the Jabal Druze and Hawran were instrumental in the success of the Arab Revolt in World War I and in the Syrian Revolt of 1925. Druze in the

Golan (Jawlan) have resisted Israeli occupation since 1967 retaining strong Syrian identities, despite the fact that in Israel Druze are considered a separate category from Arabs and are given access to greater rights as Israeli citizens than Israeli Arabs possess.

'ALAWI OR NUSAYRI

The 'Alawi or Nusayri also grew out of Shi'ism and, though no official figures exist for their numbers, they are Syria's largest religious minority. The movement first emerged in Iraq, where the founder of the religion, Muhammad ibn Nusayr al-Namiri was a supporter of the 10th Imam, 'Ali al-Hadi (868–874). Ibn Nusayr had proclaimed Imam 'Ali al-Hadi as divine and claimed himself to be the prophet which brought immediate condemnation by the Imam. When 'Ali al-Hadi died and was succeeded as Imam by his son al-Hasan al-'Askari (874–878), ibn Nusayr became his devoted follower and, according to 'Alawi traditions, al-Hasan entrusted to ibn Nusayr a new revelation that forms the basis for their religious doctrine. Ibn Nusayr briefly had the support of an important minister of state in the Baghdad court, but the radical nature of the new doctrine was not generally approved by Shi'ite or Sunni scholars.

The movement seems to have attracted some of the ethnic Persians in Iraq who introduced some ancient Persian customs into the religion such as Persian New Year, or *Naw Ruz,* and the autumn equinox festival of *Mihrgan,* which the 'Alawis celebrate as the days when 'Ali ibn Abi Talib's divine nature is changed into the sun. The movement was brought to Syria in the tenth century by Abu 'Abdallah al-Hussein ibn Hamdan al-Khasibi, a poet of his day who had worked in the courts of the Buwayhids in Baghdad and the Hamdanids in Aleppo. He died in Aleppo in 957, and his tomb is venerated by the 'Alawis today. Local missionary activities continued, and the rulers of al-Ladhikiyah, then briefly under Byzantine rule, were among those who converted. During most of the Crusader period the 'Alawi area was ruled, at least nominally, by the Principality of Antioch.

The 'Alawis and the Isma'ilis lived in much the same region, and conflicts emerged between them. Several councils were held by the two communities to resolve the conflict over land, but no concrete solutions were concluded. When the Mamluks conquered Jabal al-Ansariyah, they attempted to force Sunni Islam on the inhabitants, but they were unsuccessful. The famous Syrian Hanbali scholar ibn Taymiyah (1268–1328) issued a *fatwa* condemning the 'Alawi as heretics and allowing war against them.

The 'Alawi were subject to active persecution by the Mamluks but the Ottomans took a less aggressive stance and eased persecution. Initially the

Ottomans allowed the 'Alawis to be governed by four local lords subject to the Pasha of Tripoli (Tarabulus al-Sham in today's Lebanon). In later Ottoman times, the 'Alawi were governed by the *Mutasarrif*, or District Officer of Safita. In the second half of the nineteenth century the Ottomans gained direct control over the region and broke the power of the local 'Alawi tribes. In the twentieth century the 'Alawi were able to have themselves recognized as part of the 12er Shi'ite community due to the writings of one of their number, Muhammad Amin Ghalib al-Tawil, whose *History of the 'Alawi* helped dispel many of the popular misconceptions about their beliefs.

'Alawi beliefs, however, do differ from the mainstream 12er Shi'ites in a number of important ways. They appear to be greatly influenced not only by the pre-Islamic Persian religion but also by Christianity and Gnosticism. A number of biblical prophets, early Christian saints (including St. Peter), and 11 Imams are considered to be manifestations of the divine. 'Ali ibn Abi Talib is held to be the eternal God; the belief from which their name 'Alawi derives. They believe that the 11th Imam told ibn Nusayr his secret revelations, and ibn Nusayr subsequently was able to transcend this world becoming a star. Women are believed to be born in the devil's sin and are not allowed to attend 'Alawi religious gatherings. Today 'Alawi follow the Ja'afari madhhab, or legal code used by the mainstream 12er Shi'ites. Nonetheless, for many Muslims, the 'Alawi remain beyond the pale of Islam.

In post-independence Syria all three Muslim minorities, the Isma'ilis, the Druze, and the 'Alawi, have embraced the secular ideology and strong Arab nationalism of the Ba'ath party. For many from these groups, emphasis on a national identity regardless of religion appeals to them. Opportunities have opened up for them, particularly in government and in the military, that historically had been closed. When Hafiz al-Asad took power in 1970 he became the first 'Alawi to become the head of state and break the control of the Sunni elite; however, in order for him to remain President of the Republic, the Mufti of the State (who is always a Sunni) had to issue a fatwa stating that the 'Alawi are indeed a branch of 12er Shi'ism, and that Hafiz al-Asad was in fact a Muslim and able to remain in office. Today the 'Alawi dominate the officer corps in the military.

YAZIDI

The Yazidis form a very small group among mainly the Kurds in northern Iraq and Syria, numbering only a few thousand in total. They most likely are another Isma'ili splinter group, though little is known about their founder, Shaykh 'Adi ibn Musafir, who lived in the twelfth or thirteenth century (there are several dates for his death including dates in the eighth century). He is buried near Mosul in Iraq. The Yazidis call themselves *Dawasin* or *Dasnayi*, and the term *Yazidi* appears to be one of abuse first applied to them by 12er Shi'ites (in connection with the Umayyad Khalifah Yazid, who ordered the death of Imam Hussein).

The Yazidis are dualists and are usually accused by others of being devil worshippers due to the deep fear and respect they show to the devil, whom they call the Peacock Angel. They believe that evil is as much a part of divinity as is good, and people should demonstrate their respect for the force of evil as much as for the force of good. Yazidis appear in the first few opening scenes of the first *Exorcist* film as the Catholic priest realizes his archeological excavations have released the devil. Yazidis practice certain food taboos much to the amusement of their neighbors, such as not eating lettuce. The food taboos are a possible clue to the Manichean influence since it also subscribed to similar food restrictions. Among the popular beliefs held about the Yazidis by their neighbors is that they avoid pronouncing the Arabic letter *shin* because the Arabic word for devil *shaytan* begins with the letter. They are most likely influenced most by Manicheism (one of the pre-Islamic religions popular in Iraq) and Gnosticism.

SUFISM: ISLAMIC MYSTICISM

Islamic mysticism is called Sufism from the Arabic word *suf,* meaning wool. Supposedly the early mystics wore rough woolen clothes as a sign of their piety and austere life style. Sufism began in the early decades of Islam; some Sufis claim that Salman al-Farisi, a companion of the Prophet, was one of the first mystics. Early Sufis were, perhaps, greatly influenced by the monastic practices of Syrian and Egyptian monks who sought solitude in the desert or remote places.

Islamic mystics seek a more personalized contact with God and have developed a number of methods to reach this state of being. The different methods are called *Tariqah* (plural *Turuq*), often translated as Brotherhood, and through time a hierarchy arose within each of the Tariqahs based on the levels of understanding a person can achieve. Among the first of the Brotherhoods to emerge was the Qadiri founded by 'Abd al-Qadir al-Jilani (1077–1166), who is buried in Iraq. The Qadiri subsequently became one of the most important of the Sufi Tariqahs throughout the entire Islamic world. A number of local sub branches have subsequently been developed each with its own name from the person who founded them. In the pre-modern period many Sufi Turuq also served as craft guilds combining movement up through the ranks of both their knowledge of Sufism and in their skills. Sufi practices include what is called a *dhikr,* meaning to remember where, depending on the methods used, those attending mention God and the Prophet Muhammad. Some Turuq do this through music and ecstatic dance or trance, while others do it through quiet contemplation or reading religious texts.

Several major Sufi Turuq were well established in Syria during the Mamluk and Ottoman periods. Sufis were supported by both states that provided places for Sufi ascetics to live and study called *khanqa* or *takiyah* in the major urban centers such as Damascus, Homs, and Aleppo. Among the major Turuq in Syria were the Mawlawi or Mevlevi and the Naqshabandi in addition to the Qadiri. The Mawlawi was founded by Jalal al-Din Rumi (1207–1273), who is buried in Turkey, while the Naqshabani was founded by Muhammad Baha al-Din al-Naqshabani (1318–1389) in Central Asia. Both spread to Syria during the Ottoman period. The Mawlawi are popularly called the "Whirling Dervishes" from their practice of spinning/dancing during their dhikr. The Naqshabani dhikr rarely involves more than reading religious texts followed by discussion.

Sufism lost a good deal of popular support following Syrian independence, and some of the subsequent regimes have been openly hostile to Sufi Turuq. Seen as a major competition for the heart and minds of the people, more secular political parties have been very hostile to them. Some have also thought that the Sufis have been fronts for other religious organizations, such as the Muslim Brotherhood, which was banned for a number of years. With independence, a greater degree of control was exercised by the state over sources of income, such as property, for religious organizations, making it difficult for many of the Sufi Brotherhoods to survive. In much of Syria, Sufism suffered a good deal; nonetheless, it has survived and for the past several decades has been on the rise again. More friendly state policies have helped. Syrian Sufi groups such as the Mawlawi have participated in international music festivals; their instrumental and vocal music being well known on the international level.

ISLAMIC HOLIDAYS

For the majority of Syria's Muslims, whether Sunni or Shi'ite, the main Islamic holidays are celebrated. Sunnis as well as 7er and 12er Shi'ites follow the Islamic calendar, fast the month of Ramadan, and make the pilgrimage to Makkah at least once in their lifetime. They all subscribe to the Five Pillars of Faith (the *Shahadah*, or profession of faith; *Salat*, or five daily prayers; *Siyam*, or fast the month of Ramadan; *Zakkat*, or payment of the poor tax; and *Haj*, or pilgrimage to Makkah), and the differences between them are more about details and not in the main beliefs or spirit of the religion.

The Islamic calendar is based on lunar cycles of 28 to 30 days per month, and as such the months are not fixed in the way solar months are. The Islamic month moves forward into the solar calendar by approximately two weeks each year and in a 30-year period has passed through the entire solar year. The beginning of each new month is marked by the new moon, and for important celebrations such as the start and end of the month of Ramadan, the new moon must be sighted and reported. In the past it was possible to have different communities begin and end the month on different days depending on the ability of the responsible local person to sight the moon. Today Syrian state's religious officials have access to scientific data that allows them to know well in advance when the month will begin and end, but the official announcement is still made on television during the evening news the night the moon is sighted.

Ramadan and 'Id al-Fitr

Ramadan is the ninth month in the Islamic calendar and is a month of fasting; no food or drink may pass the lips of the faster from dawn to dusk. The day's fast is announced in most Syrian cities by a cannon, an Ottoman innovation that most Arab countries have continued. When Ramadan occurs in the summer, many people suffer from the lack of water and those addicted to tobacco or coffee often have bad tempers, though fights that occur during Ramadan negate the fast. The purpose of the fast is for all Muslims to better understand the privations faced by the poor all year round and encourage them to be generous when asked to pay *Zakkat*. In addition, the first revelations of the Qur'an came to the Prophet during Ramadan.

The end of the day's fast is also announced by a blast from a cannon, and people are allowed to eat and drink again. In Syria, those who hold to the *sunnah* of the Prophet break their fast with milk and dates and then pray the *maghrib*, or sunset prayer. Most Syrians though break their fast with a sumptuous feast called *iftar*, meaning simply breakfast. Most everyone begins by drinking a very sweet apricot drink called *Qamar al-Din*, which means Moon of the Religion, in reference to the lunar based Islamic month of Ramadan. *Qamar al-Din* is made from an apricot paste that is rolled out into thin sheets. The sheets are soaked in water until they dissolve making a thick sweet drink that helps to quickly restore energy to the fasters. Ramadan is a month of special sweets not usually eaten at other times of year, such as *qatayif, zalabiyah,* and *mushabbak*. All three of these are pastries deep fried and covered with a rose or orange water and sugar syrup. *Qatayif* is stuffed with nuts or *malban* (Turkish delight).

The first week of Ramadan most people stay at home after breaking the fast on home cooked meals but starting in the second week many people go out to restaurants and hotels that offer massive Ramadan buffets. These have become popular with many urban Syrians, who may go from one such buffet to another during the course of the month tasting the different dishes available. Some of the more up-scale establishments have initiated "Ramadan Nights," including live groups playing classical Arabic music and following the iftar with coffeehouse like services such as tea, coffee, different forms of entertainment, and water pipes with flavored tobaccos. A feature of many urban neighborhoods is special tents or areas set up to serve iftar to the poor. These are called *Ma'idat al-Rahman,* or Tables of Mercy, that are financed and supplied by either private wealthy individuals or by mosques.

Following iftar many stores reopen, and the streets of Syria's cities are filled with shoppers and people enjoying the festive atmosphere created by the holiday lights decorating shop fronts. Those who are more religious attend the night or *'ishiyah* prayer, which in Ramadan is followed by an extra prayer called *tarawih.* In the hour just before dawn people eat a light meal called *suhur* in preparation for the day's fast. The meal needs to be consumed before the dawn prayer and today newspapers publish *msak,* the time when food can no longer be consumed. In the past each neighborhood used to have a person called a *masaharti,* who would walk around banging on a drum and announcing that people should wake to eat *suhur.* Few neighborhoods still employ a *masaharti,* and it is more likely local teenage boys will go around making a tremendous noise beating on metal pots and pans in great sport to make sure everyone is awake.

The twenty-seventh day of Ramadan is called *Laylat al-Qadir,* or the Night of Power, marking when the Qur'an was first revealed to the Prophet Muhammad. Prayers offered in a mosque that night are believed to have special power because, as mentioned in the Qur'an "Laylat al-Qadir is better than 1,000 months and on this night the angels and the spirit of grace descend to settle all affairs" (*Surah 97 al-Qadir*). Men and boys spend the entire night in prayer and contemplation in mosques throughout Syria and the Islamic world. Syrian television devotes the night's program to broadcasting the activities at the main mosque in Makkah.

'Id al-Fitr (meaning the celebration to break the fast) or *'Id al-Saghir* (meaning the small celebration) marks the end of Ramadan and people celebrate it by eating a morning meal that usually includes a special short bread called *ka'k.* Ka'k is made with almond flour and is not very sweet. All males attend a special 'Id prayer held in local mosques or large open areas. The prayer is followed by the special 'Id breakfast of ka'k. Zakkat is collected after the prayer, though in Syria, like many Muslim countries, this is done through special offices attached to mosques and administered by the Ministry of Religious Affairs. In Syria official offices and many stores are closed

for three days to mark the 'Id. During this time people exchange visits and usually children are given gifts of new clothes. Like holiday time in the United States, the 'Id marks a time when many new films are released to the cinemas, and one of the newer Ramadan customs is for children and teens to go to the movies especially during the first afternoon of the 'Id. Some cities may set up carnivals offering rides and games to entertain children and young people.

Haj and 'Id al-Adha

The most important holiday in Islam is the feast that marks the end of the Haj, or pilgrimage to Makkah. The Haj takes place during the first 10 days of the twelfth month in the Islamic calendar, called *Dhu al-Hijjah,* meaning the Month of Pilgrimage. Many Muslims today try to be in Makkah or Madinah starting in Ramadan and stay there until after the end of 'Id al-Adha. The Haj requires a number of set rituals all pilgrims are to perform on specific days in Makkah and in nearby Mina, Muzdalifah, and Jabal 'Arafat before returning to Makkah to finalize it. Syrian television carries live reporting from the pilgrimage sites carrying interviews with Syrian pilgrims and with Saudi officials managing the movement of people.

'Id al-Adha (celebration of the sacrifice) or *'Id al-Kabir* (the big celebration) is celebrated on the tenth of *Dhu al-Hijjah* and commemorates Ibrahim's (Abraham's) willingness to follow the commands of God and sacrifice his son Isma'il (Ishmael) in the Islamic tradition (Isaac in the Jewish and Christian traditions). God sends the angel Jibra'il (Gabriel) to stay Ibrahim's hand and substitutes a lamb, which Ibrahim then sacrifices. The sacrifice is yearly re-enacted by all Muslim families who slaughter a sheep on the *'Id* day. Similar to *'Id al-Fitr,* the day begins with a special communal prayer held in an area large enough to hold the whole community after which heads of households slaughter a sheep. Part of the sheep is consumed on the day while part is put away to be preserved (in the past as a dried meat), while the remainder is to be donated to the poor who can not afford to buy a sheep.

Like *'Id al-Fitr, 'Id al-Adha* is a three-day holiday in Syria with all official offices and most businesses closed. Syrians use the days for visits to friends and family and feasting on roast lamb. Some shops may open on the second day and by the third day many have reopened for holiday shoppers. Restaurants and coffeehouses do a brisk business on the second and third days, though many may be closed on the first day of the *'Id.*

Mawlid al-Nabi

Mawlid al-Nabi, or the Prophet's Birthday, falls on the twelfth day of *Rabi' al-Awwal,* the third month of the Islamic calendar. The celebration of the

Prophet's birthday began in Fatimid Egypt perhaps in response the colorful celebrations of the Christian Copts for the birth of Jesus. The *Mawlid al-Nabi* spread from Egypt to other areas under Egyptian political or cultural influence, and in 1588 the Ottoman Sultan Murad III made it an official Ottoman celebration. In Syria, the day is marked as an official holiday, and all government offices and many businesses are closed. Little else is done to mark the day.

OTHER ISLAMIC CELEBRATIONS

The only other Islamic celebration marked by any official day off is *Ra's al-Sannah,* or Islamic New Year, that falls on the first day of the first Islamic month, *Muharram.* Little is done for the day other than it is a day off from work or school. The idea of taking the first day of the new year is a Western influence and very recent. For some religious scholars, it is close to *bida'* (an innovation of a type forbidden by Islam).

'Ashurah, the tenth day of *Muharram,* is not an official holiday in Syria, and there are major differences between how Sunnis and Shi'ites mark the day. For Sunnis, the day is one that follows the *sunnah* of the Prophet who observed it as an optional fast day, perhaps a borrowing from the Jewish Day of Atonement. *'Ashurah* has become more for children who traditionally would go from house to house singing. They would be given sweets, candies, and money by each house—something akin to a cross between Halloween and Christmas caroling—but the practice is rarely done now.

For Shi'ites the day is one of deep mourning for the death of Imam Hussein at Karbala' and historically was introduced as a public observance by the Buwayhids in the tenth century. The Shi'ites fast the day before (the ninth) and on the tenth hold parades where they manifest their deep grief by self mortification with chains, knives, or fists. Such public displays have often been banned by Sunni governments. In Syria, where Shi'ites are a minority, the Sunnis have generally not approved of such behavior in public. There are also plays where the death of Imam Hussein is reenacted much like a passion play. In villages where Shi'ites are the majority, such plays are often held out of doors while in urban centers, such as Damascus or Aleppo where Sunnis are the majority, the plays are held in special buildings sometimes called *Husayniyah*s.

CHRISTIAN COMMUNITIES

Christians of various denominations comprise between 10% and 13% of Syria's population; making them as a group the second largest religious minority in the country. The majority of them are ethnic Arabs, though the Armenians are a significant group who are their own ethnicity speaking their own language as well as having their own church. Syria's numerous Christian communities include some of the oldest that still exist and include those who fall under the Pope of Rome and those under the Patriarch of the Orthodox Church, while others have their own hierarchy independent of the main churches. Syria has been a place where Christian groups have been able to survive just as it has been for various heterodox Muslim communities.

During the early centuries of Christianity questions about the nature, body, and will of God, Jesus, and Mary resulted in numerous debates. Eventually the Byzantine Emperor had to become involved and judge the debates selecting the party that best presented its case, which then became the so-called official doctrine of the state. Those who did not agree with the outcome were persecuted, and their priests were replaced by those who followed the official line. The outcome of one set of debates could be overturned in another, thus, those seeking to escape official control sought refugee in the out of the way places found in Syria. The arrival of the Muslims in the seventh century helped guarantee their continued existence. As long as Christians paid their taxes, the Muslim state did not interfere in their affairs. Under the Ottomans this policy was solidified into what was called the *millet* system; each religious community was recognized by the state, and a particular person was designated to be responsible for them to state authorities.

The largest Christian church in Syria is the Eastern Orthodox. They are sometimes called the Malikites from the Arabic term *malaki*, or royal; those who followed the official church doctrines supported by the Byzantine Emperor and the Patriarch of Constantinople. When Constantinople fell to the Ottomans is 1453, the Byzantine Empire ceased to exist, but the Patriarch of the Orthodox Church remained and remains in Istanbul yet today. In Syria, the Patriarch of Damascus, whose seat is at the Monastery at Sidnaya, is the most important official of the Orthodox Church in the country and is the head of the Orthodox community. In the nineteenth century the Arabic-speaking Orthodox Church gained a good deal of control over their own affairs being able to be sure priests were Arabic speaking and that the services were also in Arabic. The assertion of local control of their church is seen as the first victory of the Arab revival, and Orthodox Christians have been part of the Arab Nationalist movement from its inception.

There are a number of small Christian Churches in Syria with historical links to the Orthodox Church but who broke away in the centuries before the arrival of Islam. These are mainly Monophysite, believing that Christ had only a divine nature, including the Syriac or Assyrian Church (sometimes called the Jacobites) and the Nestorians. They challenged the official declaration following the Council of Chalcedon in 451, and they finally split from the main body of Christianity by 600. These Churches have small followings in the country located mainly in the upper Jazirah. At one point Nestorians had a fairly large following with vigorous missionary activities in the Sasanian Empire reaching into Central Asia, China, and India. They had a favored position in the Sasanian court and much later held again a favored position with Mongol leader Hülegü Khan, whose wife was a Nestorian. There are a few Syriac or Assyrian Christians in Syria, but the Church has its largest congregations in Iraq, and now in the United States. The Assyrian Church is one of the oldest Christian communities in the world and their church leadership has good relations with the Armenian Church. Both the Nestorian and the Assyrian Churches have maintained the Syriac language in their liturgies.

Some eastern Christian Churches placed themselves under the protection of the Pope of Rome in disputes with the Greek Orthodox hierarchy. These are referred to as Uniate Churches; they follow the Catholic Pope but have kept their own liturgies. Many of these add the word *Catholic* to their official designations in order to distinguish themselves from those who are still part of the Eastern Church. The Maronites are among those who have joined the Roman Catholic Church, but they have maintained their own liturgies and practices. The Maronite Church takes its name from Mar Maron or St. Maron, who died around the year 410. From the start they were a problematic community, and his followers were persecuted by the Byzantines. They fled to Mount Lebanon, which remains their heartland. The Maronites were among the few eastern Christians who welcomed the Crusaders, and they forged strong ties with the French in particular which last till today.

The Armenians are Monophysites and are both an ethnic and religious minority in Syria. They have been part of the general Syrian population for generations; major Syrian cities such as Damascus and Aleppo have Armenian Quarters as distinct districts from the Christian Quarters. These districts date as far back as the early Islamic period. The Armenians have maintained their own language, music, foods, and even clothes worn on special occasions. The Armenian Church is broken into two branches: the older Orthodox Church, which is in communion with the Copts of Egypt and the Assyrians; and the Armenian Catholics with ties to Rome. The majority of Syrian Armenians are Armenian Orthodox. The Armenians claim to be the oldest Christian church since their king was the first monarch to accept Christianity as the official religion for the state and people, well before the year 300.

There are a number of other very small Christian groups in Syria including western Protestants. The Protestants are mainly converts from other Christian groups as a result of missionary work starting in the second half of the nineteenth century. Many of the missionaries were American or British who helped establish the first secular schools in Syria, Lebanon, and Palestine. While they were successful in getting a few converts, their numbers remain very small and when counted together with the Maronites, Assyrians, and Nestorians amount to less than 1% of the total population.

CHRISTIAN HOLIDAYS

Eastern Christians have a number of holy days, many of which require fasting or partial fasting on the part of the believer. Christmas and Easter are preceded by long fasts and partial fasts (over a month) prohibiting consumption of meat or animal products including milk. The result is that many Syrian Christians have developed a wide variety of vegetarian dishes. Most Christian holiday meals are heavy with meat, poultry, and fish, making up for the long periods when they could not be eaten.

Officially Syria recognizes the Eastern Christian Christmas celebrated on January 7. On the night of January 6, many churches have mass, which is broadcast on Syrian television. Government officials including the Mufti often attend, though the President does not. Government offices and most business do not close for the day, but businesses owned by Orthodox Christians are, and Christian employees are allowed to take the day off with no penalty. Those Syrians who celebrate Christmas according to the Western calendar are allowed to take the day, and often Syrian TV broadcasts parts of several different services. The day is thus marked, and those Syrians who belong to Western Christian Churches are allowed to take the day off.

Easter is also celebrated according to the Eastern calendar but again it is not an official holiday; government offices and most business are not closed. Syria's Christians are allowed to take the day, and most attend a midnight mass on the eve of Easter and another mass on Easter day. Easter, like Christmas, is proceeded by a fast or Lenten period that prohibits consumption of most meats (including poultry and fish) and, for some Eastern Christians, even milk and milk products are prohibited. Easter day Christians celebrate with a major feast following a high mass that lasts several hours.

Christians have a number of important Saints' Days. They also celebrate the days associated with the Virgin Mary such as the Feast of the Assumption. Many of the Syria's monasteries, such as the Monastery of St. George at Humayrah (which according to local history was built in the sixth century), have special days associated with them. St. George is a widely revered figure in Syria, Lebanon, Palestine, and even Jordan, who may have been a pre-Christian god or demi god, though he is also considered to be one of the early Christian martyrs. Within Islam, George is associated with al-Khidr Abu al-'Abbas mentioned in the Qur'an, and often Muslims and Christians

visit the same shrines. The Monastery of St. George celebrates the Feast of
St. George on the May 6 and for the Elevation of the Holy Cross on the
September 14. The Monastery is crowded with visitors on those days and
many come days in advance from not only all over Syria but from other Arab
and non Arab countries staying in the rooms the monastery has set aside to
accommodate visitors. Similarly, the Christian town of Ma'alula celebrates
the Feast of St. Tekla on September 22 and St. Sarkis on October 7. The
Church St. Sarkis contains one of the oldest Christian alters made originally
with the drain, a feature of pre-Christian altars to allow blood from an animal
sacrifice to drain off of the altar top. The door of the Church of St. Sarkis is
both narrow and short to prevent cavalrymen from riding into the building.
A number of Syria's older churches have this feature, which is a reminder of
the conflict many Syrian Christian communities had with the Byzantines.

JUDAISM

Judaism has a long history in Syria, which is sadly coming to an end. Syria's
cities have had Jewish populations since at least late antiquity. The synagogue
in the Hellenistic-Roman city of Dura Europos dating from the first centuries A.D. is one of the most interesting ever uncovered by archeology and
is the only synagogue known where Hellenistic humanist art decorated its
walls. The frescos are preserved in the Dura Europos wing of the National
Museum in Damascus.

Jews were an important part of Syria's urban merchant class during the
Islamic periods though they were never a very large minority. Syria, like
other parts of the Arab world, took in Jews fleeing persecution in Europe.
The Ottomans welcomed Jews expelled from Spain, Portugal, Italy, and
other parts of Europe. Syria's Jews played a role in the development of Jewish
mysticism, or the Kabbala, whose major figure, Shabbetai Zvi (1626–1676),
lived in the Ottoman Empire. Safad in Palestine became the major center
for the study of the Kabbala. Syria, like much of the Arab East, was also
where both Rabbinism and its rival Karaism were embraced by the Jewish
communities. Damascus was one of the major centers for Karaism, which
does not differ that much from the Rabbinical tradition, though it operates
with a different calendar and does have somewhat different set of religious
laws. Syrian Jews belonged to different liturgical rites as well; most of them
follow what is called the Babylonian Rite, while the rest follow the Palestinian Rite. Certain Jewish communities maintained Aramaic as their daily language much like the Christians of Ma'alula. During the nineteenth century
the Ottomans gave Jews and Christians equal rights with Muslims as part
of the *Tanzimat*, or Reform movement. However, large numbers of Syrian

Jews left for Latin America in the second half of the nineteenth century as a result of the collapse of much of Syria's economy due to the opening of the Suez Canal. The period between the two world wars saw the beginnings of popular anti-Zionist agitation in Syria due to events in Palestine, and by independence, only some 30,000 Jews were left, mainly in Aleppo and Damascus. Following the establishment of Israel in 1948, conditions for Syria's Jews deteriorated, and they were placed under restrictions. Certain jobs in government, the police, and the military were not open to them. While they were allowed to leave the country, Syrian governments tried to prevent them from going to Israel. If they were able to get visas for Western countries such as France, Canada, or the United States, they were allowed to leave.

Syria's Jews were concentrated mainly in Damascus and Aleppo, and some of the families had long been involved in certain crafts such making as silver inlaid brass trays, boxes, and tables. Syrian Jews have also been traditionally studied medicine or other professional degrees. During the decades of the 1970s to the 1990s Syria's Jews enjoyed a degree of improved official treatment (there were still reports of harassment that the government did not prevent), though they were not allowed to serve in the military or top government positions. As part of the post–Gulf War agreements, Syria eased regulations about emigration, and most of its remaining 5,000 Jews left for Europe, Canada, and the United States. The small numbers who remain are all that is left of a long history stretching back more than two thousand years of cohabitation with other religious groups in Syria.

POPULAR RELIGION IN SYRIA

Popular expressions of religion are often shared between Syria's different religious communities. Sunnis, Shi'ites, Druze, 'Alawis, and Christians often make visitations to the same shrines and venerate the same figures. All of Syria's religious communities share common beliefs such as in the evil eye or, more correctly, the eye of envy. Some of the expressions of such popular beliefs may connect Muslims and Christians with pre-Islamic practices.

A widely held popular practice is what is called a visitation, or *ziyarah*, to the tomb/shrine of a religious personage. These may be located inside a city or town or can be in an isolated spot far from any settlement. As noted before, some of these are shared between the different religious communities who come seeking the assistance of the person buried in the tomb, such as that of John the Baptist located in Damascus's most important mosque, the Umayyad Mosque. Sunni Islam officially does not sanction such actions since no one can act as an intermediary between a believer and God; however, many Sunnis make such visits. The tombs/shrines visited are of men and women who while they were living were known for their piety and for having God's blessings, or *barakah,* that they are able to pass on to those who come to see them, even after death. People come to ask for their blessings or to ask that they intercede on their behalf. Such popular beliefs are more common among women than men. Women having difficulties with husbands or children come and often make promises or vows sealed by leaving a padlock on the grillwork of the tomb. When the vow has been fulfilled, she returns and unlocks the padlock and takes it with her. Some may leave a personal item at the tomb or tie a ribbon either on the tomb or on a tree located near the tomb again as a symbol of the bond that ties the woman and her promise to the person buried in the tomb.

Many Christian monasteries in Syria contain the tombs of saints who are visited the year round, but many also have their own special days when the community will venerate the saint's icon or relics. The main Orthodox church in Homs is said to have among its relics the robe of the Virgin Mary, which is the focus of a good deal of special veneration. Again, women come to ask help of the Virgin making vows and promises.

Some Christian churches are believed to have miraculous icons and relics that can cure people of physical and mental illnesses. For example, a small church located the far northeast of the country near the border with Turkey is reported to have an image of Jesus appear on the wall that weeps a holy oil. According to the local priest, this oil has defied all attempts by scientific investigation to identify it. The oil is used to cure a wide range of illnesses both as a topical agent or as an ingested curative. Such sites might be visited by Muslim women as much as Christian women.

A common belief held throughout the Mediterranean is the belief in the evil eye, or more properly the eye of envy. Children, especially babies, are susceptible to the forces of envy and are protected by charms placed on cradles or pinned to their clothes. These charms may be a blue bead or blue piece of glass with an eye painted on it; small beaded triangles with geometric designs; small, flat, circular or square pieces of silver with the Qur'anic inscription for Muslims and the picture of a the Virgin Mary or a saint for Christians; or a piece of animal tooth, ivory, or coral-encased silver. In rural areas boys may be dressed as girls until they reach the age of six or seven and even have their ears pierced in order to "fool" the eye into thinking the boy is a "less valuable" girl. Children, or for that mater anyone or thing in a house, should not be admired without first invoking the name of God by saying something like "*Ma Sha' Allah*" or "What God wills," as a precaution against the evil eye.

There is a strong belief in spirits and *jinn,* or genies, which can be both good or bad; the *jinn* are mentioned in the Qur'an as one of God's creations, which all Muslims believe in along with angels. Women are more prone to the actions of these spirits since they frequently are associated with water and water sources, the home of many spirits. Women traditionally both fetch and use water in cleaning and cooking and are the ones who dispose of used water by throwing it down the toilet. Bathrooms are also popular haunts for such spirits to linger near; when angered by the action of an unweary woman, the spirits may decide to possess her. Spirit possession is dealt with by experts, often other women, who know how to contact spirits and interpret what they want or why they are angry. Such beliefs are less commonly held today, but once were rather frequent occurrences for women in unhappy marriages.

Other popular beliefs include numerology, where numerical value of letters can be used for magic. In many Syrian cities street numbers are decided by numerology as much or even more than by a systematic counting of buildings. It is difficult to use the numbers on buildings to try to find an address since what is posted on the wall may be a number selected by an expert in numerology rather than the assigned number. There are lucky and unlucky numbers, and no one wants to live in a building with an unlucky number. Such beliefs are cultural and are shared by all religions.

CONCLUSION

Syria is a country that historically has given refuge to a wide range of religions. As such, the country is host to a number of relatively important minorities, which altogether make up around 25% of the total population. Some of the minority groups, such as the Orthodox Christians, Isma'ilis, Druze, and 'Alawis, have been attracted to the nationalist ideology of the Arab Ba'ath Party, which has given them important places in government. The secular nature of the Ba ath party has reduced the importance of being a member of a specific religious community, especially that of the majority Sunni Muslims.

Religion does play a role in the identity of Syrians and has a wide-ranging influence over issues such as marriage. Interfaith marriages are still not common, and some of Syria's minority communities do not allow marriage outside of their faith. Though the state pushes a secular agenda, many Syrians are religious and perhaps are becoming more so. Muslim women are increasingly wearing the veil, despite the fact that the government frowns on such overt religious symbols and in some cases if women employees of a state agency wear the veil, they get penalized with a reduction in their salaries.

Syrian popular expressions of religion are an interesting mix of faiths bringing together pre-Christian, Christian, and Muslim practices. Cross-confessional vows and visitations are common, especially among women. At any shrine in the country it would be difficult to pick out Muslim, Christian, Druze, or 'Alawi women from among those visiting it on any one day. Such cross-confessional practices can be seen as one of the strengths of Syrian society, and while there have been dark days of religious persecution, cohabitation has been the greater historical experience.

3

Literature and Media

SYRIA HAS LONG been a center of literature from antiquity to the present. Some of the oldest literature in world has been uncovered during archeological excavations in places such as Ebla, Mari, and Ugarit. During the Hellenistic and Roman periods Syrian schools such as those in Antioch were among the most important of the time and were among the last of the classic schools to be closed by the Byzantines. Syria's position as a center for literature became even more important during the Islamic era; the political, social, and economic elite of Damascus and Aleppo were major patrons of poets and writers. Syrians are very proud of the place their country has played in the revival of Arabic literature, which started in the nineteenth century as part of what is called the Arab Awakening, and Syrians were involved with starting Arabic language newspapers and magazines, even if they worked in places like Cairo or Paris.

PRE-ISLAMIC LITERATURE

Syria produced some of oldest literary texts known to man. Excavations at the numerous tells that dot Syria, especially in the north, have uncovered massive numbers of texts including religious narratives written with a dramatic flare. Archeologists working at Mari, Ebla, and Ugarit have uncovered massive libraries with texts in a number of ancient languages, but perhaps the most significant are those written in Semitic languages, among the oldest texts written in a Semitic language to have ever been discovered. The scribes in Ugarit improved the rather cumbersome cuneiform script into an alphabet, the world's first, which made it much easier to learn to both read and write. Some of the oldest dictionaries have also been uncovered with word lists from other languages such as Sumerian with the local Semitic translations.

Syria's urban elite remained among the most sophisticated in the ancient world and with the conquest by Alexander the Great, Syrians soon developed important schools of philosophy and classical learning able to rival those of Athens and Alexandria. Antioch was the capital of Hellenistic Syria, and its school was among the last of the great so-called pagan schools to be closed by order of the Byzantine Emperor. The influence of the eastern schools is well attested to with the popularity of Gnosticism among the early Christians in Syria; Gnosticism is based as much on Hellenistic reason and philosophy as on the Gospels. The debates between the Gnostics, Monophysites, and Eastern Orthodox was the last great outpouring of Hellenistic thought in the East, but, because the Gnostics were suppressed by the Byzantines, little remains of the texts today. However, over the past several decades some Gnostic writings have surfaced in antique bookshops in Aleppo (the texts had been used in the bindings of other Christian books) and in a farmer's field in Upper Egypt, but it seems that most of their writings have disappeared or were destroyed. Among the most famous of the late antiquity thinkers was St. John Chrysotom, or the Golden Tongue. He was educated in the classical school in Antioch but used his knowledge to promote Christianity. He is truly the last thinker of the classical Hellenistic period in Syria.

CLASSICAL ARABIC LITERATURE

Syria played a major role in the development of classical Arabic literature; Syrians have contributed to all of the major branches of classical Arabic literature including the Islamic sciences (religion and law), histories, biographies, narratives, and poetry. Both Damascus and Aleppo were important centers of high culture and learning. In the early Islamic period poetry remained the highest expression of Arabic literature; a legacy of the pre-Islamic Arabs who developed poetry into a high art form. Bedouin poetry was divided into several major types, but most important here are long epic poems, or *qasidah*s, and satire, or *hija'*. Epic poems follow a set format describing a desert journey, pride in the beauty and strength of the author's horse or camel, the fine qualities of his own tribe or an attack on an enemy tribe's lack of such qualities, and the longing for his lover. Satirical poems often poked fun at specific people and their tribe using humor.

The most important of the poets from the Umayyad Period are all of Bedouin origin who followed the patterns and models developed in Arabia. The three famous names are al-Akhtal, al-Farazdaq, and Jarir, who all found royal patronage at the court in Damascus and who engaged in verbal duels, considered yet today the finest satires ever produced in Arabic. All three were born sometime around 640 and died between 710 and 730. Ghiyath ibn Ghawth al-Salt al-Akhtal was a Monophysite Christian of the Taghlib Arab tribe that was well established in Syria before the arrival of Islam. Al-Akhtal never converted to Islam, but still found favor in the courts of many of the Umayyad Khalifahs. Al-Akhtal's satirical attacks on the Bani Kulayb poet, Jarir, was supported by al-Farazdaq despite the fact that Jarir and al-Farazdaq were of the same tribal confederation and were both Muslims. Tammam ibn Ghalib al-Farazdaq was of the Tamim tribe and was born in the southern part of the Arabian Peninsula. He moved first to Iraq and later to Syria where he became one of the major supporters of the Umayyads, attacking all those who opposed the Umayyads with his scathing satires. Al-Farazdaq and Jarir ibn 'Atiyyah ibn al-Khatafah ibn Badr were from the Tamim tribe and engaged each other in a 40-year "war of words" personally attacking each other through satirical poems. After their deaths, their poems were collected into anthologies, or *diwans*, which have remained important sources for not only the Arabic language but as important insights into to the political and social conflicts of the Umayyad period.

After the collapse of the Umayyads, their successors the 'Abbasids moved from Syria to Iraq to be closer to their support base; however, both Damascus and Aleppo remained centers of learning and high arts. Among those to emerge in this period was Abu al-Tayyib Ahmad ibn al-Hussein al-Ju'fi al-Mutanabbi (915–965). Al-Mutanabbi was born in Kufah in Iraq and spent part of his youth with Bedouin tribes near his home city. He perfected his ability in Arabic as well as seems to have been influenced by the Shi'ite Qaramitah movement, which had strong support among the Bedouin. Al-Mutanabbi lived a wandering life and eventually moved to Syria, where he led a rebellion against the 'Abbasid governors of Syria and Egypt, the Ikhshidids. The rebellion was supported mainly by Bedouin but they were eventually defeated by the Ikhshidids. Al-Mutanabbi was captured, and it was during this time that he was given the name *al-Mutanabbi,* or "prophet-like," partially due to his ability in the Arabic language said to rival even the Qur'an. Al-Mutanabbi was eventually released, and he returned to Syria where the Hamdanid ruler of Aleppo Sayf al-Dawlah welcomed him. Al-Mutanabbi felt that his talents were never fully appreciated, and his difficult, demanding personality acted against him. His poems were collected into a diwan both during and after his death in 965.

Abu al-Hassan 'Ali al-Hamdani Sayf al-Dawlah became the ruler of most of northern Syria by 944 and made Aleppo his seat of government. A poet of considerable talent himself, he gathered around him as many men of letters as he could; including the already famous al-Mutanabbi. The Hamdanids were of Bedouin origins from the Taghlib tribe, and in the troubled times of the tenth century they were able to establish states centered on Mosul and Aleppo. Sayf al-Dawlah's nephew Abu Firas al-Hamdani was also a well-known poet, whose diwan includes poems about warfare as well as on the noble ancestry of the Hamdanids. The high quality of Abu Firas' works are such that even during his lifetime, his poems were compared to the finest of the pre-Islamic period. People began to collect them while he was alive, and he assisted in editing some of the volumes. Today the city of Aleppo celebrates him with a statue in one of its largest public parks.

Among the most famous of Syrians from the period marking the fall of the Hamdanids is Abu al-'Ala' al-Ma'arri (973–1058) born in the northern Syrian city of Ma'arrat al-Nu'man. Al-Ma'arri became blind at the early age of four as result of suffering from smallpox. Despite his blindness he was already composing masterpieces in poetry by age 12. He studied Islamic law and became a Shafi'i judge serving in a number of posts mainly in northern Syria. Among his numerous works, the most influential is *Risalat al-Ghufran,* or *Epistle of Paradise,* which seems to have served as inspiration for Dante's *Divine Comedy.* Al-Ma'arri's work was well-known in the Islamic world and popular in al-Andalus, or Muslim Spain, where it was translated into Latin.

Another popular genre of literature from the classical Islamic period is called belle lettre, or in Arabic *adab.* These were often in prose or rhymed prose demonstrating the author's deep knowledge of Arabic such as the ability to end every line with same letter of the alphabet. Such prose works were secular and during the high period of classical literature, love stories were popular. Bedouin love stories, such as that of the unrequited lovers Qays and Laylah, were especially popular. Some of the best of these love stories were written in Muslim Spain and exported east to Syria where they influenced a form of music as well.

Syrians wrote a number of histories and biographical dictionaries with the greatest outpouring in the twelfth to thirteenth centuries. Histories tended to follow a fairly set format starting with the age of prophets and continuing to the lifetime of the authors. Many of these histories are written as chronologies with the events of any one year recorded. Among those that are still considered to be major sources to understand their times are the works of 'Izz al-Din Abu al-Hassan ibn al-Athir (1160–1233). 'Izz al-Din was one of three brothers all of whom are known for their books on philosophy, literary criticism, or history. 'Izz al-Din authored several major works on history and was an eyewitness to the campaigns by Salah al-Din al-Ayyubi. 'Izz al-Din is best known for his history *al-Kamil fi al-Tarikh,* or *Complete History.* He drew on the earlier works of ibn al-Qalanisi (1073–1160), such as *Dhayl Tarikh Dimashq,* or *Compendium to the History of Damascus,* and ibn 'Asakir (1105–1176), such as *Tarikh Madinat Dimashq,* or *History of the City of Damascus.* Kamal al-Din ibn al-'Adim (1192–1262) was a noble of Aleppo who wrote the history of his city *Zabdat al-Halab fi Tarikh Halab,* or *Buttercream of the History of Aleppo* (a play on words as the Arabic name of Aleppo is the same as the word for milk). There are no complete copies of his history, but he was so thorough in noting his sources that even with the incomplete copies available, it is possible to get an understanding of the massive libraries Aleppo had prior to the Mongol destructions in the late thirteenth century.

Ahmad ibn Mahmud Ibn Khallikan al-Irdibili (1211–1282) was an historian and a Shafi'i judge in Damascus. He was born in Irdibil in northern Iraq but moved to Syria where he became the chief legal authority for Syria under the Mamluks. He wrote one of the most important biographical dictionaries called *Wafayat al-'Ayan wa Anba' Abna' al-Zaman,* or *Obituaries of Notables and News of the Sons of the Age.* His work included only those for whom he had definite dates of their deaths and only included verifiable information. It remains a standard for such collections of biographies to this day.

One of the most interesting Syrian authors of the twelfth century was the prince of Shayzar, Usama ibn Murshid ibn 'Ali, best known as ibn Munqidh. The Banu Munqidh were originally Bedouin Arabs who gained control over much of the middle Ghutah as allies of the Mirdasid rulers of Aleppo. Shayzar was on the frontier between Crusader-held Antioch and Saljuq and Zangid Syria. Usama was born in 1095 and grew up in the period following the loss of the Mediterranean coast to the European Crusaders. Later in life the urbane and well-educated prince wrote an autobiography called *Kitab al- I'tibar,* or *Book of Instructions,* meant mainly to teach other young gentlemen proper behavior through the example of his own life. The book gives Usama's first hand accounts of meetings with the Europeans and is a valuable source of better understanding the encounter between the two cultures. The book has been translated into English by the Lebanese historian Philip Hitti under the title *Memoirs of a Syrian Gentleman.* Usama wrote a number of other works and organized his own diwan of poetry. He produced books on history, religion, and one called *al-Manazil wa al-Diyar,* or *Book of Campsites and Dwellings,* has come down to us today. Usama died in 1188 after a long and distinguished career serving Salah al-Din among others.

Geographies are another of the classical works written by Syrians. For the Muslims of the day geographies not only included information about topographical features, but of roads and road conditions, climate, economics, and politics; information needed for merchants, pilgrims, or government officials. Geographies were often written by daily stages describing villages, towns, agricultural production, wells, streams, forts, and any other feature that would be encountered along the roads. One of the most informative of these is the work *al-Masalik wa al-Mamalik,* or *Book of Roads and Kingdoms,* by Abu 'Abdallah al-Maqaddasi (died in 1000). Unlike most of those before him, al-Maqaddasi divided the known world into zones that he defined and then presented information on the peoples, languages, religions, histories, political organizations, economic activities, as well as on the physical geography of each. He is also among the first geographers in the world to present a list of geographical terms with their definitions. Other geographies were more like dictionaries arranged by the first letter of the main entry. Each entry would include the origin of the name and its proper pronunciation; information on the people, government, history, economics; and even any mention of the place in religious or literary texts. One of the most extensive of these is the work *Mu'jam al-Buldan,* or *Dictionary of the Nations,* written by the former slave, Yaqut al-Hamawi (died 1229).

Arabic literature fell into decay in the late Mamluk period with most authors more interested in reproducing the form rather than being creative with the material. When most of the Arab world fell to the Ottoman Turks, the court language changed to Turkish and Persian. Arabic remained important in the sciences and religion, but Persian in particular was favored by the Ottomans as the language of literature. Such Arab stories as that of Qays and Laylah were translated into Persian and Turkish, and the corpus of romantic tales was added to by those of ancient Iran. Turkish was used in history and geography as much as Arabic. In the courts of the Ottoman officials in places like Aleppo and Damascus, Turkish was favored. Modern Arabic literature began with the Egyptian occupation of Syria in the decade of the 1830s when young Arabs began to rediscover their own literary past.

MODERN LITERATURE

Modern Arabic literature begins in the nineteenth century following the 10-year occupation of Syria by Ibrahim Pasha, the son of Egypt's reforming ruler Muhammad 'Ali. Ibrahim Pasha had introduced a number of government reforms while occupying the area, and though not necessarily liked by the locals, these reforms left an important impression. In addition, a number of new European and American schools were opened up first mainly for the Christians in Syria, Lebanon, and Palestine. These schools taught history, and Arab students were made aware of their own contributions to Islamic civilization. With the spread of literacy came the desire to have journals and newspapers printed in Arabic. The period from 1850 to 1900 is called the Arab Awakening as the Arab subjects of the Ottoman Sultan become not only aware of their shared past but began to be politically active.

Two of the first Arabic language journals were *al-Muqtataf* and *al-Hilal*, both founded in Cairo by Lebanese/Syrians in the 1870s. Cairo was a more receptive place for many of the first generation of new Arab intellectuals, as Egypt's rulers were willing to exploit them in their own rivalry for superiority with the Ottoman Sultan. In 1875 the daily Arabic newspaper *al-Ahram* was founded in Cairo also by an immigrant Lebanese family. One of the most influential of these immigrants was the Syrian Rashid Ridda, who founded the journal *al-Manar*. Rashid Ridda (1865–1935) was a close follower of the Islamic reformer Muhammad 'Abduh (1849–1905). The journal *al-Manar* remained faithful to the teachings of Muhammad 'Abduh even after the reformer's death.

For modern Arabic literature, Cairo was, and in many ways still is, the center of any real movement. Syrians, Lebanese, Palestinians, and others have looked to Egypt as a place to work and as a place where such innovations as the Arabic novel, free verse poetry, and theater were born. In the decades following World War I until the end of World War II, no other city in the Arab world would be able to rival Cairo as home to the growing Arab intelligentsia. Damascus was able to assert itself as another cultural center of the Arab world after World War II and able to challenge Cairo's cultural supremacy. The Syrian government has supported the arts, and in the 1960s the Ministry of Culture helped establish the National Theater of Damascus, the Itinerant Theater, and the People's Theater in Aleppo.

Damascus, and to a lesser extent Aleppo, attracts a number of contemporary poets, playwrights, and novelists. The two best-known Syrian poets are 'Ali Ahmad Sa'id and Nizar Qabbani. 'Ali Ahmad Sa'id was born in 1930 and while a student was active in Syrian nationalist politics against the French occupation. He took as his pen name Adunis (Adonis), one of the pre Islamic gods of Syria. He entered Damascus University in 1950 and began writing poems that broke with the traditional conventions of Arabic poetry and wrote on social and political themes. In 1956 he was imprisoned and exiled to Lebanon. Adunis eventually took Lebanese citizenship and remained there continuing to write poetry as well as found and edit several important literary journals, including *al-Shi 'r*, or *Poetry*, and *Mawaqif*, or *Positions*. These journals have been among the most important for what is called experimental poetry.

Nizar Qabbani was born in 1925 in Damascus and originally studied law. He had a career as a diplomat including service in China as well as in Europe and the Middle East. Qabbani gained popularity in the Arab world for his love poetry, which gave voice to the feelings of women. As his popularity grew and his writings matured, he began to write on the pressing social and political themes of his day, especially after the 1967 defeat. One such poem entitled *Bread, Hashish, and the Moon* criticizes Arab society for living on dreams and drugs rather than dealing with the realities of life.

Another well-known Syrian poet is Muhammad Maghut, who was born in 1934. Maghut is also a playwright, and is perhaps better known for his plays and television screenplays than for his poetry. His works deal with problems of injustice and totalitarian governments. His use of humor and comedy have made him a favorite with many Syrians; placing ordinary characters in extraordinary circumstances. His dialogues are full of wit and word play yet are able to make it past any form of government censorship. Other playwrights are 'Ali 'Aqla Irsan, Sa'ad Allah Wannus, and Walid Ikhlasi, whose works have been performed by the National Theater Company.

FILM INDUSTRY

Syria's film industry is relatively small though it dates back to the early twentieth century. The first known showing of a film in Syria dates back to 1908 in Aleppo, and the first film to be made in Syria was *al-Muttaham al-Bari'*, or *The Innocent Victim,* in 1928. It took its inspiration from Hollywood gangland thrillers. In 1937 Syria made a film about the Palestinian Revolt, which included a number of documentary scenes taken from Western newsreels and films. All of these efforts were private and unlike in Egypt where a strong economy allowed investment by wealthy individuals in the cinema industry, Syria's weak economy did not promote such investments. In addition, the French authorities made it very hard for Syrians to compete with the French film industry by placing numerous obstacles in the way of attempts to make movies. Following independence, the Syrian authorities did not encourage a cinema industry until after unity with Egypt in 1958.

During the brief period of unity with Egypt, the Syrians adopted a number of Egyptian institutions, including a film section of the Ministry of Culture. Under the Ba'athists the government actively supports cinema and helped found the National Film Organization. The new film organization sent technicians abroad to be trained to help improve the quality of what was being produced. In addition to the state film organization, private film companies have continued to make movies and documentaries. At first most of these tended to be historical or political in nature, and among the best of these is the film adaptation of the Palestinian novelist Ghassan Kanafani's *Rijal Taht al-Shams,* or *Men in the Sun,* the film version being called *al-Makhdu'un,* or *The Duped,* made in 1972. The story follows three Palestinians who are smuggled into Kuwait to find work. The truck is parked under the intense sun for hours as the driver deals with border-crossing issues only to find that all three have men have died due to the heat. The purpose of the film was to jolt the Arab audience and to make them more aware of the plight of the Palestinians.

The best-known Syrian actors anywhere in the Arab world, Durayd Lahham and Nihad al-Qal'i, first became known through a popular television sketch in the early 1960s. They successfully built screen and theater careers in the 1960s and 1970s, making more than 12 comedy films together such as *'Antar bin Haddad* (a play on the name of the famous pre-Islamic hero 'Antar bin Shaddad), where they play hapless and not overly bright private detectives in Cairo. In *Gharam fi Istanbul,* or *Love in Istanbul,* they again play not so clever con men trying to pass off a gypsy girl as the heiress to a massive fortune of an Ottoman princess. They have been compared, and sometimes compared themselves, to the classical American comedy team Laurel and Hardy, even looking a bit like them with Lahham resembling Laurel and al-Qal'i resembling the heavier Hardy. Since the first airing of the television series *Sahh al-Nawm,* or *Restful Sleep Hotel,* in the 1970s, they have made a number of major films featuring the characters developed in the series, the clever Ghuwar al-Turshi (Lahham) and the musician Husni Burazan (al-Qal'i). A number of other characters such as the hotel's female owner Fatum Hisbis, the neighborhood tough guy and enforcer Abu 'Antar, the somewhat dense chief of police Badri Bey, and Ghuwar's sometimes accomplice and fellow employee at the hotel Yasin (played by the Syrian character actor Yasin Bakush), and the others representing average people in Syria. Through their comic actions it is possible to find deep social and political criticism of the regime: corrupt and incompetent government officials, lack of services such as electricity in traditional neighborhoods, poor transportation system, and other issues. In the film version of *Sahh al-Nawm,* the plotting by Ghuwar to win the hand of his employer Fatum Hisbis are all to no avail and in the end not only does Fatum Hisbis marry Husni Burazan but Ghuwar and his accomplice Abu 'Antar end up in prison. In the film *Imburaturiyat Ghuwar,* or *Empire of Ghuwar,* a local neighborhood is under the control of a traditional local strongman, a *qabadai,* who is at war with the strongman in the next neighborhood. Ghawar, the local barber/traditional doctor/circumciser, is able to take the place of one of the qabadais and is even worse in his abuses. The locals are able to outwit the strongmen and bring in the government only to find that the new police captain is none other than Ghuwar, and the new policemen are the henchmen of the former qabadai.

During the 1970s and 1980s, Durayd Lahham made several other films with strong political messages. The film *al-Hudud,* or *Borders,* follows the life of a man named 'Abd al-Wadud, who loses his passport between border posts and is condemned to live in the no man's land between them. The border guards from the two countries take pity on him and help him as do taxi drivers taking people from one country to the other. He marries a Bedouin woman named Sudfah, who makes her living by smuggling goods between the countries, and eventually their plight is discovered by a young idealistic female journalist. As a result of her stories the Arab League holds a meeting at his home in the no man's land and declares him a citizen of all the countries in the Arab world. Once the delegates all leave, 'Abd al-Wadud and Sudfah once again try to cross the border but are stopped because they have no passports. In the closing scene they release their animals, which all cross the border without incident, and then in an act of defiance, 'Abd al-Wadud kicks down the border barrier and he and Sudfah start to cross. The border police all cock their rifles and shout "Stop!" and thus the film ends.

Another major film by Durayd Lahham is called *al-Taqrir,* or *The Report,* which follows the life of the one and only honest inspector general in government. He resigns over accusations of dishonesty, expecting his good reputation will get him his job back, but no one asks him to return. He and his loyal secretary set out to thoroughly document the vast amount of corruption in the government—finding it much more than they had ever thought. Once the report is ready he tries to have it presented to the people, only to find that everyone is at a soccer match. He goes to the match and tries to read it out loud, only to be trampled to death by the players and fans and the pages of the report blow all over the playing field. Like all of Lahham's films, there is a good use of comedy, making people laugh at themselves and their governments. He also uses a good deal of drama and turns of fate, such as the tragic end of the inspector general and the possible end of 'Abd al-Wadud and Sudfah.

Syria is also home to a new genre of Arab film sometimes called *al-Sinima al-Badilah,* or Alternative Cinema. This movement was born out of the 1972 First International Festival for Young Arab Cinema sponsored by the National Film Organization, which featured films from a number of Arab countries made by young directors. The films are less commercial in nature and are to express the realities of the Arabs, to develop films rooted in Arab culture, and to produce social action on the part of the audience. Story lines are taken from major works of contemporary Arab literature or from actual events. One such film made in 1974 is called *Kafr Qassim,* the name of a northern Palestinian village where in 1956 the Israeli army massacred a large number of civilians. The Israeli army had instituted an unexpected curfew and the men out working in their fields were shot as they were returning home in the evening. The film's purpose, like that of the 1972 film *The*

Duped was to awaken the Arab audience to the plight of the Palestinians, though this time for those under Israeli domination.

TELEVISION PRODUCTIONS

While Syria's film industry remains relatively small, Syrian television has burst onto the Arabic language channels in recent decades. Television began in 1960 during the period of unity with Egypt and like the influence the Egyptians had on theater, they brought with them an expertise and important institutions adopted by the Syrians. There is one major Arabic language national channel, which is under the control of the Ministry of Information. The most important use for television has been the news and the need to keep the government and its policies before the people. Syrian television does include advertising often of state-owned products for sale in the market, though more and more non-Syrian advertisements have begun to appear as Syria's markets open up more to the outside. In recent years the Syrians have opened a satellite channel, which is a bit less government and includes a good deal of entertainment programming, and there are the foreign channels that broadcast English and French language programs. All of these are controlled by the state.

Since the 1980s the Syrians have come to produce some of the best dramatic series in the Arab world. They began by tackling topics such as apartheid in South Africa, one of the very few Arab countries to deal with the issue during the height of the apartheid regime. While Syrian actors played African parts in blackface makeup and spoke their lines in classical Arabic, the fact that they took on such a topic was highly unusual. The political realities of life for black South Africans were compared in subtle ways to that of the Palestinians under the Israeli occupation.

Since the 1990s Syrians began making historical series such as the 1996 series on the life of Queen Zenobia. Her fight against the Romans took on a strong nationalist slant. Many of these programs are made specifically for broadcast during Ramadan when large viewing audiences throughout the Arab world and beyond can be assured. Recent historical dramas have been funded by Arab Gulf countries such as the United Arab Emirates, Qatar, and Saudi Arabia, and frequently include international casts of actors (Jordanians, Iraqis, Saudis, Egyptians, Algerians, and Moroccans in addition to Syrians).

Syria produced a series of dramas that began with the conquest of North Africa and Spain in the early eighth century. The series then followed history, from the founding of Umayyads of Cordoba in the eighth century, the height of the Umayyads in the ninth century, the period of the Party Kings in the eleventh century, the rise of the Almoravids (al-Murabatin) in the eleventh century, and the eventual loss of Muslim Spain in the fifteenth century. The chronicle of Muslim Spain and its eventual loss are used to criticize contemporary Arab governments and their weaknesses, both internal and in front of Western powers. The series were filmed mainly in Morocco making use of outdoor sets, as was much of the 2004 series about the life of the pre-Islamic poet prince Imru'l Qays and the 2006 series on the conflict between Amin and Ma'mun, the two sons of the 'Abbasid Khalifah Harun al-Rashid. Many of these series have modern applications easily understood by the Arab audience; problems and weaknesses of the past are being repeated today.

Another historical series broadcast in Ramadan 2006 was set in the last days of Roman rule in Syria. The series depicts how the Romans were able to keep control by pitching Arab tribes against each other. The Romans are able to capture the hero and his close companions, whom they torture with images matching the infamous photos from Iraq's Abu Ghurayb prison. There is no doubt that though set in the fifth century A.D. the series is really about contemporary issues including the American military presence in Iraq. It is clearly understood the Romans are, in fact, the Americans, and the Bedouin heroes are the Iraqi resistance. Those Bedouin helping the Romans are the current Iraqi regime. Another 2006 Ramadan series is set in Damascus during the French occupation. Set in a traditional neighborhood, the series weaves the lives of the inhabitants as they keep the French, and their Syrian agents, at arm's length. They are even able to assist the resistance in Palestine without the knowledge of the authorities, yet even while trying to keep the old order, it is changing around them.

Syrian television has also tackled issues no other Arab country has touched. Syrians have dealt sympathetically with homosexuality and AIDS. In recent television series homosexuality is not only talked about, but homosexual characters are presented in a positive way, not criminalized or seen as sexual deviants. AIDS is discussed in an intelligent manner with an attempt to both demystify the illness and teach the audience about it. Drugs and drug abuse are also discussed in Syrian television dramas including the criminal side of dealing and the destruction of families as a result of drug abuse.

The reasons for the broader set of topics included and the better acting, scenes, and photographic techniques used are because there is a good deal of competition. While the Syrian state controls the broadcast of television, private companies have arisen to make the series. Damascus hosts over 20 private production companies, each competing with the others to sell their programs to the Syrian state, as well as to other Arab television channels. The competition has helped improve the quality and as well as the quality of what is produced. Financial support from the Arab Gulf countries has made it possible to make sweeping historical dramas with large casts, as well as tackle contemporary issues state-dominated media in other countries fear to do. Syria is now able to compete in the international Arab market with the one-time dominate power of Egypt.

OTHER MEDIA

Radio has long been the most important medium in Syria, as it is able to reach a much larger audience than television. Syrian Arab Republic Radio broadcasts news and a large number of political programs including military and political music in praise of the state, of the Ba'ath Party, and of the president. In 2005 the state allowed the first private radio station called al-Madina FM but it is an entertainment station and is not allowed to broadcast the news or any political commentary. Syrian opposition abroad has been given access to a shortwave station, which they call Radio Free Syria, which is supported by the United States. Such broadcasts have little local appeal since many Syrians are able to pick up both radio and television from a number of countries including Lebanon, Israel, Jordan, Iraq, and Cyprus. With satellite television Syrians have access to channels such as the Arabic and English language versions of *al-Jazirah,* which carries non–government censored news.

Syria has a number of daily newspapers mainly in Arabic. *Al-Thawrah,* or *The Revolution,* belongs to the government and can be seen as its voice. *Al-Ba'ath* belongs to the Ba'ath Party while the other major Arabic daily *Tishrin,* or *November,* is technically independent though it follows the government line. There is only one news agency authorized in the country, the state-run Syrian Arab News Agency (SANA), which gives news releases in Arabic, English, and French. No other news agency is licensed to operate in the country and most of the news is subject to government censorship; however, access to alternative news is impacting government control.

The internet is gaining ground especially among the young. The government is trying to maintain control over access to the internet but like with satellite television channels it is harder and harder to do. The media freedom watch organization Reporters Without Borders states Syria is one of the worst offenders against internet freedom, trying to censor opposition and independent news Web sites. Government attempts to control and censor media, especially news, remains an important problem for the future.

CONCLUSION

Syria was and remains an important center for Arabic literature. Syria during the classical Islamic period produced major writers in all of the different forms from poetry to prose to history and geography. Syrians set the standards for others in many of these and the patronage given to writers by local rulers helped maintain the high standards. The Ottoman period saw a decline in the quality of the literature produced, but Syrians were in the forefront of the rebirth of Arab literature in the nineteenth century.

Syria's economy was hit hard in the nineteenth and early twentieth century making it hard for its elite to support new developments such as cinema and theater. It was not until after World War II and more so with the brief unification with Egypt that Syria began to develop their arts. It now has a small but competitive film industry, and its television programs have come to dominate the pan-Arab satellite television programming.

Syria is struggling to open itself up to greater media access. Syria is criticized for government interference and censorship. Though the country is starting to open up to new stations, it has a far ways yet to go to match the strides made in countries such as Lebanon and Jordan. A brief period of openness shortly after Bashar al-Asad came to power did not last, and there was a strong official reaction; however, many Syrians are hopeful the situation will change for the better.

4

Architecture, Traditional Crafts, and Traditional Dress

SYRIA HAS A long tradition of sophisticated urban life and therefore has developed over millennia traditions of architecture, crafts, and dress that reflect its high art and taste. Syria's urban elite have been able to afford lavish buildings, furnishings, and decorations and have been able to patronize artisans. Some of these traditions date back well into antiquity as they are attested to in the detailed sculptures from Palmyra while others are part of the development of taste and fashion up to the present day. Much of what can be seen today of Syria's urban features date from the Mamluk and Ottoman periods, yet other traditions from Syria's countryside are contemporary descendents of those that date back to the Neolithic. Like much of their culture, Syrians are proud of their contributions to world heritage in crafts and architecture. Syria's government places great value on traditional crafts and officially supports their preservation.

TRADITIONAL URBAN ARCHITECTURE

Syria boasts some of the oldest settlements in the world, and both Damascus and Aleppo claim to be the oldest continually inhabited cities in the world. Both date back to the Neolithic period though much of the older periods are buried underneath later constructions. In Damascus a few of the Roman period buildings or urban features are still evident, the most important being

part of the Temple of Jupiter, which stands just outside the main entrance to
the Umayyad Mosque and parts of the famous Street Called Straight. Other
cities in Syria also date back to early antiquity, and some have substantial
ruins still standing. The southern town of Bosra Eski Sham, for example,
boasts a large number of Roman and Byzantine period buildings, including
a massive amphitheater that was rebuilt into a fortress in the Islamic period.
Bosra is located in a volcanic region, and most of the buildings are made
of black basalt, including the roof beams where stone was used instead of
wood. Bosra has a number of early Christian churches and one of the oldest
mosques built outside of the Arabian Peninsula. The Mosque of 'Umar in
Bosra is reported to be the first to adapt the Christian bell tower into the
familiar minaret. Before that time the Muslim call to prayer was done from
the roof. With the conquest of large Christian areas of Syro-Palestine, the
Muslims adapted the square bell tower from Syrian Christian churches into
the minaret. The Mosque of 'Umar, built sometime in the seventh century, is
the oldest known mosque in the Muslim world to be built with a minaret.

One of the most spectacular ruins is the oasis city of Palmyra or Tadmur.
Until the middle of the twentieth century the contemporary village was
located within the walls of the massive Temple of Bel built in the second century A.D. Other Syrian cities include bridges, water works, temples, churches,
and other major monumental buildings from the pre-Islamic period that have
been combined into later constructions.

Syria's cities have taken on their current look as a result of over one thousand years of Islamic influence. There are a number of important urban
architectural features that mark the Islamic" city, and Aleppo's old city, or
madinah, is considered one of the best preserved "Arab-Islamic" cities in the
world. These major features include large Friday mosques, smaller neighborhood mosques, water works including public fountains and water wheels,
Islamic schools (both primary level *kuttab* and higher level *madrasah*), hospitals, specialized industries and markets, public bathhouses, trade agencies
(usually called a *khan* in Syria), and monumental tombs of religious and
political elite.

The Umayyad Mosque in Damascus marks the transition from the Greco-
Roman architecture of late antiquity to the Islamic architecture that now
dominates Syria's cities. The Umayyad Mosque is located near the center of
the old city, and the location has been a place of worship for millennia, being
first the Temple to the Syrian god Ba'al Hadad and then to the Roman god
Jupiter. After the official adoption of Christianity in the Roman Empire, it
was converted into the Church of St. John the Baptist by the Emperor Theodosius in 379. When Damascus was taken by the Arabs in 636, the Christians
were allowed to keep the building and conduct worship there. As the Muslim

population grew, the church was shared between the two communities until the reign of the Umayyad Khalifah al-Walid (705–715) who ordered that it be rebuilt exclusively as a mosque. Al-Walid purchased the building from the Christian Patriarch and work began in 708 to convert it into a mosque. The orientation of the building had to be changed so the prayer niche, or *mihrab*, was placed in the middle of the southern wall, which necessitated blocking some of the older entrances. A large dome was built in the middle of the building allowing for the change in orientation from an east-west axis to a north-south one.

The Umayyads used skilled local workers for items like stained glass windows and cut stone grill work; however, they had to bring other skilled workers from Constantinople such as those to make the extensive mosaics on the façade of the building. The mosaics show gardens, pavilions, and palaces and are among the best portrayals of late antiquity architecture anywhere in the world. From the mosaics it is easy to visualize what Damascus and other Syrian cities looked like in the eighth century.

The square minaret based on the Syrian Christian bell tower remained the main model until into the twelfth century. The most advanced model of the square minaret is that of the Great or the Zakariya Mosque in Aleppo—originally the Cathedral of St. Helen. First turned into a mosque during the Umayyad period, the Zakariya Mosque was rebuilt a number of times, and the current minaret was built between 1090 and 1092 by the Saljuqs. The tower is tall (45 meters or 147 feet) and thin, divided into four separate registers, each with its own specific design, yet all four blend into a unified whole. It is seen as the precursor of the Syrian styles that emerged in the Ayyubid and Mamluk periods that followed.

Mosques in Syria follow a general model of a large, open courtyard with a fountain used for ritual ablution before prayers and an enclosed prayer hall. The prayer hall is aligned to the south, southeast with a central dome over the prayer niche. The roof of the hall is frequently in a series of transepts supported by columns. The large domed prayer hall was introduced to Syria by the Ottomans in the sixteenth century and is a distinctive feature of Ottoman architecture. Minarets remained square until the twelfth century with the introduction of Iraqi, Iranian, and Central Asian architectural styles by the Saljuqs, Zangids, Ayyubids, and Mamluks. Minarets began to be more rounded usually taking on a hexagon or octagon form. The tops of the minarets developed the distinctive crown sometimes called a *mabkharah,* or incense burner, since the older ones look very much like the traditional incense burner. The balcony at the foot of the *mabkharah* served as the place where the call to prayer could be done, the human voice being replaced by electric loudspeakers today. With the introduction of Ottoman styles, minarets became the round, long, thin form with narrow, pointed tops often called the pencil style since they look very much like sharpened pencils.

Syrian cities have a large number of mosques built by the Umayyads, Saljuqs, and Ayyubids but the largest share are from the Mamluk and Ottoman periods. The Mamluks helped develop a Syrian style especially in the use of alternating layers of different colors of stone called *ablaq* in Arabic. They developed this into geometric mosaics of white, red, black, and yellow stone. These alternating layers of different colored stones have become a distinctive feature of Syrian architecture used in official monumental buildings, public baths, commercial centers, and private houses.

Another major urban structure found in Syrian cities often connected with mosques is the Islamic school, or madrasah. Madrasahs were introduced in Syria by the Saljuqs in the later half of the eleventh century, but the schools were supported by subsequent Sunni dynasties (the Zangids, Ayyubids, and the Mamluks), first as a way to combat the popular appeal of Shi'ism among the people and later as a means to produce competent government employees. The Islamic education system began with the local, neighborhood primary school usually called a *kuttab,* where both boys and girls were sent to learn the basics of reading, writing, mathematics, and to memorize the Qur'an. Those male students deemed to be bright by their primary school teachers were encouraged to attend the next level, the madrasah, where they would continue with what were called the Islamic sciences, Arabic language and grammar, and law. In Syria, all four major Sunni legal systems were taught even if the majority of Syrian Sunnis followed the Shafi'i *madhhab.* Once graduated from a madrasah the graduate was qualified to fill many of the lower levels in the state's administration and to serve as Imams or prayer leaders at local mosques. Those who had been able to excel in their studies were encouraged to continue at the *jami'ah,* or university connected to a major Friday mosque. In Syria the Umayyad Mosque in Damascus served as a university though it was never thought to be of the same level or international fame as al-Azhar in Cairo.

The madrasahs were large buildings able to house the students and provide meals for them. Usually built on what is called an *iwan* format, the buildings had large central courtyards with four partially covered side courts, one for each of the four Sunni schools of law. They had a large prayer hall on the side facing towards Makkah. Some of them were endowed by political or economic elite, who would set aside rooms near the prayer hall for their tombs such as that of the Mamluk Sultan Baybars in the *Madrasah al-Zahariyah* built 1277 in Damascus. Some of the Islamic schools were supported by craft guilds such as the soap makers, booksellers, perfume and incense sellers, cloth weavers, dyers, and the like. The craft guilds would provide scholarships for bright young men often from the countryside who upon graduation would be expected to assist the guild in legal matters.

Connected to both mosques and sometimes Islamic schools were places for Sufis, or Islamic mystics, to live and contemplate. These are called *takkiyah* or *khanqah* in Syria, and many of them were founded by political or economic elite. One of the best preserved is the *Takkiyatayn,* or the Two *Takkiyahs* of Salim and Sulayman, in Damascus built between 1553 and 1554 by the famous Ottoman architect Sinan Pasha in honor of the two Ottoman Sultans Salim the Grim and his son Sulayman the Magnificent. The complex includes the Madrasah of Salim, which today is used as a handicraft market. There is a small mosque (still in use), kitchens, rooms for travelers, and other buildings. Each room is covered by a dome and provided with a fireplace.

All of Syria's major cities offered special places for merchants from other cities or countries to stay and sell their wares usually called *khan*s. The khans are located near the main market areas of the old cities and included places for the visiting merchants to stable their animals, rooms for rent where they could display their goods, and upper levels where they could stay. In recent years a number of the khans have been restored and open for visitors. One of the most beautiful of them in Damascus is the *Khan Asad Pasha* built in the eighteenth century located near the Street Called Straight (also called *Suq Midhat Pasha*), which connects eastern and western gates of the city. It has a major central dome with eight other smaller domes flanking it. The walls use the Syrian decorative ablaq of alternating rows of different colored stone, in this case gray and white. There are nine other khans located in the same area dating from the fifteenth to the eighteenth century, and most of them carry the names of local notables who built them though some carry the names of the products that were brought there to be sold such as *Khan al-Zayt,* or the Olive Oil Khan, which dates to the sixteenth century.

Khans are built near or in markets or *suq*s. Suqs are also built urban spaces, and in Syria the markets of Damascus and Aleppo are among the best preserved in the Arab world. Other Syrian cities, such as Homs, Hama, and Dayr al-Zawr, also have well-preserved markets, but they are not as well-known as those in Damascus and Aleppo. The markets in Aleppo are the longest covered markets anywhere in the Islamic world running a total length of 7 kilometers or 4.3 miles and date from between the thirteenth to the sixteenth centuries. The structure of markets depends on the types of items sold with more industrial and dirtier materials separated from the cleaner types. Raw materials for weaving like cotton and linen are marketed close to the looms and where the final product is sold (in Damascus this is the *Suq al-Jumruk,* or the Customs, since some of the raw materials were imported). Other markets bare names such as *Suq al-Buzariyah* for roasted seeds and candies; *Suq al-Nahhasin* for the coppersmiths; *Suq al-Siyaghah* for the goldsmiths; and *Suq al-Sarujah* for the saddle makers. In most Arab-Islamic cities markets are located around the major Friday mosque, and the same can be said for cities in Syria. In Damascus, for example, the main street leading to the Umayyad Mosque is *Suq al-Hamidiyah* named for the Ottoman Sultan 'Abd al-Hamid II, under whose rule the local governor ordered its restoration and had it roofed. Surrounding the Umayyad Mosque are other markets for woodcraft, kitchen utensils, and, in the past, books, perfume, and incense. With the growth of tourism since the 1970s a number of antique shops have located along the *Suq al-Hamidiyah* and in the neighborhood of the Umayyad Mosque.

The *maristan* or hospital is another urban feature in many of Syria's cities. The word *maristan* is Persian in origin and was borrowed into Arabic in the early centuries of Islam following the conquest of Iraq and Iran. The ancient Persians were among the most advanced in medical sciences at the time of the Islamic conquest, and the Arabs quickly adopted the Persian model for public hospitals. They added the medical knowledge of the ancient Greeks to that of Iran and India, and for centuries Islamic medical knowledge was far ahead of that of Europe and Arabic medical texts were used in Europe into the eighteenth century. The Zangid ruler Nur al-Din was the first to build public hospitals in Syria, which he did in Damascus and Aleppo in 1154. Nur al-Din was originally from northern Iraq and the buildings he ordered constructed (such as a madrasah built between 1167 and 1172) are marked by the use of the *muqarnas,* or honeycombed domes, native to Mesopotamia. The hospital he founded in Aleppo has not survived to the present, but the hospital in Damascus has been restored and turned into a museum of Islamic sciences.

The public bath, or *hammam,* is another major feature of Islamic cities. In Damascus the *Hammam of Nur al-Din* built between 1152 and 1172 is the oldest still standing in use. Its interior has often been used for historical dramas for television and film, and in the 1990s a popular television talk show, which used the late Ottoman period for costumes and music, was hosted from the bathhouse. The *Hammam al-Nasri* or *Hammam Yalbugha* in Aleppo built in the fourteenth century remains one of the most splendid in the entire country. It was completely restored and reopened in 1985 as a tourist project. Bathhouses pre-date the Islamic period in the Middle East; they were an important introduction by the Greeks following the conquests of Alexander the Great. The Romans continued the tradition though bathhouses fell into difficulties during the early Christian period being seen as too closely connected to "pagan" practices. The Muslim emphasis on bodily cleanliness, especially for prayer, made them popular, and all urban neighborhoods supported at least one. The pubic bath was open to both males and females but because of Islamic sensibilities, men and women had different hours or days of use. When the bathhouse was being used by women, all of the bath attendants were women and for men only male bath attendants were present.

Bathhouses served a number of important social roles not only as places where people would come to be bathed and perhaps have a massage. Behavior at a bathhouse were ways to judge the manners of a family, and women on the look out for potential brides for their sons would study how young women from the neighboring families behaved: whether she remained modest: the sound and volume of her laughter; her way of speaking: and traits other than her looks that were seen as more important in a daughter-in-law. For men the bathhouse allowed them the chance to relax together and talk. Most bathhouses used to (and those still in operation still) provide coffee, tea, and even food. In some instances, the more wealthy ones included entertainment such as chamber groups playing classical Arabic music. Today the chamber group may be replaced by a television. Bathhouses are still popular places to go for relaxation though nearly all urban houses now have indoor plumbing with fully equipped bathrooms.

The town houses of Syria's urban elite are massive structures often broken into two major sections; a *salamlik,* or public area where the males of the house would receive guests and perhaps conduct business, and the *haramlik,* or private, family area of the house where the only males allowed were those of the immediate family. Homes of Christian families, however, often did not have two divisions. Syria's urban elite made use of the styles and decorations introduced by the ruling political elite (who in the past were often non Syrian), but they developed them along local lines. Two major distinct styles of town houses emerged, perhaps stretching back into early antiquity: the Damascus house and the Aleppo house. Other urban centers in Syria were influenced by these two cultural centers with those of the south (including modern day Lebanon, Palestine, and Jordan) influenced by Damascus, and those of the north (including parts of southern Turkey) influenced by Aleppo.

The Damascus town house was, and still is, a splendid building constructed of different layers of colored stonework for the ground floor, and wood and mud for the upper floors. Wealthier houses made use of not only the different colors of limestone (white, off white, yellow, and gray) and basalt (black) but also of local marbles (white, gray, black, and brown). The emphasis was on the interior the house rather than on the exterior, which was, and is, covered in a thick, monotone cover in light brown mud and plaster. Only the doorways had a monumental aspect. The doorways of the wealthier families and those of the political elite were inset into the thick walls of the house, and overhead *muqarnas* in colored stonework protected the door. On either side of the door, benches were built into the wall where servants sat in order to screen and announce visitors. In many instances the benches were not used but were ways to announce the wealth and status of the family.

Most town houses had two courtyards with central fountains. The court-yards were paved in stone, and the more wealthy homes paved them in mar-ble. The walls were decorated with stucco with insets in paste work and tiles. Damascus produced high quality ceramic tiles dating back into the thirteenth century, but the use of decorative ceramic tiles was made more popular dur-ing the Ottoman period. The use of stone mosaics, paste work, and tiles gave the home an elegance that rivaled the palaces of other major Islamic cities. In the nineteenth century the opulent Ottoman rococo style was introduced from Istanbul, and many of Syria's urban elite quickly adopted it. Ottoman rococo was a blend of European baroque and rococo with a degree of Islamic design. While it would seem to be a near impossible blend of Europe and tra-ditional Middle Eastern styles and decorative motifs, Ottoman rococo seems to work especially with the addition of lavish Syrian inlaid wood furniture.

The courtyards also served as gardens shaded by at least one fruit or nut tree. Most gardens included fragrant, flowering shrubs as well as flowers such as roses and herbs used in cooking. Most of the town houses included side alcoves, or *iwans*, slightly raised above the level of courtyard. They were fur-nished with benches or couches, tables, and even mirrors and dressers. These served as places where the family could gather even in the colder months and where women could work or visit. In the larger homes with two courtyards the second one was for the exclusive use of the family while the outer one was for guests, especially males.

Town houses in Damascus often had two or three floors, and the upper levels were for the family's private use such as bedrooms. Some of them were made to accommodate married sons and their families as well as the head of household. Indoor toilets were in use since the early Ottoman period if not before, and they too were located in the upper floor often not far from the bedrooms. Many of the homes had large kitchen areas on the ground floor though much of the preparation work was done in the open courtyards.

Ceilings were, and are, magnificent works of art. The older ones were made of wooden beams carved and painted in geometric forms. By the twelfth cen-tury these were being replaced by wooden ceilings using a variety of architec-tural features including the use of *muqarnas* to help support the four corners. Some ceilings were false domes being an interior inset rather than the actual roof. In late Ottoman times the ceilings were often flat and covered with either sculpted stucco, painted fresco, or painted wallpaper. A central light-ing fixture was suspended from the middle, which was usually a fantasy of colored glass and brass in geometrics, which cast colored shapes and shadows when lit. In the late Ottoman period Damascus artisans began making other types of wall lamps or table lamps in brass with beaded fringing along the sides. These are still popular items not only in Damascus but are in Jordan, Lebanon, and even the Gulf States.

The old city in Damascus and the towns it influences are a maze of narrow streets. Many of the streets are twisting and dead end at some one's door. The streets are made even narrower by the second and third floors, which are built to overhang the street below. Enclosed balconies, protected by elaborate wooden screens called *mashrabiyah,* also hang over the street. The edge of the balconies are so close that they nearly touch, cutting off direct light from much of the street.

The Aleppo style did not differ from that of Damascus in its basic floor plan but did in its building materials. While the Damascus style used wood and mud for the upper levels of the house, the Aleppo style used mainly stone and wood. Houses in Aleppo did not have overhanging upper floors typical of Damascus but had tall straight walls making the streets appear less twisting and cramped. Aleppo houses tended to be both narrower and taller allowing more light and air to flow between them. In the late Ottoman period the upper floors were entirely encased in wooden *mashrabiyah* such as one still finds today in some sections of the city such as Bab al-Nasr Street. Homes in Aleppo had similar floor plans to those in Damascus but were often more restrained in use of decoration such as *ablaq,* tiles, or paste work. Aleppo's old streets are described as having an air of serenity and elegance missing from the dark, twisting streets in Damascus.

TRADITIONAL VILLAGE ARCHITECTURE

Syrian villages display a variety of construction techniques and architectural styles influenced as much by the climate as the available building materials. Several distinct forms are found in Syria some of which date back into the Neolithic and the origins of settled life.

Among the most distinct of village architectural styles is that found in the northern part of the country stretching from the area just to the south of Aleppo to the east near the border with Iraq and north into Turkey. Here the buildings are best described as beehives; conical buildings built in clusters with each hive serving a single purpose. The hives are joined by an outer wall that forms the courtyard where much of the day's work is done. This type of home has been around for millennia, as found in archeological excavations in Syria's Jazirah region. The buildings are made of mud brick as the region offers little else for building materials. A variation on the mud brick house is that found in the further eastern areas near Dayr al-Zawr and the eastern parts of the Jazirah, where instead of making a series of beehive domes, houses are made in large squares with rooms around a large central courtyard. Like the beehive houses, each room is used for a single purpose, and the courtyard is where most of the work is done.

Furnishings in these houses are simple, and alcoves, storage places, and shelves are built into the walls. The floors are covered in reed mats (now mainly made of plastic) or locally woven rugs. Wealthier families might have several better quality Persian or more frequently Turkish or Kurdish rugs in the room used to receive guests. Mattresses and cushions covered with patterned cloth or local embroidery are placed next to the wall, and in the past a brass brazier was placed in the middle of the room for heat the winters. In the bedroom large, oversized dressers, mirrors, and beds with mother of pearl inlay, often made in urban centers such as Damascus, Homs, or Aleppo, were popular until into the 1980s when imported furniture became the style. The beds in the Jazirah are of particular note as they are raised high off the ground and are reached by a short ladder. The beds are built high in order to prevent scorpions from being able to climb into them. The beds are often large enough to hold the entire family and in the hottest months of the year they are often brought out into the courtyard where the night air is cooler.

Walls of the houses were, and still are, decorated with homemade hangings, decorated mirrors, and religious pictures. A Syrian specialty is painting on glass which show pictures of Qur'anic and Biblical stories, the pilgrimage to Makkah, or the famous pre-Islamic hero 'Antar bin Shaddad and his beloved 'Ablah bint Malik. These paintings became very popular in the late nineteenth century, and there is still one craftsman in Damascus producing them today. More frequently these traditional decorations have been replaced by mass-produced calligraphy in frames and cheap pictures of Makkah or Madinah in velvet imported from Pakistan and China.

In other parts of Syria, village homes are made of cut stone, rubble fill, and wood. Size of the homes and the number of associated building had to do with the wealth of the family, and the village elite lived in so-called throne houses, houses with an elevated room where guests could be received and housed. Specific architectural features often had to do with whether the village was exposed to attack by Bedouin raiders or hostile neighbors, such as those inhabited by the 'Alawi and other persecuted religious minorities. Such communities needed be build their villages as fortresses to discourage attacks. In general the stone buildings were one-room affairs again often surrounded by a stone wall. In many Syrian villages the outer gate opened up onto the courtyard, and several small, square buildings facing onto the courtyard made the house. The courtyard was shaded in the summer by one or more fruit and or nut trees. In addition many of the courtyards included a small roofed over work space called a *ma'rash,* where women did much of their daily chores in the shade or protected from rain.

The Hawran in the southern part of the country developed its own distinct style due to the amount of black basalt found in the region. Where limestone is also found the houses may have alternating layers of black and white stone, perhaps the origin of the *ablaq* style made popular in urban buildings by the Mamluks. The lack of wood caused people to use basalt stone as roof beams. The beams are narrow but not long, which limits the length possible for the roof, causing the rooms to be high and narrow. Use of interior arching or strong, square pillars allows rooms of the wealthier villagers to be expansive.

Decorations for houses in the Hawran are similar to those in other parts of the country though the Hawran is also well-known for its fine basketry. Large serving trays made of colored straw are stored by being hung on the walls of the rooms. The Hawran is also known for its embroidery, and the women still make a number of items, such as mirror covers, that are also used to decorate the walls. Floors are covered with local weaving, which, though made by village women, look much like those made by Bedouin women. They are made on the same type of narrow ground loom used by Bedouin women and then are sewn together with colorful wool yarn. The wealthier families were able to buy finer knotted carpets from Turkey or from Turkish pilgrims on their way to Makkah along the Damascus Pilgrim's Road. In recent years machine-made carpets from Belgium and China have come to replace the more traditional handmade knotted rugs.

THE BEDOUIN TENT

The tent used by the Bedouin is a form of architecture and in any discussion of the architecture of a Middle Eastern country it must be included. Syria is home to a number of important and once powerful Bedouin tribes, such as the 'Anazah confederation and the Shammar. These great tribes once dominated much of the Syrian Desert and were even able to successfully challenge government control over most of the rural areas. Tribal elites developed close ties with the important urban merchant families in Damascus, Homs, Hama, and Aleppo, as well as in smaller centers such as al-Hasakah, Dayr al-Zawr, and Dar'ah. Several of the tribal political elite established sections of their families in the cities where they hoped to influence local politics. They bought large urban town houses in order to have the space to deal with the visits by their tribesmen, as well as to entertain and impress urban elite, yet all of them retained the distinctive Bedouin tent, which might be erected in the courtyard of the house.

The Bedouin tent is made of panels of black goat hair sewn together to form a long, wide, rectangular block. The size of the tent and the importance of the person living in it are signified by the number of poles needed to hold it up. The usual size for an ordinary family is a two- or three-poled tent, while those of the shaykhs would need 10 to 12 poles in order to accommodate the space to receive guests and hold meetings. Some Syrian cities such as Homs and Aleppo still have specialized markets that cater to Bedouin needs and provide tent panels and other woven items, ropes, iron tent pegs, and household furnishing made by urban artisans. The market in Aleppo is located along the main access, the old Roman Decumanus, making it easy to find. It is still very active though not as large as it once was, as recently as the 1950s. The black goat hair tent material sold in the Aleppo market comes mainly from the nearby village of Jisr al-Shughur where men, not women, weave the panels on vertical looms. While most Bedouin tents are made by the women of the family from the hair of their own goats, for those who don't own goats (such as camel herding tribes) or for those tribes whose women don't know how to weave, the panels are bought from urban markets in Damascus, Homs, and Aleppo.

Since the 1950s the Bedouin in Syria have begun to use white canvas for tenting material, mainly during the summer months. The canvas is cheap and light but not nearly as weather resistant nor as strong as the traditional black goat hair tent. Bedouin in Jordan scoff at the introduction of canvas tenting among the Syrian Bedouin and refuse to use it themselves. Even in Syria, the use of canvas is seen as the sign of a poor family; a family too poor to own a so-called proper goat hair tent, or a family where the women lack the required skills in weaving, which is equally embarrassing for the family. Those who can prefer to use the hair tent, and tribal leaders always use the black goat hair tent.

Syria's Bedouin women are also skilled at making colorful mats called *zirb* that are used as wind breaks set up around the front of the tent, especially to shield the cooking fire. The mats are made of reeds bound together in colorful wool yarn. The yarn is tied to each of the reeds in such a way as to make geometric patterns; diamonds, triangles, and squares connected by herring bone designs. These are works of art similar to the rugs and tent dividers woven by the women in wool and camel hair. Today women often buy imported pre-dyed yarn for the wind screens in urban centers like Homs and prefer bright, even florescent colors of yellow, red, green, orange, pink, and purple. The colors are eventually softened by the sun into mellow shades more appealing to western tastes. The windscreens last only a few seasons and then need to be replaced with new ones.

In Syria Bedouin decorate the front of their tents with colorful narrow woven strips with tassels hanging along the bottom. In the past these were fine pieces of weaving done mainly in natural off-white, red, and black woolen yarn with occasional use of yellows or other bright colors to highlight designs. Today urban artisans in Damascus and Homs make the strips usually from cotton thread rather than wool yarn on semi-mechanical looms thus the pieces have the look of a machine-made item rather than that of a handmade piece. The new tent strips are often in red with black and white diamonds and triangles designs. Cotton cushion covers and rugs with the same general patterns are also made by the same artisans and found in both Bedouin tents and settled village homes.

CONTEMPORARY ARCHITECTURE IN SYRIA

Contemporary architecture in Syria is greatly disappointing in comparison with the traditional forms. Since the late nineteenth century, cement was introduced as one of the major items used in construction, and the newer sections of Syrian cities, towns, and villages lack the distinctions, and even decorative features, they were once famous for. Syrian cities did not have a flourishing colonial period in architecture as one finds in Egypt, Tunisia, or Morocco because the Syrian economy was too weak to support it. Only a few French came to Syria, and there was very little investment in the country. When Syria gained its full independence in the 1940s, urban architecture did not flourish again due to the weak economy. The Socialist orientation of the government since the 1960s emphasizes public housing along a Soviet or Nasserist model; large, multistoried housing blocs with no distinctive features. The results are uninteresting and unspectacular buildings meriting little comment. Public buildings are equally bland and even grim built in dull gray cement. Once inside an apartment or house, the visitor again finds the grace and elegance of the Syrian home. Many apartments have two salons; one with typical Syrian inlaid wooden furniture and the other with over-stuffed so-called European furniture. The European furniture is often local imitation of Louis XIV styles made popular during the late Ottoman period called Louis-Farouk after the Egyptian King Farouk I, who ruled during the first half of the twentieth century and who favored the style in his lavish palaces.

Villages have also taken on a general similar look with the use of cement. Newer homes are usually one-story square box-like structures. Many of them leave the side pillars of cement and reinforced iron sticking up above the roof indicating a desire to eventually add a second level to the house. The newer

homes may have a walled-in back garden with several fruit or nut trees, which
serves the same purposes as the courtyards in the older village homes. Cement
is not nearly as good of a building material, and the new houses are both cold
in the winter and hot in the summer, so hot that families may be forced to
sleep on the roof. Village houses provide a sitting room used to receive guests,
which is usually furnished like the traditional homes, while the village elite
may have two salons; one the "Syrian" or "Arab" room and the other the
"European" room furnished much the same way as in the urban homes.

TRADITIONAL CRAFTS

As noted above, Syria has a long tradition stretching back to the beginnings of history in fine craftsmanship. The Syrian cities of Damascus, Homs,
and Aleppo have well-established reputations for fine work in ceramics,
stone, metal, wood, leather, and textiles. Certain regions in the country are
well-known for arts in embroidery, weaving, and basketry. Syria's role as a
cultural crossroads brings together cultural influences from Egypt, the Mediterranean, the Arabian Peninsula, Anatolia, Iraq, Iran, and Central Asia. Syria
has attracted skilled artisans from other parts of the Islamic world as well as
has been a source for craftsmen who have settled in such widely dispersed
places as Spain and Central Asia. The Syrian government is well aware of the
wealth of cultural heritage the country's craftsmen represent and actively tries
to preserve them from dying out.

URBAN CRAFTS

Craftsmen in the urban centers cater to both urban and rural tastes. Urban
craftsmen have a long tradition of fine workmanship, and many of their items
were exported to Europe as luxury goods well into the twentieth century. Syrian expertise in colored glass was brought to Italy during the early Medieval
period, and Damascus steel was the world standard for the highest quality of
sword blades. The term *Damascene* describes the ability to inlay steel with
designs in fine gold thread; an art brought by Syrian artisans to Toledo in
Muslim Spain. Both Damascus and Toledo have maintained the tradition of
fine craftsmanship in steel blades and gold inlay on steel.

Damascus, Homs, and Aleppo are major centers for metal crafts. All three
have well-known *Nahhasin,* or copper smiths markets, which produce a
wide variety of copper and brass items. Copper and brass trays, boxes, and
cups are among the common items and much of what is available today is
mass-produced using machines rather than by hand. It is still possible to have
fine handcrafted pieces made by families who have been involved in business

for centuries. Aleppo is better known for its copper work while Damascus is better known for brass items inlaid with silver wire. Some of the families specializing in silver inlay work are Jewish, and both men and women of the family do the inlay work. They still make silver inlaid trays, boxes, small cabinets, and even tables. Though made by Jews or Christian craftsmen, the silver inlay work is mainly Arabic calligraphy of Qur'anic verses. Syrian metalwork emphasizes geometric designs and calligraphy, and those pieces with figurative elements are called Iraqi since the tradition of including people and animals was more associated with Mosul in northern Iraq.

The city of Homs is one of the main sources for the brass *dallah,* or coffee pot, used by Bedouin and rural people to make Arabic coffee. The Homs-made coffee pot is distinctive in its shape and can be identified as such even if the maker's stamp is no longer visible. The lid is flat, giving the pot's long, curved spout greater emphasis. The Damascene *dallah* has a conical top, which is often elongated, giving it a tall elegant look. The spout is not as pronounced as in the ones made in Homs. Both cities also make a variety of other utensils used to make coffee such as the *raqwi,* which is used to make Turkish coffee. The *raqwi* varies in size depending the number of cups of coffee to be made. It is usually open at the top and widens at the bottom. It has a long handle so that it is possible to hold it even though the *raqwi* is placed directly on the heat. Those made in Homs may have a hinge midway along the handle to allow it to be folded for storage. Those made in Damascus can be elegant affairs with a brass or copper rooster placed where the handle meets the vessel and may have brass or copper crescents suspended on chains hanging from the spout.

Damascus and to a lesser extent Homs are well-known for woodworking. Syrian woodworking is called intarsia, or the use of mother of pearl, colored-wood, or bone inlay on wood. Nearly every item from sandals worn in the bathhouse and Qur'an stands to massive dressers, desks, and chests are made using intarsia decorations. Mother of pearl and bone are cut to match the shapes carved into the wood and set by using tin. Originally the use of inlay was restrained but during the last decades of the nineteenth century well into the twentieth century, items were heavily decorated often covering the entire surface. Since the 1970s, more restrained use of the inlay allows more of the underlying wood to show. Designs include flowers, vases, trees, birds, stars, and crescents, in addition to calligraphy and geometric shapes.

A distinctive Syrian form of intarsia is the use of different colored woods cut into geometric designs and inserted into the wood base. Long, thin sticks of the colored woods are first assembled into the final shape and bound together and glued so they will stay in the pattern once cut. They are then cut with a saw with a fine blade of about one millimeter thick. The outline of the design is chiseled out of the wood base, and the entire piece is then glued into place. Rough edges are sanded down, and the whole item, once finished and sanded, is covered in a layer of varnish to help hold it all together and to give it a soft sheen. Today some of the colored woods and even the mother of pearl have been replaced by cheaper plastics.

Damascus, Homs, and Aleppo have long traditions in textiles, each with its own distinctive types and styles. Damascus still produces high quality silks and silk brocades. Silk became established in Syria and Lebanon in the sixth century A.D., and while the industry has suffered a number of setbacks especially with the introduction of cheaper silk cloth from France in the nineteenth century, the Damascus silk textile industry has been able to survive, especially through the production of brocades called damasks. The cloth produced can have up to seven different and distinct colors with one side emphasizing one set of colors and the other side emphasizing another set of colors, which often creates a contrast of dark and light shades. Damascus brocades include metal threads that are made by spinning gold or silver metal thread around a core of cotton or linen. Since the early nineteenth century the Jacquard loom was adapted to the older draw loom method of making brocades, and today most of the cloth available in the Syrian market is made on Jacquard mechanical looms. Of all of the unique artisan products of Syria, Damascus brocades are the most in danger of being lost as there are perhaps only two looms still in operation.

Damascus is also famous throughout the Arab world for a type of cloth called *ghabani*. Ghabani refers more to a type of looped embroidery pattern sewn by machines onto cotton cloth. Ghabani is used for clothes to make caftans, or more often today, to make men's turbans for as far away as Morocco and Senegal. While Syrians rarely wear items in ghabani today, there is a flourishing market both domestically and internationally for table cloths and runners in ghabani.

Homs is equally famous for its textile industry, but the main market for its cloth are Syria's Bedouin and rural peasants, who use especially the heavy silk and silk and cotton scarves called *Hamsiyah* or *Kasrawaniyah*. These are worn as headscarves and headbands by Bedouin and village women in Syria, Jordan, and Palestine. They are usually dark red, blue, or red with silver or gold metal threads making a large diamond in the center. The best and most expensive are "signed" by the maker with a symbol, such as two facing lions or a fish, that is particular to the shop where it was made. Some include the name of the weaver woven into the shop's design. Today most of these scarves made in Homs are cotton and wool rather than in silk.

Homs is also well-known for its fine quality cottons, most of which comes from the *Ghab* and the *Jazirah* areas. Homs cottons are decorated with stamped designs, usually black on white or off-white cloth. The stamps are large, heavy wooden blocks with the design carved into them. The blocks are pressed into the dye and then pressed onto the cloth leaving the design. In addition Homs and its sister city Hama are also well-known for producing tie-dyed cloth used primarily by women for dress material, though many of the pieces are tie-dyed by the women themselves.

Aleppo is the other major producer of textiles in Syria. Aleppo is well-known for a number of different types of textiles and is a major rival of Homs in making fine quality *Hamsiyah* scarves. It is best known for its silk and artificial silk scarves made using block print designs. The cloth is first treated with lime. The cloth is then printed with the block that has been treated with a lime resistant solution, which removes the lime from the areas that will then be dyed to make the designs. This type of scarf is still in high demand by Bedouin women and village women in Syria, Turkey, Iraq, Jordan, and even in Saudi Arabia. In recent years the scarves have become sought-after items in high fashion boutiques in Beirut and Europe.

Aleppo was also known for its silk and silk and cotton ikat textiles. Ikat, called *tarbit* in Arabic, is more often thought of as an Indonesian textile but historically it was produced in Iran, Turkey, and Syria. Ikat is made by wrapping or knotting parts of the yarn before dyeing, and the yarn can be used as the warp, weft, or both in order to make the designs. The main item made from ikat cloth is the wrap used at the bathhouse called *mizar al-Hammam*. Only one shop in Aleppo still makes ikat cloth, and like Damascus brocade, the future of this craft is in doubt.

Jewelry, while usually made by urban craftsmen, was marketed to village and Bedouin women as well. Damascus, Aleppo, and Dayr al-Zawr have long traditions of making jewelry in both gold and silver while the other cities in Syria do not seem to have been involved in the craft though they had shops that sold jewelry. Until the 1950s, village and Bedouin women tended to wear more silver while urban women preferred to have items made in gold. Since the 1950s less and less is being made in silver as village and Bedouin women demand that they be given gold jewelry. Generally, the goldsmith is also the silversmith as they are able to make items in either metal.

Items made for urban clients, as noted above, have generally been in gold. Earrings, necklaces, and bracelets tended to be delicate in appearance with more items made in filigree or using small rings to attach coins or pendants. Blue, red, and green glass beads, red coral, and polished turquoise pieces were often inset into the pieces. Examples of older pieces made before the 1950s show a great deal of imagination in the designs while most of the modern pieces seem more standard, lacking the inspiration of the older ones. Today the most common items found include bracelets made of fake British sovereign coins; bangles with incised designs to catch the light and sparkle as the woman moves her wrist; and large pendants of the Dome of the Rock in Jerusalem or with Arabic calligraphy. Earrings, usually rather large with pendants, are also more or less standard.

While the gold jewelry made for urban women follows contemporary fashions, the silver jewelry made for village and Bedouin women are often more traditional. Some of the forms and designs can be traced back to at least late antiquity. The funerary statues from Tadmur (Palmyra) show close detail of clothes and jewelry worn by women in the first centuries A.D. that closely resemble many of the pieces still worn by rural Syrian women today. There is a wide variety of types of jewelry worn by both village and Bedouin women: front pieces that are worn on their head cloths as well as decorated headbands; temple pieces and earrings; necklaces and chokers; pendants, charms, and pectoral pieces (attached to the back of a woman's dress); bracelets and armlets; anklets; rings; and elaborate belts of leather, cloth, and silver. Traditional jewelry has an element of regionalism with some pieces worn in certain parts of the country but not in others. In addition, some pieces are made specifically for Bedouin women, and generally speaking village and urban women do not wear them. Others are more commonly worn by village women.

Silver jewelry is made mainly using techniques such as sand casting, filigree, granulation, hammering, repoussé, and niello. These are the common techniques used by silversmiths throughout the Arab world from Oman to Mauritania. While most of these techniques are also common to working in gold, niello is unique to silver. Making niello work involves melting a mixture of silver, copper, and lead sulfide powders into an etched design. The melted mixture fixes to the silver, but it has to be high quality silver, at least 80%, or the black niello will come off. In Syria and the surrounding countries, niello has come to be associated with the Circassians mainly because much of their decorative arts make use of it. Circassian saddles, bridles, whips, daggers, and pistols have silver niello mountings. Circassian women wear necklaces and bracelets with niello work as well.

Many of the jewelry pieces worn by rural Syrian women make use of chains. The art of making these chains requires a good deal of skill as the way the individual links connect may involve either a number of them to form a round, square, or braided chain. One of the more spectacular items made with chains is the *jnad*, or shoulder chain, worn by Bedouin women in Syria, Jordan, and northern Saudi Arabia. The *jnad* is a long chain worn over one shoulder and under the other reaching to the waist. They end in a large charm or pendant often with small charms and/or bells dangling from the bottom of the pendant. The chain itself is interspersed with coins, bells, and balls suspended along its length. Another item worn by Bedouin women in northern Jordan and southern Syria is the *'arjah;* a large and complicated headpiece. It is made of one wide chain as a headband that is linked to another wide chain that runs over the top of the head from the front to the back, where it attaches to a long, wide strip of cloth that reaches to the woman's waist. The back cloth strip is decorated with silver coins and ends in several large silk or metallic tassels. The front of the headpiece is also heavily decorated in beadwork and a row of silver or gold coins. In addition further decoration in the form of temple/false earrings may be attached to the sides making the *'arjah* one of the most distinctive pieces of jewelry in Syria.

Kurdish women in Syria's northern regions and Druze women and boys in Syria's south traditionally wear a distinctive silver disk sewn to the tops of their head dresses. The disk is made by various methods but is most often repoussé or a sheet of silver is laid over a mold and then hammered, taking on the reverse of the mold's decorations. They are further decorated with silver filigree and sometimes glass or semiprecious stones are inset into the disk. The finished disk for a woman has coins or other small silver objects suspended along the edge.

*Hijab*s, or charms, are found on a number of different pieces of jewelry and can be small so they can be suspended from another item or can be a large pendent. Charms are shared by all of the different religions in Syria, and many of the charm forms are common to all of them. The blue bead to ward off the Eye of Envy (or the Evil Eye) is common to all of Syria's religions and is sewn onto the clothing of a child or worn on a chain. Charms made for boys used two teeth from a wild boar set in silver and worn on a chain around the neck. Other charms are in the shape of a square or leaf and have verses from the Qur'an etched onto them. Those for Christians have images of the Virgin Mary or a patron saint such as Saint George etched onto them or may be a miniature on bone set into a silver mounting. While silver was the usual metal for these in the past, today many are made in gold.

*Hijab*s are also part of women's jewelry in form of cylinder pendants called *hirz,* or square boxes with verses from the Qur'an, Bible, or Torah placed inside. One shared by all religious groups is called a *samakah,* or fish; a pendant in the shape of a fish, which seems to have once been a symbol of fertility though it has no significance today. Other animal forms used as charms include salamanders and frogs, both symbols of long life. Different-colored stones and beads set in silver mountings are worn by women: blue against the Evil Eye; red for good health; and white for better lactation. Among Bedouin a green stone with red flecks that comes from the Hijaz of Saudi Arabia shaped into a heart is believed to bring good fortune.

VILLAGE AND BEDOUIN CRAFTS

Unlike urban crafts, which are the domain of male artisans, village and Bedouin crafts are the work of women. Village and Bedouin women still produce beautiful works in embroidery and weavings. Most of the items they make are for practical use in the home or to wear. Women embroider the clothes they wear; weave trays and baskets in colored straw; and weave tents, rugs, and cloth for cloaks as well as camel and horse equipment from wool and camel hair.

Embroidery in Syria is distinctive and it is possible to know the village or set of villages a woman is from by the designs and colors used to decorate her clothes. The most elaborate embroidery comes from a number of northern villages including Saraqib, Khan Shaykhun, and Ma'arrat al-Nu'man, and the eastern oasis of al-Sukhnah. The women from Saraqib, Khan Shaykhun, and Ma'arrat al-Nu'man make a particular type of embroidered dress that is made out of black cotton cloth; the front yoke as well as the back yoke of the dress are worked in large geometric designs, mostly in reds with some use of yellow and white. The seams of the dress are also fully embroidered, and the sides have wide patterns while back panels have wide, open designs from the waist to the bottom. Some of the designs are made to look like the silver jewelry worn by the women, and there seems to be a close link to the jewelry depicted on funerary statues from ancient Tadmur. Women from the villages of Mhardah, Kafr Tashrim, and Qala'at Sam'an embroider an outer coat using more restrained patterns that concentrate on the front chest, sleeves, cuffs, and along the bottom. Some are made so that the embroidery on the outside of the coat picks out the design that on the inside is done in appliqué. These coats are made so that they flop open while walking to show the inside appliqué. The coats from Mhardah are distinctive because one side of the front of the coat is heavily embroidered while the other is only lightly embroidered.

Dresses, coats, trousers, and skirts from al-Sukhnah are heavily embroidered with red, yellow, purple; green, blue, orange, and white thread on black silk or satin cloth. The embroidery covers much of the surface of the clothes in geometric designs, mostly diamonds, and what is called date palms and cypress tree motifs. Unfortunately the art of making these unique embroidered items is being lost, and few if any women in al-Sukhnah now make them.

Women in other parts of Syria also embroider their clothes as well as mirror cases, tobacco pouches, money pouches, curtains, and wall hangings. Embroidered dresses from the southern part of the country emphasize the seams, cuffs, and sleeves of the dresses. Some of the dresses have embroidered removable sleeves that can be added for holidays or celebrations. While most of the embroidery in the north is half cross stitch and cross stitch, the embroidery done in the south includes chain stitch, couching, and satin stitch. Both use herringbone stitch for seams.

Village women in the Hawran are famous for their basketry in colored straw. They make large serving trays with a variety of imaginative designs such as spirals and rows of triangles or diamonds in yellows, reds, greens, and blues. More elaborate ones have added edges made from wrapped and dyed straw in the form of triangles; the tip of the triangle points away from the tray while the two corners attach to the side. Others, used for major events, are edged with black ostrich feathers or colored wool yarn. In addition to trays, women in the Hawran make straw baskets in a wide range of sizes. One of the most attractive of these is the sewing box made of colored straw, which is often decorated with silk or wool yarn tassels. While these are more commonly made by rural Palestinian women, they are also found in southern Syria.

Bedouin women are the masters of weaving wool and goat and camel hair into beautiful yet practical items including tent panels, tent dividers, saddle bags (for camels, horses, and donkeys), and rugs, as well as decorative panels for tents, camel trappings, and saddle covers. Both Bedouin women and village women weave on the traditional narrow ground loom. The ground loom has no moveable parts, and the change between the weft and warp, the shed and counter-shed movements in the weaving process, are done by the women separating the threads and physically moving them up and down through their own strength of arms. The ground loom is simple to construct and is staked down to the ground in order to hold the tension. The woman weaving on the loom slowly proceeds along the length of the piece sitting on what she has already completed. Since the loom is narrow, no more than a meter and a half wide or about four feet, any wider item such as a rug or tent divider is made of several pieces sewn together.

Designs are made using two different methods; warp patterns and twined weft patterns. Warp patterns run the length of the piece using the colored yarn only when needed in the pattern, leaving it running loose along the underside otherwise. Twined weft weave requires that two or three yarns are wrapped around individual or several warp yarns to make the design. The warp is fully wrapped, leaving a space or a slit between the design and the next warp thread; thus, this type of weaving is also called slit tapestry weave. In most items made by Bedouin women, there is an attempt to minimize the length of the slits by using overlapping designs.

Conclusion

Syria's architecture and arts are as varied and rich as is the population of the country. The major cities of Damascus, Homs, and Aleppo cater to the sophisticated tastes of the country's urban and urbane elite, who demand both high quality and fashion for the items they buy. Syrian artisans have developed skills that rivaled those of imperial capitals such as Istanbul. Throughout Syria's history it has been an important player in international trade; both a receiver of ideas and concepts as well as an exporter to other areas. As a result, Syrian architecture and crafts are a blend of Arabia, Central Asia and Iran, Anatolia, Egypt, and the Mediterranean.

Syria's rural women also produce beautiful objects of art, although the objects are generally made for everyday use. Masters in the arts of embroidery and weaving, Syria's rural women make items that are collected as much for their artistic value as for their ethnographic value. Rural crafts still mark certain regions of the country where they are made, though the introduction of cheaper machine-made items has already had a negative impact on craft production.

Syria's architectural and handicraft heritage is in danger of being lost despite government attempts to give them value. Many of its famous crafts, such as Damascus silk brocade, is being lost as fewer and fewer young people want to enter the professions. In recent years the local market has been flooded with cheap items made in places like China that are simply less expensive than the local crafts. While the government is making every attempt to keep these traditions alive, simple economics has placed their future in question.

Statues from Tall Halaf form the portico of the National Museum in Aleppo. The Aramean culture of the first millennium B.C. tried to copy previous Hittite models, but were considered to be inferior to the originals. Courtesy of the author.

Above left: Dayr Sam'an or Qasr Sam'an marks the place where St. Simeon or Simeon Stylites sat atop a pillar between 425 and 459. During his lifetime pilgrims began to come to visit the place and after his death the pillar continued to be an important pilgrimage site for Eastern Christians. Courtesy of the author. *Above right:* Umayyad Mosque of Damascus. Courtesy of the author.

Ma'alula is one of the small number of villages where Aramaic is still spoken. The population is divided between Greek Catholics and Greek Orthodox. Courtesy of the author.

Above left: The Temple of Ba'al Hadad-Jupiter in Damascus was rebuilt by the Roman Emperor Septimius Severus (193–211). It was later converted into the Church of St. John the Baptist and then the Umayyad Mosque. Courtesy of the author. *Above right:* Palmyrene sculpture from a funerary tower depicting a family. It now rests in the gardens of the National Museum in Damascus. Courtesy of the author.

Waterwheels at Hamah on the Orontes or al-'Asi River are over 60 feet (20 meters) in diameter. The waterwheels were originally installed it the late Roman period but the current ones (still in operation) date from between the thirteenth and fourteenth centuries. Courtesy of the author.

Above left: Small village church in the northern Jazirah near the border with Turkey and Iraq belongs to one of many such Christian communities who survived Byzantine persecution by being so remote. The bell towers on such churches served as models for the earliest minarets. Courtesy of the author. *Above right:* Shrine of St. John the Baptist in the Umayyad Mosque in Damascus supposedly contains the head of the saint. The Emperor Theodosius converted the Temple of Ba'al Hadad-Jupiter into a church and the Umayyad Khalifah al-Walid (705–715) converted it into a mosque. The shrine was rebuilt in Ottoman rococo style after the fire of 1893. Courtesy of the author.

Above left: Umayyad Mosque in Damascus showing the minaret named Madhanat al-'Arus, or the Bride's Tower. The lower register is the remains of the original bell tower for the Church of St. John the Baptist and the upper part dates from the Mamluk period. Courtesy of the author. *Above right:* The Umayyad Mosque showing the Qubbat al-Khaznah or Bayt al-Mal meaning treasury, which was built raised above the ground for security. The mosaics date from the thirteenth- or fourteenth-century restorations of the earlier 'Abbasid period structure. Courtesy of the author.

The Madrasah and tomb of Nur al-Din in Damascus was built between 1167 and 1172. The honeycomb or muqarnas domes are unusual in Syria and were introduced from Iraq by the Saljuqs. Courtesy of the author.

Above left: Doorway to the governor's palace in the Citadel of Aleppo was built in 1230 by the governor al-'Aziz is an excellent example of the ablaq style of stone work that has come to be a major characteristic of Syrian architecture. *Above right:* The Takkiyatayn of Salim and Sulayman was built by the famous Ottoman architect Sinan (not the same as the governor also named Sinan) between 1553 and 1554. It served as a retreat for Sufis and later Sultan Salim II had a madrasah built in the name of his father, Sulayman. Courtesy of the author.

Houses in old Damascus. Many of these old houses are being torn down to make way for more modern ones. Courtesy of the author.

Old houses in Aleppo were built differently from those in Damascus. Upper stories are most often wood with wooden screens but rarely are built out over the street as they are in Damascus. Courtesy of the author.

Contemporary mud brick house built to house the excavation crew at Tall Tunaynir follows traditional Jazirah style. Note the large bed in the courtyard that is used in the summer when it is too hot to sleep indoors. Courtesy of the author.

The Hijaz Railway Station in downtown Damascus is an example of Ottoman rocco style. Courtesy of the author.

This street in the southern suqs of Damascus connects to the famous Street Called Straight or Midhat Pasha today. The minaret of the Mosque of Hisham (1426–1427) is seen on the right. The large poster of former President Hafiz al-Asad is a common part of Syrian political iconography. Courtesy of the author.

Suq al-Saruja or Saddle Makers Market in Damascus still makes and sells items for horses, mules, and donkeys. Courtesy of the author.

Shop in the Suq al-Bidhariyah in Damascus that sells spices, candies, and roasted seeds (as the name of the suq indicates). Courtesy of the author.

Inlaying silver wire into brass wares such as this tray is an art once associated with Jews in Damascus. There are still a few Jews working in the craft; skills passed on from one generation to another. Courtesy of the author.

Above left: Maker of 'aqal or the head rope used to secure the man's head scarf or kuffiyah in the section of the Damascus suqs where traditional men's clothing is made. Courtesy of the author. *Above right:* Commercial cloth weaver using a Jacquard loom in Damascus. Such looms are used to make nearly all cloth with the exception of the fine silk brocades that requires using a hand loom. Courtesy of the author.

Covered suq in the Euphrates River town of Dayr al-Zawr date from the late Ottoman period. Courtesy of the author.

Street vendor in Suq al-Bidhariyah in Damascus selling freshly baked goods. Courtesy of the author.

Street vendors in Damascus selling 'araq sus, a licorice flavored drink. Courtesy of the author.

5

Traditional Cuisine and Costume

SYRIA'S FOOD AND dress, like its arts and architecture, include both sophisticated urban traditions as well as those of its rural peoples. Damascus and Aleppo have been political and economic capitals a number of times throughout history, and their elite have indulged their taste buds and their desire for fashion. The rural regions have equally produced a large variety of foods and traditional clothes that in no way lack imagination or taste.

TRADITIONAL FOODS OF SYRIA

Syrian food is famous throughout the Arab world as being one of the finest cuisines in the Middle East. It is the dominant type of the eastern Mediterranean and differs little from the foods of Lebanon. Syria exercises a cultural influence even today over Jordanian and Palestinian foods and is a rival of Turkish and Greek cuisines. It is often a matter of national pride for the different countries in the eastern Mediterranean to claim to be the original home of a large number of shared dishes. Many of these foods have ancient origins and with the extensive trade between peoples of the Mediterranean, it is hard today to say where a particular dish may have been invented. Nonetheless, the kitchens in Damascus and Aleppo are deservedly famous for their fine cuisine.

Syrian cuisine, like that of most of the Mediterranean region, is based on olive oil and wheat. Olive oil is the primary cooking ingredient; bread is also dipped it in, and it is poured over the top of many other dips and salads. Black and green olives are served as appetizers at lunch and dinner and are an important part of most people's breakfasts. Olive oil is used in pickling or preserving vegetables, such as carrots, cucumbers, and cauliflower. Wheat is made into numerous types of bread dough most of which do not use yeast or any other form of leaven. In addition, Syrian cooking uses wheat in the form of cracked wheat, or *burghul,* in salads, soups, stuffing, or mixed into ground meat for the different forms of *kibbah* (usually pronounced *kibbi* in Syria and Lebanon).

Syria's climate encourages a number of fruit and nut trees to flourish, and their produce are part of the taste experience in Syrian cuisine. Walnuts, pistachios, and almonds are used mainly in deserts but along with roasted and salted seeds such as pumpkin and sunflower are common snacks. Roasted almonds and pine nuts are frequently used to garnish salads, dips, and meat and rice dishes. Bitter green almonds are sold on the street in the spring and eaten with a pinch of salt to help cut the bitter taste. Fruits include grapes, figs, pomegranate, oranges, lemons, limes, apples, pears, peaches, and apricots. Citrus juices and grated peel are used as spices in many meat, poultry, and fish dishes, and pomegranate seeds are used as garnish. Dates and dried figs or apricots are part of Ramadan foods, such as the drink *qamar al-din* made of apricot leather melted in water. Syrian deserts are often large bowls of mixed fruits and melons of the season, especially in the summer months.

Syrian cuisine, both urban and rural, makes use of fresh vegetables, and most Syrian cities are surrounded by truck gardens that supply the markets on a daily basis. Tomatoes, eggplant, potatoes, cucumbers, squash, pumpkins, okra, artichoke, beans, peas, peppers, cabbage, lettuce, cauliflower, and numerous other vegetables are available either in a specific season or year-round due to hothouse production. In addition to the fresh vegetables, there is a wide selection of dried legumes such as lentils, fava beans, and chickpeas available all year. Syrian foods make use of fresh and dried vegetables through salads and dips. One of the easiest salads is often simply called *salatah 'arabi-yah,* or Arab salad, made from finely chopped green peppers, tomatoes, and white onions tossed with an olive oil and lemon juice dressing spiced with black pepper, cinnamon, and allspice. Another simple salad is called *khiyar bil-laban,* or cucumber and yogurt salad, made from chopped cucumbers in a yogurt sauce flavored with garlic and mint. Other salads such as *tabbuli* are made of cracked wheat with chopped tomatoes, both green and dried onions, parsley, and mint, topped with the olive oil, lemon juice, cinnamon, and black pepper dressing.

Syrian cuisine, like all of the Levant, has a number of dips made from vegetables or yogurt often served as appetizers as part of a *mazzah.* Mazzah is usually served with lunch and can include up to 90 different hot and cold appetizers. Many people in the west are familiar with *humus;* a puree of chick-peas, sesame paste, lemon juice, garlic, and cumin served with a dash of olive oil and garnished with *summaq,* a sour purple spice from the sumac tree. In Syria, this is usually called *humus bil-tahini,* as there are numerous other dishes made from humus such as *humus bil-lahm,* or humus with fried or grilled chunks of meat and pine nuts scattered over the top. Another dip well-known in the west is *Baba Ghannuj* made from eggplant, garlic, and sesame paste blended together. A similar type of eggplant dish found in Syria is called *m'tabbal,* meaning spiced. Its basic ingredients are the same as Baba Ghannuj but the use of different spices including a pinch of red pepper makes it a more interesting dish. Yogurts are also made into dips of which the most common is called *labnah,* which is similar to a sour cream. *Labnah* is usually served with a sprinkle of crushed dried mint and a dash of olive oil to keep it moist and soft during the meal.

Breads come in a variety of shapes and types. The most common type is called *khubz 'Arabi,* or Arabic bread, or sometimes *khubz Suri,* or Syrian bread. It is familiar to most people in the west as pita or pocket bread, though the taste of it fresh from the baker's oven is much better than the packaged bread bought in stores. Arabic bread is used at every meal in Syria for dips, salads, and to help with picking up mouthfuls of meat, fish, or poultry with the hands, and bread is the staple of the eastern Mediterranean diet. There is a wide variety of breads available from the paper thin *shrak* or *marquq* popular among rural people to a thick type made with leavening. Other bread-based foods include much of what could be called Syrian street foods such as open-faced meat, cheese, or spinach pies made on bread called *kmaj,* which is like pizza dough. A popular morning street food is *manaqish bil-za'tar,* made of a bread base spread with a thin layer of olive oil and then with *za'tar* (a mixture of thyme, marjoram, summaq, and salt), which is then baked. In addition to the open-faced pies are a number of closed pies called *fatayir,* which are stuffed with ground meat, pine nuts, and onions. A popular on-the-go breakfast is a bread called *ka'k,* which is not too unlike a bagel though it is baked rather than steamed. *Ka'k* is sold by street vendors who also sell small packets of za'tar and hard-boiled eggs that are eaten along with the bread. Croissants were introduced by the French during the Mandate period and were quickly adapted to the Syrian taste by stuffing them with za'tar or the same salty white cheese used to make the open-faced pies.

Syria has a long tradition of street foods but the most well-known is no doubt the hot sandwich called *shawarmah.* Shawarmah is made by cooking thin slices of meat or chicken on a spit and as the meat cooks, the outer layers are sliced off. The sandwich is made with a warmed pocket bread; slices of

meat or chicken; sliced tomatoes and onions that have been allowed to cook
a bit; pickles; and a dash of thin sesame paste sauce. Shawarmah stands usually also have stuffed kibbah, and together they can make a good lunch along
with a glass of fresh orange or lemon juice from the juice stand next door for
those on the go.

Syrian cooking makes use of a wide variety of spices that came to be
common and affordable at a very early period. One of the oldest archeological finds of a clove, which grows in Indonesia, was at Tall Brak in northern
Syria and dated back to perhaps the Bronze Age. By late antiquity Syrian
markets boasted clove, cardamom, cumin, different types of cinnamons, allspice, nutmeg, black pepper, and saffron as well as local coriander, parsley,
summaq, za'tar, thyme, sage, marjoram, and mint. Since the discovery of the
Americas, red peppers have been grown locally. Sugar, honey, rose water, orange blossom water, as well as lemon and orange peel, are also used to flavor
foods. It is beyond a doubt that the tastes in Syrian cuisine are the result of its
strategic location on the spice trade for millennia. Syrians came to appreciate
the subtlety in tastes spices can produce and learned what combinations can
create a better dish.

The traditional Syrian breakfast is very healthy and emphasizes fresh products. It generally includes one or more types of fresh bread dipped into a
dish of olive oil then dipped lightly in another dish of za'tar and perhaps a
second one of summaq. There are usually dishes offering different fresh, raw
vegetables such as sliced tomatoes, carrots, red radishes, and cucumbers in addition to pickled cucumbers, carrots, and cauliflower. A small but tasty type
of green olive is usually included. A variety of white goat and/or sheep cheeses
that are salty or mildly sweet are cut up and served along with fresh, sour yogurt (*laban*) and sour cream (*labnah*). Breakfasts often include falafal, which
are small cakes of chickpeas that are deep fried then dusted with a covering
of sesame seeds. Scrambled eggs or more likely omelets are served as well.
Some people prefer a bowl of steamed chickpeas flavored with a bit of onion
and salt for breakfast. Fresh juices of the season such as grape, mulberry, or
orange are poured into large juice glasses. Juice may or may not be included,
but glasses of sweet tea are a must. The first glass of tea often is more than half
sweetened condensed milk and for each succeeding glass the percentage of tea
increases until the last glass is all tea and no milk.

The Syrian lunch can be a massive affair and includes meat, poultry, or
fish in addition to salads, dips, and yogurt dishes. Lunch is when mazzah
are served, especially if there are guests and the host wants to demonstrate
the hospitality and generosity of the house. In addition, mazzah provide the
women of the house an opportunity to display their talents in the wide variety of choices available in addition to the individual taste of each dish.

Mazzahs always include various vegetables such as tomatoes, green peppers, hot peppers, potatoes, or vine or cabbage leaves stuffed with a meat and rice mixture, which are steamed or baked for what are called *mahshi,* meaning stuffed.

Various types of kibbah can be made and served at lunches. Kibbah is made with cracked wheat, ground meat, onion, cinnamon, allspice, and black pepper, which can be shaped into balls and stuffed with pine nuts, ground meat, and onions or layered to make something like a casserole and baked. It can be baked with fresh, sliced tomatoes or covered in a sauce made from sesame paste and lemon juice. *Kaftah* refers to ground meat that has been spiced with chopped onions, parsley, cinnamon, allspice, and a bit of black and red pepper, and salt. Baked kaftah is called *kaftah bil-saniyah,* and there is no end to the different ways this can be done but two favorites are *kaftah bil-banadurah,* or kaftah with tomatoes, and *kaftah bil-tahini,* or kaftah with sesame paste. In addition, kaftah can be shaped around kabob skewers and broiled in the oven but more commonly they are barbequed over a charcoal brazier.

Main meat dishes can be a roast of lamb or beef, or more commonly the meat has been cut into small pieces and placed on skewers with alternating pieces of liver, green pepper, onion, tomato, and animal fat to help it cook faster. This is known to westerns as kabob but is usually called *shishlik* in Syria. A form of this with marinated chunks of chicken rather than red meat is called *shish ta'wuk.* Chickens can be baked, grilled, or broiled, and those from Aleppo are famous throughout the country for both the large size of the birds and the use of red pepper in the seasonings. Chicken is often served with a ground garlic sauce to dip each piece before eating. Fish is more common along the Mediterranean coast where good supplies of freshly caught sea fish are available every day. Fish can be stuffed, baked, or grilled.

Along with bread, lunches frequently include rice. Rice is usually made by first sautéing it for a short time in olive oil or butter before adding water and salt and leaving it to steam. A favorite way of preparing rice is to include some vermicelli, which is first browned in olive oil or butter. Then rice, water, and salt are added and left to steam until both the rice and the vermicelli are soft. Any type of rice will do, but generally people prefer the long grain types from India such as Basmati over the shorter, sticky Chinese rice. Rice is served with the meat, poultry, and fish dishes, or the rice itself can be made with meat, poultry, or fish and vegetables cooked with it.

Traditionally water is served to drink along with lunch or glasses of soured buttermilk, called *rayib.* In Aleppo, known for its hotter spiced foods, a drink made from powdered rock hard yogurt, or *jamid,* and then mixed with water is served. The drink is salty and tends to ease the heat of the spices without smothering the taste of the hot peppers. Today in Syria most people serve some type of commercial soft drink along with lunches though many Syrians prefer fresh juices or milk.

Dinners traditionally are not as large as lunches. Dinners include a number of different stews usually served with rice and bread. In winter, soups may also be part of both lunch and dinner along with salads. Before refrigeration was common, dinner stews and soups were a good way of dealing with leftovers from lunch. Today this is not a problem, and dinner has come to resemble more a European three-course meal for many Syrian families.

Syria's Christians have developed a large number of vegetable main dishes for the Lenten fasts required by their faith. Eastern Orthodox Christians have over 100 days in a year when they have food restrictions, such as no meat and/or no dairy products. Many of these dishes are based on high protein substitutes such as lentils and chickpeas and may include eggs when not forbidden by the rules of a particular fast. Other ingredients include eggplant, fava beans, cabbage, okra, green beans, and cauliflower. For flavor, garlic, onion, cumin, and lemon are the most commonly used to spice meatless dishes.

Syrian deserts are justly famous for being among the best in the Mediterranean. Many are made with layers of highly buttered filo dough and stuffed with pistachios or almonds or sweet cream called *qishdah.* The list of this type of pastry is long but the best known is *baqlawah,* or baklava, which in Syria has a number of different forms. Baqlawah is made layers of highly buttered dough with a stuffing of sugar, cinnamon, allspice, and crushed almonds, walnuts, or pistachios. Most Syrian pastries have a light sugar and rose water or orange blossom water syrup poured over them. If poured over while the pastry is fresh and hot from the oven, the syrup seeps into every part of it. While many pastries are associated with holidays such as Ramadan, 'Id al-Fitr, Christmas, or Easter, most are available all year long from Syria's numerous pastry shops.

In addition to the long list of filo pastries Syria has a number of cookies. *Ma'mul* cookies are stuffed with ground walnuts, almonds, or pistachios or date paste. Before being placed on a cookie sheet to be baked, the ball of stuffed dough is pressed into a wooden mold that leaves a decorated imprint. When the cookie is baked, the designs are hardened into place. Other types of cookies include a thin sesame and pistachio wafer called *baraziq* and an almond cookie called *ghraybah.* Macaroons have come to be part of Syrian deserts; they are spiced with the local touch of anise seed to give them a bit of a licorice flavor.

Syria may be the original home of ice cream and one of the oldest ice cream parlors in the world is located along the famous Hamidiyah Suq in Damascus. Traditional Syrian ice cream, or *buzah,* is pounded into a paste with large wooden pestles; a process to slow down the rate of melting on hot summer days. The ice cream is served with a sprinkle of crushed pistachio nuts on top. It is not hard to believe that ice cream could have been invented in Syria given that *sharbat,* or flavored ice, dates back into the early Islamic period if not before. Ice brought from the Mountains of Lebanon was flavored with fruit *sharbat,* or syrups; and, in fact, the words "syrup" and "sherbet" come from the Arabic word *sharbat,* as it was borrowed into European languages during the Crusades.

Any discussion of foods in Syria must include coffee. Coffee is a social affair in Syria as it is in the rest of the Arab world. There are two main types of coffee: Turkish coffee that is found in the cities and coffeehouses, and Arabic coffee that is found in the rural areas, though more among the Bedouin. Turkish coffee is thick and black and can be bitter (*sadah,* or plain, no sugar) to very sweet (*ziyadah,* or with extra sugar). It is usually made in a special copper or brass with a long handle called a *riqwi* or *kanakah.* The size of the pot depends on the number of cups to be made from 1 up to 10, as does the number of teaspoons of finely ground coffee—one teaspoon of coffee grounds and usually one teaspoon of sugar per cup to be made. The coffee is boiled from two to three times, especially if sugar has been added. Once it has boiled the second or third time, it is ready to be served in a small demitasse cup.

Arabic coffee is green in color rather than black. Arabic coffee is made by first roasting an amount of beans on a special roasting pan over open fire. The beans are then allowed to cool before being pounded into powder in a wooden mortar called a *mihbaj.* The coffee is then boiled in a brass coffee pot with a long curved spout along with cardamom pods, which give it the green color. Once finished the coffee is served in tiny handless cups made specifically for Arabic coffee. For the Bedouin, all major meals should end with several rounds of Arabic coffee, which is believed to help with digestion.

TRADITIONAL COSTUME IN SYRIA

Men's Clothes

Syria's traditional costumes vary a good deal from region to region and from urban to rural. Some ethnic communities such as the Kurds have distinctive garb to help distinguish themselves from their Arab neighbors while the Druze have adopted special dress to set themselves apart from their Muslim and Christian neighbors. Nonetheless, most of the traditional dress, especially that for men, shares more common features than not.

In general, men's costume in Syria consists of a tight waist-length coat and vest, matching baggy trousers that reach to about mid-calf (this type of trouser is often referred to as Turkish in English), and wide silk or silk blend sash or cummerbund, a hat or turban, and leather shoes or high-topped soft leather boots. The quality of the cloth used for the clothes and the amount of embroidery on the vest, coat, and trousers served as a means to know the status of the man. Those from the urban elite wore tailored clothes with a high amount of fine embroidery often in silk or cotton silk floss. The sash or cummerbund for the wealthy was made of a long and wide strip of silk folded in two and then wrapped around the waist, while for the others the sash was made of lower quality silk or silk and cotton blend (which today is more often an artificial silk). Turbans worn by men of the elite were made of the highest quality *ghabani* or silk brocade. If wearing a felt *tarbush,* a strip of expensive cloth was wrapped around its base. In the later part of the nineteenth century and into the twentieth century, fewer men wrapped cloth around their *tarbush* unless they were Muslim scholars, who still use a narrow strip of fine white cotton to mark their status as men of religion. In the last half a century of Ottoman rule, many urban men adopted the black frock coat with black tie and white shirt made popular by the Ottoman reformists.

Men from poorer social classes wore less flashy clothes, though tailored, if they could afford it. Instead of fine quality types of cloth, their clothes were made of plain cotton or cotton and wool blends. Most of the urban working class and rural farmers preferred trousers made of black cotton, which didn't show the dirt as much. Those from the rural regions might prefer to wear a plaited woolen and leather belt, a specialty of Damascus craftsmen, rather than the broad silk sash preferred by urban men. Rural men as often as not wore a *kufiyah,* which is wide, square cotton cloth usually white or with black checkers in Syria. The more familiar red-checkered cloth, though worn in Syria, is less common than the black checkered kufiyah. The cloth is worn by folding it into a triangle and the placing it on the head so that the tip of the triangle is in the middle of the back. The kufiyah is held in place by a double rope of plaited goat hair called an *'aqal* or tied in place by taking one of the two wings and tying it around the head. Many of the kufiyah available in Syria are made in Aleppo, while Damascus is a major supplier of 'aqal. In Syria, most rural men and Bedouin prefer their 'aqal to be very thin and to fit around the crown of the head rather than around the whole head.

Druze set themselves off from others by wearing mainly black with a contrasting white cotton shirt. The belted their trousers with a plain black leather or dark-colored silk brocade belt. Druze still wear a shorter version of the *tarbush,* which is covered with an all-white or all-black kufiyah. As an over cloak, they wore the wide-sleeved *bisht* of fine camel hair, usually in dark colors such as black or dark brown and trimmed with gold thread embroidery; the same as those worn by the Bedouin. Druze boys used to wear a short tarbush capped with a silver disc, which they would exchange for the men's type once they reached puberty. The men's simple black and white costume makes a definite impression especially when seen in large numbers such as at a holiday gathering.

Kurdish men in Syria rarely wear traditional clothes except for holidays or special occasions today. Traditional Kurdish dress consists of a short, tight waist-length jacket with minimal or no embroidery; long ankle-length trousers that flare out midway but narrow to be tight fitting at the ankle; a wide, cloth cummerbund; and a large, cloth turban. The edge of the turban cloth has long fringe so that when it is bound around the head, the fringe hang down from every fold. The cloth can be a number of colors or color combinations, but frequently they are black and white not unlike the usual rural *kufiyah*. Today most Syrian Kurds have adopted western clothes and blend into the general Syrian population, and some now wear the Arab kufiyah and 'aqal rather than the distinctive Kurdish turban.

Most Bedouin wear a long ankle-length shirt called a *dishdashah* or *thawb* over a pair of plain white cotton trousers. Bedouin prefer their trousers to be straight-legged reaching to the ankle because they are better for riding than the more baggy type. The wealthier Bedouin have their dishdashah's richly embroidered around the collar and down the front with silk or cotton thread, and in the past they often had very long wing sleeves for added elegance. Ones for the winter are made of a cotton and wool blend usually in dark colors while those for the summer are cotton or cotton and linen blends in lighter colors. The Syrian style of dishdashah is open a short distance up the side seam in order to allow better movement when walking or running. The dishdashah can be belted with a leather belt or bandolier that goes over one or both shoulders. For festive occasions, the belt and bandolier can be further decorated with colorful silk cord that ends in several large tassels which hang down along one leg.

Bedouin men wear white, white and black checkered, or red and white checkered kufiyahs of cotton or cotton and silk blends. The best are cotton and silk blends that used to be a major craft in Aleppo, but most of them worn today are made in Korea or Japan for the Arab market. Aleppo still produces many of the all-cotton ones available in the markets in Syria and Jordan. The kufiyah is held in place with the double head rope, or 'aqal, and, as noted above, most Syrian Bedouin prefer ones that are very thin and fit around the crown of the head. They like the 'aqal to have one long tassel reaching to the middle of the back with a delicately made end design such as star and crescent or even an animal such as a camel. This is in contrast to those worn in other nearby Arab states such as Jordan and Palestine, where a thicker 'aqal with a number of long back tassels is preferred.

As an overcoat, Bedouin men wear a bisht made of camel hair and trimmed with gold or silver thread embroidery especially down the chest. The finest

bisht are so light that they are see-through, and these are usually worn only
in the summer months. In the winter, heavier ones are preferred including
those made of wool and hair that are decorated with woolen yarn embroidery.
Some of the heavier ones are made with a wide vertical strips of undyed wool
or hair. Bisht are off white, tan, dark brown, or black in color depending on
the color of the hair or wool used to make the cloth. In the winter Bedouin
men wore, and still wear, a heavy, wool coat with sheep or lamb skin lining
called a *farwu*. The outside of the coat can be rather plain with mono-color
cloth appliqué decoration or can be highly embroidered. The more embroidery the higher the price and some cost as much as $500 U.S.; too expensive
for the average Bedouin to buy. Since the 1980s, a cheaper variety using
synthetic (imitation) wool linings have been available in the local markets.
Another less costly version consists of two wool blankets sewn together and
cut into the coat, which many Bedouin women can make at home.

Women's Clothes

Traditional women's costumes in Syria have developed over time yet some
of the elements found even today in village or Bedouin women's clothes can
be found in the detailed funerary statues of women from first century A.D.
Palmyra. Not only do some of the same items of jewelry exist today but
some have been translated into other media such as dress embroidery. Urban
women, especially those of the elite, have been subject to the changes in
court fashion for generations and in the Ottoman period were not distinguishable from women's fashion in Istanbul or Cairo. Following World War I,
European fashion entered into local taste, and Syria's urban women are as
progressive as any in the world. Yet, even today the most colorful and varied women's costumes are those of Syria's rural women. Regional styles,
forms of decoration, and even jewelry are still part of everyday life. Village
and Bedouin women maintain many distinctive traditions though in some
places difficult embroidery is giving away to easier and less time-consuming
machine-made versions.

The main element in a woman's wardrobe is the full-length dress usually
called a *fustan*. Most of the dresses worn by village and Bedouin women are
long, loose fitting, and ankle length. The women from the northern villages
prefer to use black cotton cloth for their dresses as it makes a good background for the intricate embroidery designs they apply in red, white, yellow,
and green silk or cotton floss. The villages around the towns of Saraqeb,
Ma'arrat al-Nu'man, and Khan Shaykhun are famous for their embroidery
work that covers the chest panel, the shoulders, and back of the dress in
geometric forms mainly in red. Some of the motifs imitate jewelry forms
such as necklaces and dorsal pieces still worn by them and Bedouin women.

The seams of the dresses are also embroidered as are the hem, side, and back panels, which, in some pieces, can reach nearly up to the waist to the dress.

Women form the northern villages around Qala'at Sam'an and Kafr Tasharim decorate an outer coat of black cotton using both appliqué and embroidery. The chest panel is embroidered in fine small designs usually in red and yellow as are the shoulders of the sleeves and the cuffs. The bottom of the coat is made to flap open when the woman is walking to reveal the inner cloth appliqué, which is echoed in colored embroidery on the outside of the garment. Women from the town of Mhardah make a distinctive coat that is heavily embroidered down one side while the other is left with a minimal amount. The seams are also embroidered in order to emphasize the cut. Unfortunately many women from these towns no longer make their own clothes, and their coats are now more often than not items purchased by antique collectors.

The oasis of al-Sukhnah has perhaps some of the most distinctive traditional women's clothes in all of Syria, and some of the most heavily embroidered. Women from al-Sukhnah nearly covered their black cotton or velvet coats, dresses, and skirts with embroidery in red, purple, yellow, blue, green, and orange silk floss. The women favored certain motifs taken from the oasis's environment, such as palm trees and wild flowers, in addition to a number of geometric designs, such as squares and triangles. The women of al-Sukhnah were among the few in Syria who traditionally wore long skirts in addition to the more common full-length dress. Unfortunately fewer local women wish to spend the time needed to make these embroidered pieces, and they too are quickly becoming collectors' items in Aleppo's and Damascus's antique shops.

Women from the region near Homs and Hama decorate their dresses by tie-dying rather than embroidery. The cloth is usually white cotton, and the woman creates the design by tying knots with silk floss. The cloth is dyed in each of the colors to be used and the knots, or part of the knots are untied to expose the area to be dyed a specific color. Women in the region tie-dye not only their dresses but also their veils in what are called plangi patterns, designs made by a series of different colored dots.

Village and Bedouin women in the southern Hawran wore long dresses again made primarily of black cotton but they used a very different form of embroidery to decorate them. The dresses were embroidered in long narrow horizontal strips below the waist and around the arms. The floss was used to hide the underlying black cloth, and the designs were made by allowing certain parts of the cloth to show through. Other strips make use of colored silk or artificial silk cloth sewn on like appliqué, and the again the design is formed by cutting out shapes in the overlaying piece. The chest panel is left plain or has minimal design made with purchased ricrac material. This type of embroidery is shared with some of the village and Bedouin women in northern Jordan and northern Palestine.

Many other village women in Syria wear dresses that fit between the calf and ankle. Most of these are belted or are made to show the woman's waist. They are not as heavily embroidered though many may have embroidered wing sleeves that can be attached for special occasions. Rather than with embroidery, they may be decorated with cloth appliqué or couching while the dress cloth is colorful artificial silk, velvet, or cotton. The trousers worn underneath the dress come down to the ankle, and the lower leg is embroidered or may end in a lace cuff that serves to cover the wearer's heal. Druze women wear a dress that has a low-cut front, a distinct waist, and an apron. She wears a shirt underneath the dress and tucks the ends of her head scarf into the open front.

Bedouin women from the Syrian Desert region used to wear the huge double dress which was nearly twice and long as the wearer's height. The extra cloth was brought up and folded over a belt and the huge wing sleeves were secured behind her back or over her head and tied in place by a headband. The dress had minimal embroidery work on the cuffs, seams, and hem, as well as on the chest panel mainly as a means of reinforcement. This type of dress fell into disuse in the early part of the twentieth century and was replaced by ones more or less like those worn by many village women. The dress worn today is a simple affair of black cotton with half sleeves tied around the back and with minimal embroidery on the chest panel. Many Bedouin women buy their dresses already made by tailors in cities such as Dayr al-Zawr or Hama, who use sewing machines to make the embroidery. One of the most distinctive pieces of dress worn by Syrian Bedouin women today is the full-length coat, usually called a *sabunah*. It is slit down the sides allowing it to be used to secure bundles such as purchases, firewood, or even children on the back. It is often richly decorated in metal thread or cloth appliqué, with the best ones being reserved to wear for special occasions.

Women's dresses could be belted or left to hang straight. Those that were belted usually used wide leather belts with large silver buckles in imitation of Ottoman court dress. Other belts were more like jewelry, being made of a number of chains with square silver links, often times inlaid with cornelian, agate, or red or blue glass beads made by urban silversmiths. Other women wore braided leather or tablet-woven belts made by special craftsmen in the major cities, though most were made in Damascus.

Women in Syria traditionally wore head coverings no matter their religion, and it was oftentimes hard to identify a woman's religion simply by her clothes. Head coverings can be a simple scarf to a more elaborate headpiece that is as much a piece of jewelry as a means covering a woman's head and hair. One of the most elaborate headpieces is the *tantur* worn by Druze women. The tantur is made of a tall silver or silver-plated metal cone, which is placed on top of the woman's head. It is held in place by connected side pieces that fit by her ears and then secured by the cloth headband, which was often made of silk or silk brocade. Once the piece is in place, a large white silk or brocade cloth is placed over it reaching to the middle of the wearer's back. The origin of this headpiece is unknown, but it may have been introduced in the thirteenth century by the Mongols. The tantur is rarely worn today but has come to be one of the national costumes of Lebanon. Instead of the tantur, most Druze women wear a short tarbush that is decorated in gold thread or has a large silver disk attached to the top over which they wear a large white cloth that is tied at the chin and tucked into the front of the dress.

Many Bedouin and village women in Syria's south wear the *'arjah* for special occasions. The *'arjah* is also as much a piece of jewelry as a headpiece in that it is made of silver chains that form a headband with another that runs from over the top of the head to hold it in place. It is decorated with a strip of beading and coins along the forehead and has a tail that falls down the back to nearly the waist, covered in silver coins, silver charms, and ends in large silk or gold thread tassels.

Most rural women wear the *shambar* as at least one element of their head cover. The shambar is usually made of black crepe material, and in Syria it is often dyed red at the ends with long red fringes or is embroidered with mainly red silk floss. The piece is worn around the head and neck and is usually held in place by a cloth headband, and the ends are either thrown over the shoulders or tucked into the front of the dress to protect the woman's neck. Bedouin women from central and southern Syria wear brocade Homsiyah cloth as a turban or tie colorful cotton print cloth into a high cone shape, while those from the north are fond of the silk and artificial silk prints from Aleppo. Kurdish women also wear several Aleppo silk prints combined together as a head cover.

In the past a number of different decorated caps and hats that were covered with a cotton, linen, silk, or brocade cloth were part of women's costume. These caps and hats could be embroidered or made of patterned silk and usually had rows of silver or gold coins along the forehead. Jewelry and costume blend in many ways in Syria and among the interesting pieces are dorsal chains attached to the woman's back. These are still found today, though they are no longer common among younger women. The chains end in hooks that attach to the woman's dress and are decorated with silver coins or small silver charms. Other dorsal pieces worn by rural women are made of silk and cotton tassels with buttons, glass beads, and metal sequins.

CONCLUSION

Syria's rich cultural heritage is well represented in both its cuisine and costume. Syria's climate gives it a wide variety of natural agricultural produce for its basic food stuffs, and its long connection to the spice eastern trade gave rise to the sophistication of its tastes in former imperial capitals as well as among rural farmers. Syrian food can compete with any other Mediterranean cuisine in variety of dishes and imaginative use of spices. Similarly, the traditional costumes reflect not only the country's position as a major center of administration and urbane sophistication but also the diversity of its people and the skill and ingenuity of its women. Both food arts and costumes are primarily the work of women, though men do take part in making both food and clothing. Yet, the realm is mainly that of women; and, through their art, the full richness of Syrian culture can be best appreciated.

6

Gender, Marriage, and Family

SYRIAN SOCIETY, LIKE that of other countries of the Mediterranean, is characterized as having strong patriarchal tendencies. Family forms the basis for Syrian society and was used by the early Ba'athist theoreticians as the primary source for their version of socialism. In some ways the figure of a strong national leader such as Hafiz al-Asad (and now his son Bashar) is the embodiment of the father figure as the head of the household. As one takes care of his family, the other takes care of the nation.

FAMILY

The family is the core of traditional Syrian society. In the past, and to a certain degree today, large families were looked on as a measure of a man's success. Men were to be the providers and protectors of their families, which were composed of several generations living together under the rule of the head of the house. Men were expected to take care of their parents, especially of their mothers, their sisters, and of course, their wives and children. Households were large and adult sons and their families often continued to live with their parents under the guidance and control of their fathers until they were able to establish their own households or till their fathers died at which time the eldest son took over the role of head of household.

Large families were encouraged to assist with work not only in rural settings but also in the urban areas. The work load was gender divided with defined male and female tasks. Girls often began assisting with the hard housework at an early age, especially if they were the older siblings. They were expected to watch and care for younger children as well as assist the women of the household with tasks such as fetching water, doing the wash, cleaning, and cooking. In the traditional society girls were expected to be accomplished at household tasks before the time of puberty, when they could then expect to marry. In addition to the heavy work, girls were expected to know how to preserve foods (vegetable and fruit pickles, jams, and jellies; and canned or dried fruits and vegetables) as well as be skilled in such handicrafts as weaving rugs, making baskets or pottery, sewing, embroidering, and other finer arts of an accomplished young woman. Girls from wealthier families who could afford servants for the harder work still needed to know how cook, sew, embroider, and perhaps weave, as well as organize and manage large households.

Boys were allowed to spend more time at play than the girls. They were allowed to be out in the streets or in the countryside where groups of them could organize games. In the past, boys in rural areas were expected to also help their fathers in agricultural work such as plowing, planting, irrigating, harvesting, and threshing, as well as with taking care of cattle, sheep, goats, and donkeys. Poultry and rabbits were not seen as men's concerns and were left to the women of the house to raise.

In urban areas boys from the poorer districts were expected to work or be apprenticed to a craftsman to learn a trade if they weren't working with their fathers. Many trades such as weaving, dyeing, woodworking, fine copper and brass metalworking, silver and gold working, and masonry were passed down father to son. Some high-skilled crafts such as inlaying silver wire in brass and copper are still family crafts in Damascus. In the past some of the craft guilds were also associated with Sufi brotherhoods and a boy would be taken on as an apprentice both to the craft and to Islamic mysticism. Today the craft guilds have been replaced with workers unions, and there are laws about child labor. Still, boys may be apprenticed to learn a craft or skill such as auto mechanics, electrical works, or plumbing, but they are supposed to also attend school.

Boys were to learn to be men by observing the adults around them and through their roughhouse games. Syrian culture places a high value on bravery but also on generosity, hospitality, and good manners. Boys are given the responsibility of watching, caring for, and defending their sisters, even those older than them, when outside of the house. In traditional Syrian society, boys are required to take on the role of absent adults; that is to act as de facto head of the house when their fathers are not home.

In the traditional society of the past, children become adults quickly, and there was no time for adolescence. Today this has changed at least for many urban youth. Yet, the old values are still in place with strict codes of honor, but boys and girls are allowed time to talk to each other before and after school. Places such as street stands selling fresh fruit juice or walk-in fast food restaurants (called hamburger bars) serve as honorable places where teenage boys and girls can meet and talk. The teenagers are in full view of the public, and respectful distances can be maintained not to damage the girls' reputations. In recent years cyber cafes and even English language centers have become places where youth can gather and not cause too much concern for their parents.

In the traditional family, the father is the undisputed head and is the decision maker. This role is embodied in the term *Si Sayid,* or Lord and Master. There is little room for discussion once a decision has been made and to challenge a decision is not tolerated. A usual response to an announced decision is for the other members of the family to obey, which is frequently embodied in the statement, "my opinion is your opinion." Mothers play a major role in both decision making (discussions taking place beforehand in the privacy of the bedroom) and in modifying decisions, but never in such a place as to challenge the position of the father as the head of household. The family works with top-down orders by the father, which can be modified by the mother during private discussions behind the closed doors of the bedroom, away from children or anyone overhearing. Children know that if they do not like a decision, they appeal to their mother to speak to their father on their behalf. Their mother or their grandmother are more likely to get an order changed than anyone else.

Women gain power in the house by having sons and with age. Traditionally a woman takes the sobriquet "Mother of" the name of her eldest son; thus, if the first son is named Marwan she is henceforth called Umm Marwan (it must be noted that fathers also take on the sobriquet "Father of," thus in this example Abu Marwan). The more sons she has, the stronger her position grows because there is a very strong bond between mothers and their sons. Sons are to defend their mothers, even against their fathers if need be.

Likewise there are strong bonds between brothers and sisters, in fact in the traditional family the bonds between brothers and sisters are the strongest. Brothers keep their role as protectors of their sisters even after their sisters have married. Women do not change their names and join their husbands' lineage (as is done in the West) but keep their own names. Husbands can not ban their wives from visiting their brothers, and women seek refuge with their brothers should there be trouble in the marriage. Even today women know that they can always count on their brothers for support.

Bonds between fathers and daughters are also very strong. Despite the cultural bias for boys, men often have conflicts with their sons. High expectations are placed on sons, and if they fail to meet them, their fathers feel as if their own honor has been given a blow. On the other hand, girls, especially if born later in the sequence of children, are the special favorites of their fathers, indulged and pampered inside the household.

Birth

The birth of a new child is an important event, and in the past, all births were expected to be a boy. Traditional Syrian society, like that of the Mediterranean region as a whole, places a higher value on boys than on girls. Pregnancies were always expected to produce a male, an heir to carry on the family name and honor. There was a great deal of pressure on women to have boys, and if a woman continued to have girls and not produce a male, she could be divorced by her husband. While girls did not have the same high value as boys, many women would wish for girls to help them with their work.

Births of boys were celebrated events. Neighbors and family members were contacted, and congratulations were passed to the couple. The births of girls were heralded with less public acclaim yet messages of congratulations were also exchanged with the couple.

About a week after the birth of the child, whether boy or girl, a ceremony is held to formally introduce the child to the community called the *Sabu'ah*. Sabu'ah comes from the Arabic word for seven, or *saba'ah,* and for week, or *usbu',* and the celebration is usually held seven days after birth. The celebration itself seems to be of ancient Egyptian origin and has become well established as both Muslim and Christian custom throughout the Arab world. The Prophet Muhammad is known to have held such celebrations for the births of his daughters. The celebration takes different forms in the different Arab countries; Egyptians maintain many of the original Pharonic features not found beyond the Nile valley.

The celebration in Syria usually includes inviting family and neighbors for a large meal, usually at midday. The child is dressed up to be presented to the community, and the name is officially announced. For this reason the sabu'ah is often translated into other languages as a naming ceremony. The child is told to obey his or her parents, to grow quickly, and to be strong. Some families may include certain symbolic representations and actions, such as striking the side of a brass mortar with the pestle to enforce the admonition to listen to his or her parents. A pot with freshly sprouted wheat represents the new birth and wish for quick growth. There are a number of songs that mainly the women sing for each of the different parts of the ceremony.

CIRCUMCISION

All Muslim and Jewish boys are circumcised according to religious obligation. For Jewish boys the circumcision is done by a rabbi when the child is 40 days old. For Muslim boys circumcision can take place at a much older age. In the past, boys could be allowed to be uncircumcised to as late an age as 10, though generally they would be circumcised at a much earlier age. Boys need to be circumcised before they can be allowed to handle the Qur'an, thus most have the operation around the time they would be enrolled in the local Islamic school to begin memorizing the holy book.

Circumcision is still today accompanied with a celebration to mark the event. In the past the local neighborhood barber was also the person contacted to do the operation. The boys were dressed up for the event and told not to worry and that it will not hurt. Family and neighbors came to the boy's house, where, following the operation, they will be served food, fresh fruit juice or sherbet drinks, coffee, tea, and pastries. The boy would be taken to a room already set up for the operation where the barber would be waiting. The boy would be distracted in some way by the men in the room, and the barber would quickly remove the extended foreskin. While this was happening, the women and guests waited outside singing, clapping, and ululating. Once the operation was over, the boy and the men emerged from the room for the boy and his family to receive words of congratulations.

MARRIAGE

Syria has a number of regions with strong local traditions that vary somewhat from one place to another. In addition, the different ethnic groups and religious minorities have customs that are unique to them. Traditional marriage customs vary a good deal in their details but there are general customs that are shared by all. Many of these customs are still practiced by rural Syrians as well as by more conservative families in the cities.

In the past most marriages were arranged between the families of the bride and groom, and it was not unusual for the couple to have never seen each other before the wedding. Young men would usually come to their mothers to tell them that they were now ready to get married and for their mothers to start the search for an appropriate bride. Mothers could enlist a wide range of female friends and relatives to look for a good match, and among the urban families, the neighborhood hammam, or bathhouse, was a good place to find a possible bride. In the hammam, it was possible to observe how well behaved the young woman was, how well mannered, how modest, and how she laughed. It would also be necessary to ascertain if the girl in question has had other suitors or if her father's brother's son has given up his first claim to marriage. Customarily, the preferred marriage partner is the girl's first cousin (to maintain family property when she inherits), and he had a first claim to her. However, if she let it be known that she did not want him or that he had given up his right to marry someone else, she was free to marry whom she chose.

Arranged marriages are not confined to the Muslim population of Syria, but similar practices are found among the Christians. Christian mothers will look for possible brides for their sons not only in the hammam but also while at mass. The Eastern Christian mass has a different format from that of the Western Churches, and much of what is done by the priests is behind a screen out of view of the congregation. While the mass is going on, there is plenty of time to converse with other women and a chance to see how the girls are behaving and how they are dressed. Through the conversations, it is possible to know who has a daughter of marriageable age and even if there is any gossip (good or bad) about the girl and her family.

Once a possible bride was found by the women of the house, the mother would approach the father to inform him. The father and the young man would dress in formal clothes and call upon the father of the possible bride. Seeing the formal attire, the bride's father and brothers would guess the nature of the visit and perhaps put on a bisht over their clothes to receive the guests. Coffee would be served but the guests would refrain from drinking saying instead they have come on serious business. The father of the groom would announce his son's desire to marry the girl, and until the father of the bride responds, no one will touch the coffee. Usually the father of the bride would ask to be excused so that he can ask his daughter if she is willing to marry the suitor, but most often he would consult with his wife. If the women of the family agree, the father of the bride will come back to his guests and invite them to drink the coffee, a sign the answer has been yes.

The engagements are still announced by a party held at the groom's home. The party is usually held in the afternoon; an unofficial way of letting guests know that though food will be served, it will not be a full meal. The groom will be seated in one room where he will receive the congratulations of the guests while the other male members of the household will be making sure that all of the guests have tea, coffee, juice, food, and cigarettes.

Marriage in Islam is a legal contract between the two parties, and the contract can spell out conditions both for the marriage and for a possible divorce. The parties are considered legally married once the contract has been signed before witnesses. Signing the contract is called *katab al-Kitab,* or writing the book, which is done before an Islamic judge or legal authority, called a *ma'dhun,* and the required number of witnesses. Some of the legal schools require the girl be present and be asked by the legal authority if she is entering into the contract of her own free will. She has to convince him that she is before he will continue. Other schools allow her father, brother, or other male family member to act for her and she may not be present at all. Once the contract has been read and signed, it is sealed by a recitation of the first chapter of the Qur'an followed by words of congratulations. Once the "book has been signed," the marriage can be broken only by divorce.

Traditionally the signing of the book is preceded by weeks of preparation and a number of evening parties at the bride's home. Women of the family and her friends gather to help her make and embroider her wedding clothes as well as prepare the things she will take with her to her new home. As it moves closer to the wedding day, the bride will be given a henna party where her hands and feet will be decorated with designs made using henna paste. In order for the designs to take on a deep reddish brown color, the paste must be allowed to dry for several hours. In the meantime, the bride will be entertained by the other women who sing, clap, play drums, and dance. She will also be bathed, made up, perfumed, and dressed the day of the wedding before she is taken to the home of the groom.

The groom's house will also be active getting ready for the wedding as it is the groom's family that pays for it and hosts the massive wedding day meal. Women of the house may need to ask neighbor women to lend a hand in preparing the foods that will be served. The groom will be taken to the hammam by his friends, where he will be bathed, shaved, and dressed. The groom will proceed back to his house while his friends serenade him. The bride will be brought to the groom's house in a large procession bringing with her *jihaz* (the items that she contributes to her new home) along with her clothes and jewelry. In the past she was brought on horse back while the rest of the procession walked but today it is done by a long line of cars honking their horns as they make their way to the groom's house. Again, in the past, a child might ride with the bride as a symbol of the children she will bring, and today some families place a large doll on top of the car the bride is in for the same reason. In cities such as Damascus and Aleppo, the bride's procession is preceded by two or more men with swords and shields, who stage mock fights as musicians play on a large double-sided drum called a *tabl* and play a reed instrument called a *mizmar*.

Once the bride arrives she is quickly whisked away to a part of the house reserved for women while the men sit with the groom. Both the bride and groom are entertained with music and dancing. Members of the groom's family move about making sure that the guests have food, drinks, and cigarettes. The bride and groom are eventually escorted to the bedroom to consummate the marriage while family members wait outside to take proof the bride was a virgin and display it before the gathered company. Should a bride not be a virgin, the marriage can be called off on the spot, and the family of the bride is disgraced before the whole community.

Today many marriage parties are done in major halls rented for the occasion by the groom's family, and the guests usually sit at arranged tables as families rather than separate into gendered spaces. Wealthier weddings feature hired musicians, who perform Arabic popular songs as well as more traditional wedding pieces. The bride and groom wear Western clothes, the groom usually in a black formal suit, and the bride in the large white dress familiar to a western wedding. The bride and groom are placed in large throne-like chairs next to each other on a raised stage facing the room full of guests. They will stay seated while everyone else eats and dances. After several hours they will be escorted out of the hall to a waiting car to take them to a hotel or to the groom's house where the marriage will be consummated in private.

DIVORCE

Divorce is allowed in Islam and Judaism, but some of the eastern Christian churches do not allow it. The Syrian state offers couples the option of a religious marriage or a state marriage, and laws regulating women's rights in marriage and divorce are different depending on the type of marriage. Many couples opt for a state marriage even if they also have a religious ceremony. For Muslims and Jews this poses no real problems, but for some Christians it does. If they marry under the state, women are allowed divorce, alimony, and child custody rights, while under the church they have no right to divorce, and if the couple does divorce, it is not recognized by the church and any subsequent remarriage is forbidden. For a woman who may remarry and have children with her second husband, according to the church, the children are born of sin and will not be recognized or allowed baptism.

Divorce is allowed in Islam, and women have the right to divorce her husband but under very specific circumstances. Divorce is considered a bad action and allowed only after all possible means for reconciliation have failed. Women are allowed custody of their children up to a certain age, then as members of the husband's family, they should come to live with him. Women have the right to demand child support if the husband is unwilling to take them to raise or if he is unwilling to comply with other things she stipulated in the wedding contract. Women can insist on the right to divorce in the wedding contract but are often discouraged from doing so because it may cause problems with the groom's family.

The Syrian state provides a number of legal protections for women but in order to get them she may have to take her husband to court. Court cases can be long, and it may be more convenient to allow him to get away with not upholding his obligations. There are women's organizations that can help, but again family pressure to help preserve their honor may persuade women to not pursue her rights.

DEATH

Like marriage, the different communities in Syria deal differently with death. For Muslims the burial should happen as soon after death as possible, and there is no viewing of the body or wake. Christians, on the other hand, have more elaborate services for the dead, and burial may take place several days after death.

Muslims wrap the body of the dead in the simple white garment they wear as pilgrims to Makkah. The body is first washed often by the women of the family, who then wrap it in the shroud. The body is then taken by the men of the family and the neighborhood to a mosque, where prayer is said over the corpse asking for God's mercy. Immediately after the prayer, the body is carried by the men to the cemetery as rapidly as they can. As the procession passes, everyone stands and takes off anything on their head as a sign of respect or joins in to the back of the procession. Once at the cemetery, the body is placed in a grave that has somewhat of an *L* shape with the body placed to the side of the *L* then slabs of stone are placed to protect the corpse from the dirt that is replaced back in the hole. Some Muslims, such as the Shi'ites leave a "breathing hole" at the side of the grave, where during visitations it is possible to "talk" to the dead. Once the body has been buried, the company says another prayer, then everyone returns to their homes.

Visitation of graves is not encouraged by Sunni Islam but the practice is tolerated. Visitations are done mainly by women. Women have little place in the fast pace of the Muslim funeral but may accompany the procession staying at the end of the line. Because they do not have that much involvement in the funeral, women may come to the grave site to sit and mourn the dead. Women may make it a weekly or monthly practice to visit the grave, usually on a Friday.

Mourning is marked by wearing black for most, though for Muslim widows, they first wear white then after a certain time period they will put on black. The family will receive visitors who come to pay their respects; men will gather in one room and women in another. Men of the family will sit or stand near the entrance, where they will both greet and say goodbye to the visitors. The male visitors when they enter will find a place in a long line of chairs where they will take coffee and either sit silently or converse in low tones with the persons next to them. After a respectful time, they will leave and in the meantime others have arrived. In the women's side grief is more openly shown with crying and gestures of deep sorrow such as slapping the face, pulling hair, or tearing their clothes. It is also customary now to send a telegram of regret to the family, which will be delivered to the door. While the family is in mourning, neighbors make the effort to not make too much noise or play music too loudly. Those who do are quickly told to stop by other neighbors. Deep mourning continues for a 40-day period at which time there is another gathering, though more for the women of the family. Once this is over, it is possible to start returning to a more normal life.

Christians have a similar cycle of mourning though it is longer. Christians have a service or mass in the church and unlike Muslims do not necessarily wrap the corpse in a shroud. Christians use coffins and in some denominations, it is possible to have an open casket at the service. Once the service has ended, there is a slow procession to the cemetery to bury the coffin where once again prayers are said. Certain Christian groups have adopted more western practices and do not separate men and women. While the mourning period for Muslims is usually 40 days, for Christians, especially for eastern Christian churches, there are multiples of 40 that are also days of mourning where the grief is relived up to a year after the death. Christian theology has no issue with visiting graves. Women are the main ones who participate in visitations, just as with Muslims, and for some eastern Christians certain holy days are marked with visiting family graves.

CHANGING CONCEPTS OF GENDER

The governments of post–World War II Syria have strived to improve the situation of women in the society. Professions once seen as appropriate for a man have been opened to women. There are women ministers of state, in the parliament, military, police, and in other professions including medicine, engineering, and law. Education has been available for nearly all Syrians, and since the 1950s, there has been a growing middle class. The ruling Ba'ath Party supports secular policies and has even supported punitive, discriminatory actions against open display of religious affiliation, such as veiling by government employees. The result has been to change some attitudes about gender and gender roles; nonetheless, the long-held conservative ideas are still strong.

Syria has made significant advances in education with over 75% of the people literate, though its level of literacy is not as high as its two neighbors Jordan and Lebanon. Significant effort has been made by the government to promote education among girls, especially in high schools and universities. Though universities do not practice any gender discrimination in selection for degree programs, cultural and family constraints still influence choices by girls with fewer of them enrolling in more so-called male programs, such as certain kinds of engineering. Women tend to choose degrees in education, languages, humanities, social sciences, computer science, and medicine, which fit better with more conservative attitudes about so-called acceptable jobs.

The two youth organizations of the Ba'ath party also promote education and wide career choices for both boys and girls. The Vanguard, or *al-Tali'ah,* is the Ba'ath party's organization for children who are in primary school. Its weekly television program is modeled after the Mickey Mouse Club with very talented children able to sing, dance, and demonstrate their abilities in a number of games and situations. Similar to the Mickey Mouse Club, both boys and girls are included in equal numbers and freely mix together. The Youth of the Revolution, or *Shabibat al-Thawrah,* is for teenagers and, again, its weekly television program is modeled after similar western shows highlighting teenage talent. The young presenters of the Youth of the Revolution show dress in military uniforms part of the time, and the organization has a strong political/nationalist orientation. Girls are seen wearing uniforms and going through paramilitary training along with the boys, in fact, in some instances, in direct competition with them. Girls go along on such training as field camp and parachute jumping. Both youth organizations function much like the Boy and Girl Scouts, though they are promoted in the schools and have a strong political connection, making them more like the old Soviet Young Pioneers. While it can be argued such programs and youth organizations are countered by more conservative home life, nonetheless, they do demonstrate the fact that officially nearly everything is open to women.

The Syrian government also uses historical figures to help promote policies about women's participation in both politics and economics. The pre-Islamic queen of Palmyra or Tadmur, Zenobia, is often used to promote a sense of women in Syrian history. Her face is on Syrian currency, and her story is well-known to all Syrian citizens being taught in school as an example of a Syrian who stood up to imperialism, in her case Roman imperialism. Many Syrian schools take their students on field trips to Palmyra, and Zenobia has been the subject of numerous books, plays, and television series, which have been popular throughout the Arab world.

Women are very present in Syrian public life, being 33.7% of the workforce (statistics for 1991), with sectors such as agriculture and community services having the highest proportion of female workers. Many women are employed in the public sector, where they tend to hold more traditional support positions such as secretarial staff rather than decision makers, but there are women ministers of state as well. Women work in a number of jobs in factories, mainly in textiles and tobacco (for example they represent 25% of textile workers), that are owned by private companies or by the state, though again they tend to be workers and floor managers rather than top management. There are also a growing number of women professionals in fields such as law, medicine, and engineering.

Women are taking advantage of the economic openness that began in 1980s. While the number of women-owned companies (both large and small) is still small, only slightly over 3% compared to Egypt, where they are over 17% of the total; nonetheless, many are opening business in tourism, textiles, food processing, and the like. Tourism and its many side businesses, such as restaurants, hotels, transportation, is one of the quickest growing industries in the country and would take off should there be better political stability in the region as whole. Events such as the American invasions of Iraq and Afghanistan and the Israeli invasion of Lebanon have quick and devastating effects on tourism.

Syrian women are well represented in politics and make up 9.6% of Syria's parliamentarians, a percentage that was surpassed in the Arab world only by pre-war Iraq. Women are also well represented in the different ministries of the government and in some ministries, such as the Ministry of Education, Ministry of Health, Ministry of Social Affairs, and the Ministry of Tourism, women make up about one-half of all employees. In addition Syria has had several ministers of state who were women. Women are also well represented at the level of professors in the country's universities. They make up one-half of the teaching faculty in chemical and petroleum engineering at al-Baʿath University; 10% of the faculty of veterinary sciences at al-Baʿath University; 20% of the faculty of agriculture at Aleppo University; and 10% in economics at the University of Damascus.

The impact of the rapid changes in education and the economy has impacted the Syrian family. Urban families tend to be smaller in size with two or three children. Children are not expected to work, and it is rare to find an urban family that does not send all of the children to school; figures for 2000–2001 indicate that over 90% of all primary-aged children attend school. Rural families may still depend on children for at least part of their labor needs, but even in the rural areas, girls are being educated at least to the end of primary school. Young women make up around 50% of the university students at Tashrin and al-Baʿath Universities and between 25% to 30% of the students at Aleppo and Damascus Universities respectively. More and more women are working outside of the home and many younger Syrian women are pursuing full-time careers. As a result, women may decide to postpone getting married, and many want to balance their careers with their marriages. In 1985 Syria's legislature passed a labor law that gives relatively long maternity leaves, allows for breast-feeding at work, and forbids women be employed in jobs that will harm the fetus. Women are also forbidden to work at jobs that require carrying, pushing, or pulling heavy weights. Women are also not allowed to work at jobs at night with certain exceptions such as doctors, nurses, restaurant workers, in media (television, radio, and the like), and other specific jobs that require working at night. Syrian law requires periodic medical checkups and other such protection for workers, many of which are specific to women.

CONCLUSION

Syria's post-independence governments have pursued policies of gender equality in education and employment, and many women have been able to take advantage of these policies. Nonetheless, Syria is still a conservative country with strong family controls. Girls (and boys) seldom choose their careers on their own, but their parents make the choices for them. Girls have greater freedom of movement than in the past, but conservative cultural values limits who they speak to and where. Most working women fit in the age group of 20 to 24 years old, and once they are married, they may quit their jobs or cut back their hours to part time. While law may encourage women to stay in their jobs, women may be passed over in promotion, because it is expected that family life and duties will interfere or that women employees will leave once they are married. The values of honor and shame are very strong yet today, even among the educated elite. It is still considered to be polite for two brothers when talking about their mother to say a more impersonal "your mother" rather than "our mother." Things are changing but it will be a long time before many of the conservative attitudes of the people change, whether Christian or Muslim, Arab, or Kurd.

$$7$$

Social Customs and Lifestyle

SINCE THE RISE of the Ba'ath Party to power in the 1960s, Syria society has been pulled in two different directions. The Ba'ath Party's policy of secularization is in direct opposition to the strong conservative nature of Syria's traditional society, whether Muslim or Christian. The Ba'ath Party has tried to champion the numerous minorities in the country, whether they are religious or ethnic minorities. The result has been a degree of tension within Syrian society as the two forces find accommodation with the other.

CONSERVATIVE TRADITIONS AND THE SECULAR STATE: CONFLICT OR COMPROMISE?

Among the basic concepts of the Ba'ath Party is equality between all members of Syrian society no matter religious affiliation. The founders of the party emphasized the common cultural traditions held by all Arabs, whether Syrians or not, and the basic social organization of the family. The party tries to deemphasize religion, especially the differences between religions. Instead, it tries to emphasize the family as the basic social unit not only of the Arabs but of the other peoples in the Middle East; Kurds, Armenians, and Turks. As such, certain traditional values are seen as positive and part of a secular orientation of the party and the state such as respect for elders and the strong role of the head of the family.

Respect for elders is a traditional value that is also stressed by the party. In traditional society, children need to show respect for their elders by kissing their hands or foreheads when greeting them or when saying goodbye. Children should not interrupt their elders and when told to do something, should immediately jump to the task. Children should be quiet and listen or leave the room while elders discuss important matters. In the more traditional families, women are often secluded and do not join groups that include men who are not closely related to them.

While the party ideology tries to use the traditional Arab family as its social model, it does have differences about the treatment of women, for example. The party has tried to include women more and more in the work force outside of the home and to push for universal education. Women have been promoted in the government including into positions as ministers of state. Women are encouraged to pursue any field of education they are interested in and to take an active role in society. Unveiled women are rewarded while those who chose to wear the veil can be subject to discrimination including lower pay. This is in direct conflict with more traditional values that protect women through seclusion.

In traditional society women are seen as the main source of a family's honor and possible shame. Women are subjected to far more social control than men and in Syria's major cities, Damascus, Homs, Hama, and Aleppo, traditions reinforced by conservative religious interpretation kept women in seclusion. Girls under the age of puberty were given more freedom of movement and often were even allowed to play with boys. However, as a girl grew older and closer to puberty she would be required to start wearing a scarf to cover her hair and be more involved in household chores with her mother. At puberty she would no longer be able to go out alone or unveiled. In the house she would be restricted to the private sections should there be male visitors. The family would try to be sure that she was married as soon as possible in order to ensure her honor, and that of the family, would not be compromised. The best possible spouse would be a cousin, and the most preferred was her first cousin, the son of her father's brother, or *ibn 'Amm*. Such close marriages were seen as positive and helped preserve inheritance within the family.

Rural women had greater freedom of movement since they were involved in daily work that required they leave the house. Nonetheless, in the rural areas honor and shame were also linked to the actions and words of the women more than to the men. Rural women, especially among the Bedouin, had a stronger voice in decision making than urban women. Bedouin women could chose to join guests or not or could join the conversation through the woven panel that separated the private family section of the tent from the public section. Bedouin women had a much stronger voice in accepting offers of marriage and could demand divorce. Older Bedouin women, those no longer of the age to bear children, regained a good deal of freedom of movement and could even smoke in public and speak their minds at tribal councils. Such freedoms were not part of the more conservative urban attitudes.

Rural women were rarely completely veiled as it would interfere with needed freedom of movement for work. Rural women wore—and many still wear—a black crepe cloth that covers the front and back of the neck and hair called a *shambar,* which is held in place by another cloth worn as a headband, or *'asabah.* The *shambar* can be brought up over the mouth and nose if the woman wants to conceal herself from the looks of a stranger. Urban women, on the other hand, wore a large enveloping outer garment much like an over-coat, and her face was totally covered by a sheer black cloth that was attached to the top of her headscarf. Nothing could be seen of her with the exception of her hands, which could also be hidden by gloves. Various versions of this are still worn by many women in Syria. In some urban areas the face veil is made by pinning the wings of her headscarf over her mouth with several long straight pins. Others have kept the older version and need to lift it when try-ing to look at something.

Many of Syria's ruling Ba'ath party elite are from small towns or rural backgrounds including former President Hafiz al-Asad. They come from tra-ditional families but where women had greater freedoms than the old urban elite who ruled Syria for centuries. The conflicts between the two elite are more fundamental than over the veiling of women, but the conflicts are often played out through women and women's choices such as to veil or not.

The Ba'ath Party has taken the ideal family patriarch as the model for the head of state. This is not a new idea with the Ba'ath Party but is something used by many Middle Eastern states. In the traditional family the head of the household has control over every other member. His word is law, but he is also supposed to be the protector of the family. His concern is not only to enforce discipline within the family but to defend it from any outside threat. He is to be kind, but firm; generous and hospitable, even if it means his fam-ily might suffer as a result; strong, but just; and brave ready to face any threat. These are also the characteristics of the good leader and in much of the politi-cal discourse the president is referred to in the same sorts of terms used for the head of the household. He is to be the "good shepherd" and protect his "flock" from harm. Even his term of rule is called the period of "his shepherd-ing," or *taht ri 'ayat,* literally "under the shepherding of."

Such concepts of the good ruler do not conflict with the traditional values associated with the traditional patriarch. There is little resistance to the con-cept, though for the old Sunni urban elite, they do have issue with the rural and minority nature of the Ba'ath Party elite. Their conflict has less to do with the ideal but with the person. The urban elite are coming to terms with their position in the country, and while they may be nostalgic for the old days when they were in power, they do not form an active antigovernment bloc.

The Ba'ath Party has been moderately successful in spreading its socialist ideology among Syrians. They have had to make major compromises in the country's economics, for example, and socialism exists along with moderate capitalism. They have been more successful in extending public services such as health care and education throughout the country and with extending a number of rights to the numerous minority communities, but they have not made much head way with the conservative nature of the Syrian people. The Syrian Ba'ath has taken a more practical approach than was taken in Iraq and has been willing to make compromises with tradition on a number of issues.

HOSPITALITY AND GENEROSITY

Syrians are a very hospitable people and both hospitality and generosity are core cultural values. They are virtues of Arab society as a whole, and Syrian society is no exception. Syrians see themselves as so-called true Arabs and take their obligations as hosts very seriously. It is easy to get an invitation in Syria even after a brief chance meeting. Such invitations may cause problems for the family as a whole because they may be forced to quickly rush out to buy cold drinks, pastries, fruit, or other items to serve, and the women may be required to cook a major meal which is beyond the family's budget. Despite what may be a real hardship for the family, it is worse to not accept such an invitation since Syrians place such a high value on being good hosts.

Generosity is another core value that is often linked to hospitality. A good host provides lavishly for his guests, and there should so much to eat that it is not possible to clean off the plate. Guests will be constantly urged to eat more, and it is always hard to bring a meal to an end. Guests signal the meal is over by saying they have eaten their fill and evoke the name of God. The host will then bring out coffee or tea and perhaps fresh fruit juices, fresh fruit, and pastries as snacks while engaging the guest in conversation. It is also hard to take one's leave after a meal; the host will offer a place for a nap or even offer a place to spend the night if the hour is late.

Syrian hospitality and generosity is too often abused by low-budget travelers who accept the frequently offered invitations but contribute nothing to thank the family for their effort. Traditionally such gestures of hospitality will be repaid in kind with invitations from the guest to his host. Should this not be possible, it is polite to bring a gift of some kind and present it to the host. The gifts can be a box of pastries, fresh fruit or melon, sets of tea glasses or coffee cups (demitasse for Turkish coffee or small handless cups for Arabic coffee), sets of tall juice glasses or something that the family can use. Among the more Europeanized urban families, bouquets of flowers are often brought by the guests.

COFFEEHOUSES, RESTAURANTS, AND FAMILY OUTINGS

Coffeehouses in Arab society have long played a major role serving as neighborhood men's clubs. Coffeehouses are more than a place where a man goes for cup of strong Turkish coffee; it is a place to read the newspaper, listen to the television news with a close circle of friends, engage in political discussions, play cards or backgammon, or simply to relax in good company. Coffeehouses are frequented more or less on a daily basis by the same clientele, and many are situated to receive customers from nearby administrative offices, businesses, or within a neighborhood. Customers have their established times, tables, and often order their coffee the same way everyday. The waiter is as much a friend as he is a server and feels no problem interfering in the conversations at the tables. Coffeehouses serve what is called Turkish coffee, or *qahwah Turkiyah,* which is different from Arabic coffee, or *qahwah 'Arabiyah,* in the way it is made, its color, and its aroma. Turkish coffee is made in a specially made brass pot, called a *riqwi* or *kanakah.* The pot differs in size depending on the number of cups it can make from a small, individual pot to those that can make 10 cups. There are a number of ways to make Turkish coffee depending on when the sugar is added and how often the coffee is allowed to come to a boil. Generally speaking the coffee is made by adding one heaping teaspoon of coffee (that has been ground till it is like a powder) per cup to be made to one demitasse of water per cup. Usually sugar is added, one heaping teaspoon per cup, for what is called *mazbut,* or just right. Extra sugar can be added for what is called *ziyadah,* or just a touch, for what is called *al-rihah.* Some people prefer it with no sugar at all, in which case it is called *sadah,* meaning plain or black. The men who work at the coffeehouses often times have their own designations for how the coffee is to be made; a poetic code used between him and the person who makes the coffee.

Coffee was introduced as a drink first by Sufis mainly of the Shadhili Brotherhood to help them stay awake during all night rituals. It became generalized for the urban population in Cairo in the late fifteenth century and became a well-established urban institution in Egypt and Syria by the sixteenth century. It is noted that the first coffeehouses in Istanbul were both opened in 1554; one by a man from Damascus and the second by a man from Aleppo. Coffee was introduced to Europe sometime in the early seventeenth century as were other items from the East India trade. Following the Ottoman siege of Vienna in 1683, when a large number of bags of coffee beans were left behind, coffeehouses opened in Vienna serving sweetened coffee topped with whipped sweet cream. During the sixteenth century tobacco from North America was introduced to the Middle East and quickly caught on in the Ottoman Empire. Coffeehouses became places where it was possible to smoke in public as well as have a cup of coffee. At first tobacco was smoked in long-stemmed pipes made of clay but these were replaced with the introduction of the water pipe, or *narjilah*. Coffeehouses are still places where it is possible to order a pipe along with a cup of coffee.

Coffeehouses were also places for evening entertainment where poets and storytellers performed. Popular tales, often in rhymed prose, were among the most common forms of entertainment and the exploits of the pre-Islamic Bedouin hero 'Antar bin Shaddad and the Mamluk Sultan Baybars al-Bunduqdari were the favorites in Syria. Storytellers would assume the roles speaking in different voices and even if the audience were very familiar with the tales, the abilities of telling the story were highly appreciated. Storytellers kept their central role in the coffeehouses until the arrival of first the radio in the 1920s and eventually television, in the 1960s, which replaced storytellers. The Syrian government is trying to keep the art of storytelling from dying out completely and helps subsidies those coffeehouses where storytelling is still done. The most famous is the al-Nafurah Coffeehouse near the Umayyad Mosque in the heart of old Damascus. Here storytelling is still offered and the audience's favorite tales of 'Antar are still being recounted several evenings a week.

Coffeehouses are men's spheres and women rarely enter them. In many traditional neighborhoods the coffeehouses are really for the men of the neighborhood, though any one is welcome to stop for a coffee or any of the other drinks offered. There are usually several tables located on the outer fringe of the house or inside tucked away near where the drinks are prepared where so-called visitors are seated. This way they do not interfere with conversations and business of the regulars. Syrian women did not go to coffeehouses in the past, but today some include sections set aside for families and women.

Syrians do enjoy going out to restaurants, and the old cities all offer excellent restaurants with huge menus of Syrian foods. Some of the more upscale ones offer live entertainment in the form of chamber bands that play classical Arabic music. Those that are more like cabarets may provide not only live music but also a belly dancer; dancers usually appear late in the evening. Others cater mainly to families and are open more for lunch than for dinner. They may provide live entertainment but with a more folk orientation to better entertain children.

Those that cater mainly to families are often located outside of the towns and cities and are built on the idea of the Islamic garden. The tables are set up along the outer perimeter under a vine covered arbor or a roof keeping the

sides open. In the center is the garden with running water, usually an elaborate fountain, and flowering trees and bushes. Some of these restaurants in
the Jazirah deal with the blazing hot summer months by flooding the whole
establishment with water. Customers take off their shoes, roll up their pants,
and the flooded floor not only helps keep the whole atmosphere cooler, but
the customers can cool off by keeping their feet in the cold water. Others,
such as those near Damascus, make use of the higher elevations offered by the
Anti Lebanon Mountains. Again the establishments are built around a central
garden with running water and flowering trees and bushes but are also in a
rural setting surrounded by orchards. These restaurants specialize in Syrian
foods, often times providing such massive *mazzah*s that main dishes are not
needed.

Syrian families are also very fond of weekend picnics in the countryside.
Residents of Damascus make use of the large oasis that surrounds the city
to find places to stop and have a restful lunch among orchards and gardens.
Along the seacoast people can picnic on the beach, but many prefer to go
inland up into the mountains that rise up close to the coast. Syrians, even
from the urban centers, enjoy getting away to more natural settings especially
where it is possible to hear the sounds of running water and song birds and
smell the scents of flowers such as roses or citrus blossoms.

In addition to restaurants, Syrian cities boast some of the oldest ice cream
parlors in the world. These are places where women and families have always
been accepted. Traditional ice cream, fruit sherbet, fruit drinks, and thick
puddings (both sweet and sour) are served, and such shops provide comfortable places for people to stop and rest while shopping. Some of the older ice
cream parlors are huge places, much larger than coffeehouses, with indoor
gardens and fountains and decorated in turn of the twentieth century style
furniture, mirrors, and paintings. They remain very popular with Syrians
even after other types of ice cream and pastry shops appeared.

Syrians have long made use of fast food stalls that are located throughout the cities. Many serve foods such as *ful,* or chickpea dishes, *shawarmah*
sandwiches, *kibbi,* or open-faced breads toped with meat, pine nuts, and
chopped tomatoes or salty white cheeses. For many working people, meals
from fast food stalls replace home cooked breakfasts or lunches. In addition
to the fast food stalls are fresh fruit juice stands where it is possible to stop
for chilled fruit or vegetable juices. These are often located near the fast food
places. One of the traditional occupations was that of a wondering juice
seller, who specialized in a thick, black, anis-flavored drink called *'araq sus* or
lemonade. The juice is dispensed from a large glass or brass container worn
on the back of the seller who has small glasses or cups suspended on a leather
bandolier or wide belt. The juice container oftentimes has large chunks of

ice stuffed into the top and is heavily decorated with colorful items such as plastic flowers and garlands. Other itinerant street sellers specialized in cookies, Napoleons, or *ka'ak*. In recent years enterprising sellers have set up street sales of Nescafé and Turkish or Arabic coffee for the morning fast-paced office worker who does not have time to stop at a coffeehouse for the usual morning coffee and newspaper.

Since the 1970s a new type of fast food place has become popular with mainly students and white collar workers. These are the so-called hamburger bars where it is possible to get a Western-styled hamburger, French fries, and soft drink. Some of them also offer a few of the more traditional fast foods such as *kibbi* and salads such as *tabuli*. Most of these places do not offer full sit down service but may instead have a long countertop where it is possible stand or sit on a high stool to eat the meal. They are made for fast in and out but have become popular with youth as a safe place for boys and girls to meet and talk.

MIDDLE CLASS AND MIDDLE-CLASS VALUES

Syria has a small but growing middle class of mainly government employees and administrators of the small number of private companies. The middle class tends to be well educated and some have finished their higher education abroad. They tend to not live in the more traditional neighborhoods but in the newer housing districts built after World War II. In many families, both parents have careers, disrupting the usual family pattern of working father and housewife mother. Women are unable to spend the long hours needed to prepare traditional dishes that may take hours for one dish. Instead families may hire maids to do the cooking and cleaning, or the woman may buy already prepared foods on her way home from work. There is less direct oversight of the children, who when not in school may be a neighbor's house or other places where they are allowed to hang out. All of this has brought change to the family.

Working women is one of the major changes; and one that is supported by state policies. Women are encouraged to have full-time careers yet society still judges women by how well they manage as wives and mothers. Women are expected to have two careers; one at the office and one at home. While there are rather generous maternity leaves, women feel the pressure to fulfill their traditional roles of wives and mothers. Success is still measured more at home and how well she cooks, manages the household affairs, and raises her children. When there are problems, especially with children, she is the one who will get most of the blame.

Husbands may have rather open attitudes to their wives working, but few are willing to help with the household chores or in raising the children. Men who do lend a hand with household work are subject to scorn not only by their male friends but by their families who see it as proof the wife is not a capable woman or the failure of the man as the husband. Househusbands have been the subject of Syrian television programs, but most have been comedies exploiting the cultural bias against men helping with housework.

Attitudes may change as more and more families face the issues of working women and women who may earn more than their husbands. Children as of yet do not have positive images of men doing household chores or even assisting with child rearing. Nonetheless, more and more Syrian children are being educated to higher levels and more and more female students are interested in full-time careers other than being housewives. Education is the best vehicle for lasting change; however, the strong conservative nature of Syrian society has yet to be effected by the rising middle class. The middle class holds many of the same ideals as the more traditional segments of the society, and working women are an economic necessity rather a cultural ideal.

Conclusion

Syrian society has undergone a good deal of change since the beginning of the twentieth century. Syria was a center of the Arab Awakening and subsequent Arab Nationalism that gave rise to the Ba'ath Party in the 1940s. Syria's turbulent post-independence history has moved it politically to the left yet it remains a strongly conservative, Muslim society. Even the large numbers of Christians are greatly affected by the same sort of conservative attitudes about family. The middle class, which is composed of the more educated, often Western-educated professionals has not changed the basic core values of the country nor have the ideologically dedicated members of the Ba'ath Party. Syrians remain strongly conservative, but this does not mean that they are dour or frown on having fun. Men (and women) enjoy going out, seeing friends, and talking. Syrians are very comfortable with who they are—whether Arabs or Kurds or other ethnicities; Muslims or Christians—and are proud of their shared history, culture, customs, and way of life.

8

Music and Dance

SYRIAN MUSIC AND dance, like its literature, has a long history of high art connected to royal patronage. There are depictions of court musicians playing various string, wind, and percussion instruments dating back into early antiquity. Long-necked lutes, lyres, harps, flutes, and a wide variety of drums are shown in wall art and statuary indicating sophisticated court music as well as more rustic folk music of peasants and pastoral nomads. Many of these ancient instruments are easily recognizable in their contemporary forms; some of which have not changed a great deal over time.

During late antiquity and into the Classical Islamic period, music was well developed in the courts and homes of the wealthy families of Damascus, Aleppo, Homs, Hama, and Antioch. Though orthodox Islam takes a somewhat negative view of music and dance, the Umayyad court in Damascus was well known for both musical performance and dance as were the homes of its rich merchants. Stories such as that of Sallamah, a young slave woman with a fantastic voice who lived in Damascus during the early Umayyad period, have been passed down and in 1945 the famous Egyptian singer Umm Kalthum played her in the movie version of her life. The Hamdanid court of Aleppo was not only famous for its patronage of poetry but of all fine arts including music. Syria has two of the major centers where classical Arabic musical forms developed, Damascus and Aleppo; the others being Baghdad, Cairo, Fez, Tunis, and Cordoba.

CLASSICAL MUSIC

Classical Arabic music developed from the combination of Hellenistic and Persian forms with those of Arabia. Instruments and modes or musical scales from all three sources were combined into a new format that can be called "Islamic." Eight major modes or *maqamat* (singular *maqam*) were developed each has several submodal scales. A performance is begun by an instrumental piece usually called a *bashraf* in Syria from the Turkish word *pesrev,* which simply means introduction, and the use of the word is an indication of the close connection between classical music in Syria and Saljuq and Ottoman court traditions. Musical performances follow set patterns of progression similar to a western suite moving from one mode into another often punctuated with instrumental interludes referred to as *taqasim* (singular *taqsim*), or a divider or division. The instrumental interlude introduces the next mode being used and sets the melodic line. The entire suite may take hours to complete and, in the past when it was preformed at the courts of princes, parts were accompanied by a type of expressive dance (not too unlike western modern dance routines) done by troupes of young women.

Most classical music is composed for both instruments and voice and in Arabic music the voice dominates the instruments. Vocal styles emphasize the wide range of a singer and while the melody is set, the singer and instrumentalists display their abilities by individual improvisation. For many western listeners such improvisations are difficult for the ear and seem to lack the harmonic unity they are used to. For the Arab listener, each improvisation is judged on how difficult it is to execute without interrupting the rhythmic flow of the piece. Arab listeners never grow tired of the delicate balances within a piece of music, and they are assured that no matter how old the piece is or how many times they have heard it, each live performance will be a new experience in improvisation.

Classical music is supposed to produce a state of ecstasy in the listener called *tarab.* Voice is the most expressive element in Arabic music and the best singers are called *mutribin* (males) and *mutribat* (females) meaning they can induce states of *tarab* in their audiences. Those who are truly capable of creating such states of total ecstasy are called *sultan*s or *sultanah*s and in contemporary Syria the singers Sabah Fakhri and Maydah al-Hinawi have such talents. Ordinary singers are called *mughanniyin* (males) and *mughanniyat* (females) meaning that while they have good voices, they are not able to induce the emotional state of *tarab.* Some musical instruments are also able to produce such responses in listeners, such as the *'ud* or lute, the *qanun* or plucked zither, the *kamanjah* or violin, and the *nay* or reed end-blown flute.

The classical orchestra or *takht* is composed of a small number of instruments and can be best compared to a chamber orchestra in western music. In addition to an *'ud,* usually played by the lead singer, the *takht* includes a *qanun, kamanjah,* a *nay,* and for percussion a *darabukah* or an hour-glass shaped drum with a single head and a *riq* or tambourine. Some *takht* groups may also include a long necked lute called a *buzuq,* which is similar to the Greek bouzouki (the Greek name may have derived from the Arab instrument). The *buzuq* has metal strings rather than the gut used for the *'ud.* The orchestra is small because they were originally used to entertain at indoor gatherings or in palace gardens, and the instruments are to support the human voice rather than over power it.

The so-called king of instruments in Classical Arabic music is the *'ud,* which is often referred to as the *amir al-tarab* or "prince of ecstasy" in Arabic because of its importance in music. The *'ud* is one of the instruments introduced by the Arabs to the cultural mix of the early Islamic period and has a wide, pear-shaped body with a rather short neck and five (sometimes six) double-gut strings. The neck has no frets making ornamentation easier for a skilled player who traditionally uses a quill pick. Today plastic picks are generally used except by the purists to whom the difference in the sound produced by plastic picks is unacceptable. The *'ud* is both a solo instrument and one that accompanies voice. When played by a true virtuoso, such as the late Farid al-Atrash, the *'ud* can be made to sound like two or three instruments being played together or even like an organ due to the fact that the lower range strings are able to create harmony or a base drone effect. The *'ud* is the lead instrument in any classical orchestra and most pieces of classical music are first composed on it.

The *qanun* is the only real rival for the *'ud* in producing states of *tarab* in the listener. As noted above, the *qanun* is a plucked zither with 24 rows of triple-gut strings. It is played with it placed flat on the performer's lap or on a table; some of the ones made today come with removable legs to make the table. The performer uses both hands and the picks, made of metal or horn, are affixed to the forefinger by a ring or thimble worn just below the nail. The instrument needs to be tuned with a key that is fitted over the peg for each string. Some of the modern-made instruments have tried to deal with the need to retune for each mode by an internal system that raises and lowers the strings and thus changes how taunt they are.

The *kamanjah* or sometimes simply called *kaman* is similar to a violin, and today the term is often used for the European violin that was introduced in the nineteenth century and for the most part has replaced the older model. The traditional *kamanjah* is played with a bow while the instrument placed on the performer's knee rather than under the chin. The *kamanjah* has two or three horsehair or gut strings and has a small, round sound box made of wood or a coconut shell with a skin cover. It usually has a long spike at the bottom and a long, thin, unfretted neck. The strings are bowed over the sound box or above it. The *kamanjah* differs from the *rabab* found in rural Syria and among the Bedouin, which has a wide but thin sound box made of wood with a skin cover and a rather short neck. The *rabab* has one or two horsehair strings and, like the *kamanjah,* is bowed while resting on the player's knee but generally has a smaller musical range and is therefore rarely included in the more sophisticated *takht* orchestra.

The *nay* is an end-blown flute made from a cane stem. The *nay* can be overblown to produce a second, higher octave, but generally *nay* players have a number of different flutes of different sizes to produce the needed ranges for the different modal scales. The *nay* is an ancient instrument, and the *nay* played in the *takht* orchestra does not differ in make from those shown in ancient wall art or those used by shepherds to while away the time watching their flocks. While the best sounding *nay*s are made from cane, today many players use ones made from metal. The metal ones are rarely used in performances of classical Arabic music but are used by folk groups and with folk dance groups since the metal produces a sharper and louder sound. The cane flute is soft and breathy, making it perfect for the needs of the *takht* setting.

The quiet setting for classical music requires that the percussion instruments used not be so loud as to overpower the other instruments or the voice, but they need to produce the complicated rhythms that note the changes in mood in the suite. The *darabukah* has an hourglass shape, and the better sounding ones have a clay body (though they can be metal or wood) with a single skin head. The best sound is produced by shark skin, which is thin (see-through) but tough. Other skin, such as from lamb or goat, produce heavy and less distinct sounds and is not used by professionals. Clay bodies produce the best sounds; metal gives a hallow sound while wood is often too rounded and mellow for the sharper tones that may be needed. The *darabukah* is played by striking the center for the deeper sound called *dum* and close to the rim for the sharper tones called *tik* and *tak*. Rhythms have names and when learning them the player learns the combination of *dum, tik,* and *tak*. The *riqq* or *duff* is similar to a tambourine and is played by holding it in such a way as to allow the fingers of both hands to strike the head. It is struck with the same combinations used with the *darabukah* as well as being able to play the brass jingle pairs that are placed all around the edge of the instrument. Sometimes a large round, single-headed drum called a *tar* is added to the percussion section for deeper sounds than is possible with the *riqq*. The *tar* looks much like the *riqq* but does not have the brass jingles though some of them may have a series of metal rings around the inside rim which produces a buzz similar to a snare drum.

Syrian classical music makes use of a number of different types but was greatly influenced by the development of the *muwashshahat* (singular *muwashshahah*) at the Umayyad court in Spain. The *muwashshahah* was introduced by the famous singer and *'ud* player Ziryab, who left Baghdad in anger and made his way to Spain in 821. He introduced a number of innovations including adding the fifth set of strings to the *'ud.* The *muwashshahah* makes use of classical or literary Arabic for the main poetic line but the refrain or chorus is in spoken Arabic. The format became very popular in Muslim Spain and influenced early Troubadour music in Spain and France. The *muwashshahat* were introduced to the rest of the Arab world and quickly became popular in Syria. Aleppo developed a Syrian version called *qadud al-Halabiyah,* which also makes use of spoken Arabic for much of the words. Such songs are usually presented in a seamless succession so those who do not understand the words rarely notice that the singer has moved to the next song. Syria's great singer of the classical tradition, Sabah Fakhri, will move from Andalusi *muwashshahat* to Aleppine *qadud* and back without stopping; moving from mode to mode in such a smooth stream of sound that induces a state of *tarab* in even those who do not understand Arabic well or fully comprehend what is happening around them. This method of performance is called *waslah,* meaning connected and was introduced into classical music in the nineteenth century in both Cairo and Damascus. There is no greater singer in the whole Arab world today who can match Sabah Fakhri's ability as a *Sultan al-Tarab.* Any performance by Sabah Fakhri is an experience in the best of classical Arabic music.

POPULAR MUSIC

Syria is tied closely to Lebanon and both are important centers for popular Arabic music. The recording industry began in the Arab world in 1904 first in Egypt, but Beirut and Damascus had their own companies soon afterwards. Recordings made it easier for Arab singers to become better known outside of their own countries and the Lebanese cabaret owner and performer Badi'ah Masabani noted in her memoirs that in the decades of the 1920s to 1940s she constantly ran into other Arab entertainers doing concert tours from Tunis to Baghdad. Most singers moved to Cairo, the center of Arab culture, where the government encouraged the arts and where there were enough people with money to provide financial backing for artists.

Two of the main stars of the Arab world moved from Syria to Cairo following the Syrian Revolt of 1925, the brother and sister Farid al-Atrash and Amal al-Atrash. Amal later took the stage name of Asmahan. Farid and Amal were the children of the Druze lord Sultan al-Atrash and were considered to be Druze royalty. In Cairo they were encouraged by their mother to learn the 'ud from two of the foremost masters of the instrument. Both Farid and Amal were exceptionally talented and Amal began her career in 1939 when the great Egyptian singer and composer Muhammad 'Abd al-Wahhab asked her to sing in his film Yawm Sa'id or Happy Day. She turned down the offer to play the female lead opposite of Muhammad 'Abd al-Wahhab himself but did lend her voice to one of the songs. In 1941 Farid and Amal, under her stage name of Asmahan, starred in the musical film Intisar al-Shabab or Triumph of Youth, which was the first musical to be a hit without the major Egyptian stars Umm Kalthum or Muhammad 'Abd al-Wahhab.

Asmahan had a short career of only seven years because she died mysteriously in 1944. She was brilliant but she was constantly surrounded by rumors. She was married several times, twice to her cousin Prince Hassan al-Atrash as well as to several Egyptian music and film personalities. Her last husband, the Egyptian director Ahmad Salim, tried to murder her before she divorced him in 1944. Asmahan was rumored to be a spy for the British during World War II using her position as a film and musical star to make visits to Vichy held Lebanon and Syria. She died when her car plunged off the road into one of the main Nile canals where she drowned. Rumors ran rampant at the time of her death and even the great Egyptian singer Umm Kalthum was rumored to have had the car's brakes tampered with out of jealousy of the growing star. Others suspected one of her husbands of plotting her death while others thought agents for the French or Germans killed her. Her legacy is immense; a woman of noble birth who broke numerous social conventions (including marrying men who were not Druze) and greatly changed public attitudes in the Arab world towards women entertainers.

Farid al-Atrash became one of the Arab world's biggest stars and went on to make 30 films before his death in 1974. Farid al-Atrash made films with leading ladies such as the Lebanese singer Sabah and the Egyptian idols Shadiyah, Tahiyah Kariokah, and Samiyah Gamal. Many of his films are with his long-time love, Samiyah Gamal, who was one of Egyptian cinema's major dancers. They never married because Samiyah was a Sunni Muslim and Farid a Druze and neither family would allow one or the other to convert for marriage, or so it is rumored in the fan magazines of the day. Farid al-Atrash was not only an actor and master of the 'ud, but he composed most of his songs and those sung by his sister Asmahan. With his compositions he made the move from classical forms to more popular song types that had developed in Egypt during the late nineteenth century and first half of the twentieth century.

Other Syrian singers have become popular in the wider Arab world, and with the rise of Beirut as a major recording center following World War II it was no longer necessary to go to Cairo to become recognized. In addition, it was no longer necessary to sing using the Egyptian dialect; songs in Syrian/Lebanese dialects were also popular and could have a wide audience in the whole Arab world. Lebanese singers such as Sabah, who returned from Egypt to her native Lebanon, and Fayruz sang in their own dialect, which encouraged others to do the same. The Syrian singer Fahd Balan, for example, became well known starting in the 1950s and 1960s as did others such as the so-called Bedouin singer Samirah Tawfiq, though she is often considered to be Jordanian. Samirah Tawfiq sings in the Bedouin dialect common in Syria and Jordan, and in films she often plays the part of a Bedouin or Gypsy who, though uneducated and rural, in the end has the last laugh on more sophisticated urbanite due to her honesty and honorable behavior. Most Syrian popular singers are still part of Lebanese pop and it is often difficult to know if a particular singer is Lebanese or Syrian. Milhim Barakat and George Wassuf are both Syrians who sing what would be called Lebanese pop and are not distinguishable from the array of Lebanese pop stars.

Lebanese pop derives its sound from two major sources, the most current fashion in Egyptian pop (still the most influential music in the Arab world) and the rural music of Lebanon and Syria. Egyptian pop has developed the *Ya Habibi,* or my love, type of song, often about lost or impossible love; the lyrics are simple and the melodic line is also simple. Electronic instruments are used including synthesizers and canned clapping from a sound machine rather than real clapping. A small number of rhythms are used, making many of the songs sound very much alike. With the introduction of music videos based on those of MTV more time is spent on promoting the song through video releases over the numerous Arab music satellite TV channels and less on real substance in the music. The Columbian/American pop singer Shakira, who is of Lebanese origin, greatly influenced many female Arab pop singers, who try to imitate her hair, clothes, and dance actions in their videos. Shakira's use of her hips is already part of Arab dance called *raqs baladi,* or belly dance, that nearly all Arab girls know how to do.

RURAL MUSIC

Rural music in Syria (and Lebanon) makes use of certain instruments and rhythms associated with the popular folk dance called *dabkah.* The instruments such as the double reed *mizmar* (an early relative of the oboe), metal *nay,* and the large double-headed drum or *tabl* (similar to the base drum) are loud and can be easily heard out of doors where dancers need to hear the beat to stay in time. The rhythmic patterns are those associated with the dance's stomps and kicks rather than those of the *raqs baladi* hip and shoulder actions. Interludes of rural sounds in Lebanese and Syria pop songs help set them off from Egyptian pop.

Rural music is not only to accompany folk dance but there are also types of more plaintive songs where instruments form a drone background. These are called *mijanaw* after the word that is frequently repeated. They are a type of *mawwal* or vocal improvisation where the vocal range of the singer is tested to the limits. Given that most folk performers are untrained amateurs rather than professional singers, their ability is often astounding. This type of song is more known among the settled villagers in the mountains and is shared with villagers in Lebanon. *Mawwal*s usually precede other more lively songs, and it is common for folk singers to include a number of *qadud al-Halabiyah* in their repertoire.

Villagers have a number of work songs that are sung to help make the work day go by faster. There are songs for harvesting olives, wheat, and other such hard labor. Women also have work songs to help pass the time when working alone but more often when work includes a number of women. Few instruments are used other than perhaps a *nay*, drums, and clapping. Songs help keep work teams in time with each other and can make use of the natural rhythms of work actions such as cutting wheat with a sickle or winnowing with a wooden shovel. Even the sounds made by the actions may help with the words of the songs. Some of the words are lighthearted and humorous in order to help lessen the monotony of the work. Many of these work songs are quickly being lost with the introduction of machines that make the work less time-consuming. Some ethnographers have tried to collect them before they are completely lost.

Rural music includes Bedouin traditions that are centered around the *rabab*. The *rabab* is often called the *rabab al-sha'ir* or the poet's *rabab* given its close association with recitation of poetry. As noted above the *rabab* has one or two strings made of horsehair that is played with a bow also of horsehair creating a somewhat scratchy sound. It has a short neck, has a limited range of notes, which serve as a support for the singer or person reciting poetry, and is rarely played as a solo instrument. Songs are often plaintive in nature, which the sound of the *rabab* helps emphasize. Most Bedouin camps have at least one person who plays well enough to entertain guests, and tribal leaders have someone in his retinue who is expert in playing the *rabab* and reciting poetry and tribal history, who is called upon whenever he has important guests.

Shepherds contribute to rural music with songs played on the *nay*. The *nay* can be made of metal; many are made from used pipes or even gun barrels, or of a piece of reed with either six or seven holes depending on if one has been put for the thumb or not. The melodies are simple, and many are unwritten compositions made up by the shepherd as he whiles away his time watching his flock. The music helps with the herder's boredom as well as helps calm the flock. The shepherd may also be thinking of new melodies to introduce at the next wedding where he may be asked to help provide the music for a *dabkah*.

While village music is often with instruments, Bedouin song is as often as not unaccompanied. Bedouin sing a number of songs accompanied only by clapping or perhaps a drum. Bedouin use the large *tar* more than the other types of drums found in the region and for certain dance may use a large number of them played by a group of men who move and sway together as they play. The drums may be decorated with large red, yellow, green, and blue woolen tassels attached all around the rim that add to the colorful nature of the drumming, as they swung side to side and up and down to the rhythms. All the while men, and maybe women as well, are singing and clapping their hands. Other Bedouin song is sung while riding a camel and follows the rhythms of the camel's step.

DANCE

Dance, like music, can be divided into two main types, classical dances associated with the high arts patronized by the ruling elite and folk dances associated with the common people and folk traditions in the villages and desert camps. Dance as a high art no longer exists other than as part of historical dramas while folk dances are a vibrant part of any celebration whether in the cities or in the country side.

Classical court dances, as noted above, involved troupes of well-trained young women who danced in unison to instrumental interludes during long musical evenings or parties. Their movements were expressive and could be compared to modern dance in the West where the dancer tries to convey a story, emotion, or mood through body movement. Movements were fluid and stately though they could also involve shaking hips or shoulders as well. Individuals might perform brief solos, but in general the group performed choreographed movements together.

Perhaps one of the oldest dances is the *raqs baladi* (local or country dance) or *raqs sharqi* (eastern dance) often called belly dance in the West and may be the modern descendant of the temple dances frequently attacked by Old Testament prophets. Most Arab girls know how to move their hips, shoulders, and torsos to the lively drum beats by watching older women at weddings and other such celebrations dance. In the past, professional women dancers called 'awalim were usually asked to perform at celebrations and through their dances help young brides understand how to have sex with their husbands (though this explanation is not held by everyone). The 'awalim were able to break a number of social conventions, crossing back and forth between men's and women's sections at celebrations, speaking loudly and even swearing, and smoking in public; things most women would not do.

In the late nineteenth century and early twentieth century a number of the better known 'awalim in Cairo began to open their own cabarets where they would perform before adoring audiences of mainly male admirers. Cairo was able to support a number of rival cabarets because Egypt had more wealthy patrons, thus the city attracted dancers not only from Egypt but from Lebanon and Syria too. The Lebanese Badi'ah Masabani moved to Cairo and opened up one of the more successful cabarets. Following World War II Beirut was able to compete with Cairo as a cultural center; Lebanese and Syrian dancers no longer had to go to Egypt to become famous. Beirut's casinos, hotels, and restaurants attracted wealthy patrons from Iraq, the Gulf, and Saudi Arabia as well as from Lebanon. The Lebanese Civil War that started in 1975 forced many of these places to close or scale back their entertainment, and dancers needed to find other venues. Syria was able to take advantage of the problems in Lebanon to a degree and a number of hotels, casinos, and the like opened offering live entertainment. Syria is less able to compete with Cairo simply because there are fewer wealthy people who can afford to patronize such places, and Syria's tourism industry is still too small to depend on foreigners. Gulf States such as Kuwait, Bahrain, and the United Arab Emirates can still attract more professional entertainers to its hotel complexes than those in Syria.

RURAL AND FOLK DANCE

The main folk dance in Syria is the line dance called *dabkah*. This type of dance is found in all of Greater Syria; Palestine, Lebanon, Jordan, and Syria. The dance is part of rural and urban traditions and there are numerous forms of it; some are very energetic and vigorous for young men, and others are slow and stately for women. Line dances are also shared with much of the eastern Mediterranean including Greece, the Balkans, Turkey, and Iraq and between different ethnic groups including Arabs, Turks, and Kurds.

Dabkah is done by a line of people who either join hands or place their arms over the shoulders of the person or persons standing next to them; women usually hold hands while men place their arms on their neighbors' shoulders. The line is led by either the first person in the line or by someone who will be in front of the group who gives the dancers directions. The leader may hold a baton made of wood, an embroidered handkerchief with colorful silk floss tassels at each corner, or by a set of prayer beads in his free hand. He leads the group in the dance movements with both verbal calls but also by the movement of the object in his hand. For many of the all-male *dabkah*s the leader will detach him self from the group and come out to be in front of the line. His movements are signaled by the baton or handkerchief and the men in the line will follow his lead and repeat what he has done. If a group practices together it is difficult for a casual observer to note the signals given by the leader, and it seems to be an incredible fluid connection between the leader and his group. Women's versions are less athletic and emphasize instead the grace of the dancers and the swaying of their dresses. In Syria, as in Palestine and Lebanon, men and women were allowed to dance the *dabkah* together; usually with the line being led by a man and men and women alternating along the length of the group. Music for the *dabkah* is usually provided by a metal *nay* for its sharper sound or by a double-reed *mizmar* accompanied by a large, double-sided drum called a *tabl* beaten on both sides with sticks and a *darabukah.*

Dabkah steps are a combination of step movements to the side, stomps, and kicks done in complete harmony with each member in time and step with everyone else. Professional dance troupes have been able to extend the use of the folk dance into incredible shows of athletic prowess. Professional Syrian folk groups tend to continue to seek authenticity, keeping as close to the original dances as possible while the Lebanese troupe Caracalla (named for the Roman Emperor whose mother was a priestess from Baʿalbak) have taken the dance to its furthest limits. Following models from the former Soviet Union where ballet, gymnastics, and folk dances were combined into fantastic demonstrations of a dancer's ability, groups such as Caracalla have been able to use *dabkah* to tell stories from Classical Arabic literature, folk tales, or even Arab history as well as maintain strong connections to the folk origin of the dance. One such dance routine tells the story of the Arab Revolt of 1916 to the Syrian Revolt of 1925.

Syrian Bedouin have a number of dances that are shared with other Bedouin in Jordan, Iraq, and the Peninsula. Bedouin have a form of *dabkah* that is more stately than energetic and where the men dancing sway back and forth as step to the side. More specific to the Bedouin are the dances one would see at a wedding where men stand shoulder to shoulder and sway as a group side to side clapping their hands in time with sung poetry. In front of the group one or more men will step forward and taking the two ends of their wide robe or *bisht* will move in swoops, dives, and prance in front of the line. They may take up a sword or a camel prod and position themselves directly in front of the group. The group will follow the moves of the sword or camel prod as the person holding it brings it up and down or from side to side. The movement will get faster and more frenzied as the men in the line begin to say "ah-hee" in time to their clapping. In some instances an older woman will put on the *bisht* and take up a sword in her hand to do the same thing. While the dance is being done, other men will step forward and shoot so-called joy shots with a pistol or rifle whose sound punctuates the clapping and singing.

Another Bedouin dance is the war dance or *al-'ardah*, which means display. In the *al-'ardah* men form facing lines standing shoulder to shoulder and holding a sword or camel prod in the right hand. Drummers stand between the two and begin to beat out slow rhythms, which the dancers take up with their movements bringing the sword up and down in unison. The song is started by the leader of one side, and the others in his line repeat it while the leader of the other line will take up the theme and rhyme with his own words, which his side will then repeat. The words are about the warlike nature of the men of the tribe, beauty and stamina of their horses or camels, and other such themes. In some of the dances, one side, the side that "loses" shows they have lost by lowering their swords, placing the tip into the ground, bowing their heads, and, as a group, they slowly bow to the other side in rhythm with the drums.

The Kurds, Turks, and Armenians have their own forms of folk dance though they are similar to the *dabkah*. Kurds, Turks, and Armenians oftentimes allow both men and women to dance together in the same line, and many of the Turkish dances interweave men and women's lines ending with them coming together. Some Kurds, however, do not allow men and women to intermingle and have complete separation with different men's and women's dances that are even held in separate places. Kurds, Turks, and Armenians use many of the same instruments as their Arab neighbors though Armenians tend to use wooded *darabukah*s as do Iranians. The main Turkish and Kurdish instrument is a long-necked lute with metal strings called a *saz.* It is the instrument of the wandering minstrel singing folk tales, as well as the lead instrument in most orchestras. The *saz* is similar to the *buzuk* but has sympathetic strings used to create a background drone to the musical line played on the higher strings. Northern Syria, where many of the Turks and Kurds live, is an interesting musical mix of the Syrian, Turkish, and Kurdish culture, and it is possible to hear all musical styles being played in a walk along the streets in Aleppo.

CONCLUSION

Music and dance in Syria have long histories of classical forms as well as the more folk types. The Syrian cities of Damascus and Aleppo are among the major centers where classical Arabic and Islamic music developed. They helped with the development of the modal scales; contributed to the development of different genres of music; and contributed to the written scholarship on music and musical instruments. These are not old or "lost traditions of the past" but are a living part of Syrian music today with such artists as Sabah Fakhri, who is as famous and sought after in even non-Arab countries as he is in his native Syria. He has performed in nearly every Arab country as well as in the United States.

Syria's folk music and dance can be traced back to some of the oldest representations found by archeologists. Folk music and dance are part of both urban and rural traditions as well as encompass the different ethnic communities of the country. Arabs, Kurds, Turks, and others have similar line dances and use more or less similar musical instruments, yet, music and dance are among the means to demonstrate ethnic or community identity. In Syria's cities where such different populations live, it is easy to hear the different musical traditions emanating from shops along any street.

Syrians appreciate a wide range of musical types beyond their own. Since the late 1970s, music and singers from Saudi Arabia and the Gulf have become popular with many. Music satellite channels have brought a wide range of Arab musical styles to nearly every home in the Arab world. In the early 1990s Algerian Rai became known in the Arab East with first the hit *"Didi"* by Shab Khalid and subsequently singers such as Shab Mami and Rachid Taha have become well-known.

Western music has been an influence in contemporary Arab popular music since the 1930s and 1940s when Latin American rumbas and the like were first heard in Hollywood films such as *Flying Down to Rio*. Western instruments were introduced and adapted to the quarter tones used in Arabic music. In the 1950s the powerful radio station from Monaco broadcast a wide range of music from Arabic to contemporary western pop moving from one to the other in a steady stream of sound. The introduction of satellite television channels have brought with them the MTV type of video clip and American or American-inspired European rap and hip hop. The Syrian viewer has a full range of musical styles to choose from and will listen as much to Sabah Fakhri or Fayruz as to the most recent release from French rapper MC Solar or Shakira or Madonna.

Glossary

Ablaq   Alternating layers of light and dark stone used to create a decorative wall space.

Adab   Literature; belle letters; manners.

Al-'Ardah   Literally display; war dance of the Bedouin.

Amir   Commander in the Mamluk armies; prince.

'Aqal   Head rope worn to hold the **Kuffiyah** in place; usually made of tightly twisted goat hair.

'Arjah   Headpiece worn by women in southern Syria and northern Jordan. It is both an elaborate piece of jewelry and a head cover.

'Asabah   Head band oftentimes made of a colorful cotton print, silk print, or silk brocade cloth.

'Ashurah   Tenth day of the first Islamic month *Muharram;* a major day of mourning for Shi'ites who commemorate the death of Imam Hussein; a child's holiday for Sunnis now rarely celebrated.

Atabek   A Turkish term meaning literally "father protector"; a political position appointed to oversee the education of young princes during the Saljuq period.

'Awalim   Women professional singers and dancers who often were hired to perform at weddings.

Ba'ath   Renaissance; chosen as the name for a political party that came to rule Syria and Iraq; major ruling party of Syria with strong Arab nationalist ideology.

Badawah   Nomadic pastoralism.

Badiyat al-Sham Syrian Desert.

Badw The Arabic plural for Bedouin; singular *badawi*.

Barakah Blessings of God; the quality can be passed on from one generation to another.

Bashraf An instrumental introduction to a classical suite; from the Turkish *pesrev*, which means introduction.

Bida' Innovation in religion that goes against the original intent or spirit of the text, actions, or words of God and his Prophets.

Bilad al-Sham Land of the Left Hand. The older Arabic name for Syria, Jordan, Palestine, and Lebanon.

Bisht Outer cloak worn mainly by Bedouin men today.

Burghul Cracked wheat; used in a wide variety of foods in Syria.

Buzah Originally a Turkish word and borrowed into Arabic, the traditional type of ice cream that is pounded with a wooden mallet until it has an elastic consistency to reduce melting. It is usually served with a sprinkle of crushed pistachio nuts.

Buzuk Long-necked lute with a rounded, wooden sound box; more often used with folk music than in classical Arabic orchestras; could be the ancestor of the Greek bouzouki.

Dabkah Most common folk dance in Syria, Lebanon, Jordan and Palestine; a line dance involving combination of side steps, stomps, and kicks.

Dallah Traditional brass coffee pot usually used to serve Arabic coffee.

Darabukah An hour glass-shaped drum made of clay, wood, or metal with a single head struck by the player's fingers.

Dhikr Remembrance of God and the Prophet Muhammad; used by Sufis as part of their practices.

Dishdashah Ankle-length shirt worn by men in much of the Middle East.

Diwan Collection of poems or works by an author.

Farw Literally an animal pelt; a heavy winter coat made of sheepskin with the wool used as the lining; worn by Bedouin and rural men.

Fatwa Legal decision based on the principles accepted by the major Schools of Islam.

Ghabani Type of cloth decorated with loop stitch designs; used in the past by urban men for turbans.

Hadith Sayings of the Prophet Muhammad and among the main sources for Islamic law.

Haj Pilgrimage; for Muslims the term is used for the once in a lifetime obligation to go to Makkah, which is one of the five pillars of faith; for Christians the term is used for visitation to Jerusalem.

Hammam Public bathhouse.

Hamsiyah Type of brocade cloth made in Homs and Aleppo worn by Bedouin and village women in Syria and Jordan; also called *Kasrawaniyah.*

Haramlik Private part of the traditional house; term is of Turkish origin.

Hija' Satirical poetry often attacking another person or tribe.

Hijab Charm or talisman; term is also used for a headscarf worn by Muslim women.

Hijrah Literally the migration noting the move of the Muslim community from Makkah to Madinah in 622; start of the Muslim calendar.

Hirz Elongated pendant.

Ibn 'Amm Cousin; father's brother's son. In much of the Middle East and North Africa he is the preferred marriage partner and has the right of first choice.

'Id Holiday, festival, feast.

'Id al-Adha Feast of the Sacrifice marks the end of the **Haj** rituals; also called *'Id al-Kabir,* or the major feast.

'Id al-Fitr Feast of Breaking the Fast marks the end of Ramadan; also called *'Id al-Saghir,* or the lesser feast.

Iftar Breakfast; first meal of the day; during Ramadan, *iftar* happens after sundown.

Ijma' Consensus; one of the major sources of Islamic law.

Imam In Sunni Islam he is the person who leads prayer; in Shi'ite Islam the term is only used for the head of the Islamic community, a direct descendant of the Prophet Muhammad and his cousin 'Ali ibn Abi Talib.

'Ishiyah Night prayer, occurs some two hours after the **maghrib** prayer; one of the five daily prayers required in Islam.

Iwan A space that is open on one side to a courtyard that are often with an arched roof.

Jami'ah University; the highest level in the traditional Islamic education system; the term is used for secular institutions of higher education as well.

Jazirah Literally, island, but used to mean the fertile region between the Euphrates and Tigris Rivers. The *Jazirah al-'Arabiyah* refers to the Arabian Peninsula.

Jinn Plural of *jinni;* mentioned in the Qur'an, jinn were created by God of smoke-less fire with no will of their own and can be good or evil.

Jnad Long chain looped over one arm and ending in a large pendant; worn by Bedouin women in Syria and Jordan.

Juhhal Literally the ignorant; term is used by the Druze for the general member-ship who have limited knowledge of the religion.

Kamanjah Also *Kaman;* a two to three string fiddle played with a bow; today the term is also used for the European-style violin introduced during the nineteenth century.

Khalifah Arabic term for Caliph; successor to the Prophet Muhammad as the head of the Muslim community.

Khan   An urban structure that allowed merchants from other cities have a space to sell their merchandise and a place to stay.

Khanqa   Term for a place set aside for Sufis to gather, study, and live; usually associated with buildings dating from the Mamluk period.

Khilafah   Arabic term for the Caliphate.

Khubz   Bread.

Khubz 'Arabi   Arabic bread; pita bread; also called *Khubz Suri* or Syrian bread.

Kuffiyah   Traditional head cloth worn by Bedouin and rural men in Syria.

Kuttab   Islamic school; the primary level where children learn to memorize the Qur'an and basic reading, writing, and math skills.

Mabkharah   Incense burner; term is also used to refer to the top of a minaret because the earliest of them looked like an incense burner.

Madhhab   School of Islamic law.

Madinah   City; *al-Madinah al-Munawwirah* or the Enlightened City, new name given to Yathrib following the **Hijrah.**

Madrasah   Islamic school; the second level in the traditional Islamic education system; students studied law as well as Arabic grammar, poetry, history, and other subjects.

Maghrib   Sundown; one of the five daily prayers required by Islam.

Mahdi   The expected one who will precede the end of times; the concept has been accepted in Sunni Islam but plays a more central role in Shi'ism.

Maqam(at)   In music the term refers to a major modal scale that has a number of submodes; in literature the term refers to a type of rhymed prose popular during the height of the classical period.

Maristan   Hospital; the term was borrowed into Arabic in the early Islamic period.

Masaharti   The person employed in the neighborhood to announce the last meal of the night before the day's fast begins during Ramadan.

Mashrabiyah   Small pieces of turned and finished wood fitted together to make screens.

Mawlid al-Nabi   Birthday of the Prophet Muhammad.

Mawwal   Vocal introduction to a piece of classical or folk music where the singers range and ability are displayed.

Mazzah   Large number of dips, salads, and other appetizers served before a major meal. Mazzahs can contain up to 90 different dishes.

Mihbaj   Large wooden mortar and pestle used for grinding coffee beans in the preparation of Arabic coffee.

Mihrab   Niche in the wall of a mosque noting the direction of prayer.

Mizmar   Double reed instrument most often used in folk music; ancestor of the oboe.

Msak   Time to stop eating or to gather up things; occurs about 15 minutes before the dawn prayer during Ramadan.

Mufti   An Islamic scholar able to write a legal decision or **fatwa;** today a state official who makes sure the laws of the state do not conflict with Islam.

Mughanni(yin) male/Mughanniyah(at) female   Term for a singer who despite having a good voice is not able to produce the state of **tarab** in the listeners.

Muqarnas   Use of triangular wedge shapes to create the transition from a square room to a domed roof or for decorative effect.

Mutrib(in) male/Mutribah(at) female   Term for singer whose voice is so expressive and the range so great as to be able to induce the state of tarab in the audience.

Muwashshahah (at)   A type of song first developed in ninth-century Muslim Spain where the main body of the poetry is in classical Arabic, but the refrain or chorus is in colloquial Arabic.

Narjilah   Water pipe for smoking usually flavored tobaccos.

Naw Ruz   Persian and Kurdish new years.

Nay   An end-blown flute made of cane or metal.

Qabadai   Local strong man (plural *qabadayat*); an urban institution that ran most neighborhoods well into the twentieth century in most Syrian cities.

Qadud al-Halabiyah   Syrian development of the Andalusian **muwashshahat,** where the main body of the song is in classical Arabic but the refrain or chorus is in colloquial Arabic. Some of the *qadud* are more folk-like in composition with more use of colloquial language in the words of the songs.

Qanun   A large plucked zither with 28 rows of triple strings; one of the main instruments in a classical orchestra.

Qasidah   Epic poem.

Qiyas   Analogy; one of the major sources of Islamic law.

Rabab   A one or two sting fiddle often used to accompany recitation of poetry; main instrument used by the Bedouin.

Raqs baladi/sharqi   Literally local or eastern dance; belly dance. It was the main dance performed by the **'awalim.**

Riqq/duff   Tambourine.

Riqwi   Brass coffee pot with an open top and a long side handle used to make Turkish coffee.

Sabu'ah   Naming ceremony held seven days after a child is born to publicly introduce to the child to the community.

Sabunah   Long outer coat worn by Bedouin women in Syria.

Salamlik   The public part of the traditional house; term is of Turkish origin.

Salat   Prayer; one of the five pillars of faith in Islam.

Saz   Long-necked lute with a rounded, wooden sound box with metal strings including several low register ones that produce a drone background for the higher range ones used in the melody; main instrument in Turkish and Kurdish music.

Shahadah   Proclamation of the main doctrine of faith in Islam, "There is no god but God and Muhammad is the Prophet of God." One of the five pillars of faith.

Shambar   A light cloth usually made of a crepe material used to cover a woman's neck and hair. In Syria they are often times embroidered in red silk floss or dyed red along the bottom of the cloth and may be fringed.

Shami   The term is used to mean Syrian or Levantine in a general sense and Damascene in a more specific sense.

Shi'ite   From the Arabic *shi'atu 'Ali,* or partisans of 'Ali; lineage follows the succession of leadership within Islam from the Prophet Muhammad to his cousin 'Ali and then through the direct descendants of 'Ali; lineage does not recognize the legality of the succession of the Rightly Guided Caliphs, the Umayyads, and the 'Abbasids.

Siyam   Fasting for the month of Ramadan; one of the five pillars of faith in Islam.

Sufi   Term used to refer to Muslim mystics.

Suhur   Light meal eaten before sunrise during the month of Ramadan.

Sultan   Political position that arose during the 'Abbasid period; the person who possesses real political power or *sultah.*

Sunnah   Actions of the Prophet Muhammad; major source of Islamic law

Sunni   Follower of the **sunnah** of the Prophet; largest sect of Islam.

Suq   Market place.

Surah   Chapter of the Qur'an.

Suriya al-Kubra   Greater Syria. The term has a more political connotation and includes Syria, Jordan, Palestine, and Lebanon.

Tabl   Large double-headed drum played with sticks; similar to the western base drum.

Takkiyah   Term for a place for Sufis to gather, study, and practice; usually associated with buildings from the Ottoman period.

Tantur   Tall headpiece worn by Druze women in Syria in the past. It is now part of the national costume of Lebanon.

Tanzimat   Reform; the term was used for a number of political, social, economic, and military reforms during the nineteenth century in the Ottoman Empire.

Taqsim (taqasim, pl.)   Division within a piece of classical music most often as an instrumental interlude that introduces the next mode and melody line.

Tar   Large round single head drum similar in shape to a tambourine; some have metal rings along the inner rim to create a snare-like effect.

Tarab State of ecstasy created by a singer or instrumentalist in the audience; it is the highest measure of success in classical music.

Tarawih Extra prayer that occurs after **'ishiyah** during the month of Ramadan.

Tarbush Tall red felt hat with a black silk tassel. The tarbush was introduced during the later Ottoman period to replace the more traditional turbans worn by urban men. It is rarely seen in Syria today.

Tariqah Path (plural *Turuq*); in Sufism the term is used to mean the particular way to better understand the nature of God attributed to a particular founder.

'Ud Literally wood in Arabic; string instrument with a large, pear-shaped body and short neck; ancestor of the lute.

'Uqqal Sages or wise men; the term is used by the Druze to refer to those who have been initiated into the secrets of the religion.

Wali A political position; used to mean a viceroy or a governor.

Waslah A means of performing a number of songs in a progression where they flow from one into the other; developed first in Cairo during the nineteenth century it became a popular style in Damascus.

Wazir Minister of state; the term was borrowed from Persian to Arabic during the 'Abbasid period.

Zakkat Alms usually paid at the end of Ramadan; one of the five pillars of Islam.

Zirb Wind screen made of reeds bound together with colored wool yarn.

Ziyarah Visitation to a Muslim, Christian, or Jewish "saint" or holy person's grave or place where he or she has been seen. There are usually set steps for a visitation to be considered to be complete.

Bibliography

Bacharach, Jere. *A Near East Studies Handbook.* Seattle: University of Washington Press, 1976.

Beaumont, Peter, Gerald Blake, and Malcolm Wagstaff. *The Middle East.* London: John Wiley and Sons, 1976.

Beck, Lois, and Nekki Keddie, eds. *Women in the Muslim World.* Cambridge, MA: Harvard University Press, 1978.

Blunt, Lady Anne. *Bedouin Tribes of the Euphrates.* Boulder, CO: Best Publishing Co., 1960.

Burns, Ross. *Monuments of Syria: An Historical Guide.* London: I. B. Tauris, 1995.

Bushnaq, Inea. *Arab Folktales.* New York: Pantheon Books, 1986.

Chadwick, Henry, and G. R. Evans, eds. *Atlas of the Christian Church.* New York: Facts on File Publications, 1987.

Chatty, Dawn. *From Camel to Truck: The Bedouin in the Modern World.* New York: Vantage Press, 1986.

Cleveland, William. *A History of the Modern Middle East.* Boulder, CO: Westview Press, 1994.

Creswell, K.A.C. *A Short Account of Early Muslim Architecture.* Cairo: The American University in Cairo Press, 1989.

Darwish, Mustafa. *Dream Makers on the Nile: A Portrait of Egyptian Cinema.* Cairo: The American University in Cairo Press, 1998.

Eickelman, Dale. *The Middle East: An Anthropological Approach.* Englewood Cliffs, NJ: Prentice-Hall, 2001.

Gibb, H.A.R. *The Damascus Chronicle of the Crusades (of ibn Qalansi).* London: Luzac, 1967.

Hinnebusch, Raymond. *Syria Revolution from Above.* New York: Routledge, 2001.

Hitti, Philip. *History of the Arabs.* London: St. Martin's Press, 1973.

Hopwood, Derek. *Syria 1945–1986: Politics and Society.* London: Unwin Hyman, 1988.

Hourani, Albert. *A History of the Arab Peoples.* New York: Warner Books, Inc., 1992.

Hudson, Michael. *Arab Politics: The Search for Legitimacy.* New Haven, CT: Yale University Press, 1977.

Jabbur, Suhayl. *The Bedouins and the Desert: Aspects of Nomadic Life in the Arab East.* Translated and edited by Lawrence Conrad. New York: State University of New York Press, 1995.

Jayyusi, Salma Khadra. *Modern Arabic Poetry.* New York. Columbia University Press, 1991.

Kalter, Johannes, ed. *The Arts and Crafts of Syria.* London: Thames and Hudson, 1992.

Keenan, Brigid. *Damascus Hidden Treasures of the Old City.* London: Thames and Hudson, 2001.

Khoury, Philip. *Syria and the French Mandate: The Politics of Arab Nationalism 1920–1945.* London: I. B. Tauris, 1987.

Khoury, Philip. *Urban Notables and Arab Nationalism: The Politics of Damascus 1860–1920.* New York: Cambridge University Press, 1983.

Lewis, Bernard, ed. *The World of Islam: Faith, People, and Culture.* London: Thames and Hudson, 1976.

Lewis, Norman. *Nomads and Settlers in Syria and Jordan, 1800–1900.* New York: Cambridge University Press, 1987.

Lunde, Paul. *Islam: Faith, Culture, History.* New York: DK Publishing, Inc., 2002.

Mardam Bey, Salma. *Syria's Quest for Independence 1939–1945.* Reading, UK: Itahca Press, 1997.

Ma'oz, M. *Syria under Asad.* London: Croom Helm, 1986.

Province, Michael. *The Great Syrian Revolt and the Rise of Arab Nationalism.* Austin: University of Texas Press, 2005.

Racy, A. J. *Making Music in the Arab World: The Culture and Artistry of Tarab.* Cambridge: Cambridge University Press, 2003.

Rajab, Jehan. *Palestinian Costume.* New York: Kegan Paul International, 1989.

Roaf, Michael. *Cultural Atlas of Mesopotamia and the Ancient Near East.* New York: Facts on File, 1990.

Robinson, Francis. *Atlas of the Islamic World Since 1500.* New York: Facts on File Publications, 1987.

Sabbagh, Suha, ed. *Arab Women: Between Defiance and Restraint.* New York: Olive Branch Press, 1996.

Salibi, Kamal. *Syria under Islam: Empire on Trial 634–1097* A.D. Delmar, NY: Caravan Books, 1977.

Seacombe, I. J. *Syria*. Oxford: Clio Press, 1987.

Seale, P. *The Struggle for Syria: A Study of Post-War Arab Politics 1945–1958*. London: I. B. Tauris, 1986.

Shafik, Viola. *Arab Cinema: History and Cultural Identity*. Cairo: The American University in Cairo Press, 1998.

Shoup, John. *Culture and Customs of Jordan*. Westport, CT: Greenwood Press, 2007.

Smith, Dan. *The State of the Middle East: An Atlas of Conflict and Resolution*. Los Angeles: University of California Press, 2006.

Sweet, Louise. *Tell Toqaan: A Syrian Village*. Ann Arbor: University of Michigan, Anthropological Papers no. 14, 1960.

Van Dam, Nikolas. *The Struggle of Power in Syria*. New York: St. Martin's Press, 1979.

Weiss, Walter, and Kurt-Michael Westerman. *The Bazaar: Markets and Merchants in the Islamic World*. London: Thames and Hudson, 2001.

Zuhur, Sherifa. *Asmahan's Secrets: Woman, War, and Song*. Austin: The Center for Middle Eastern Studies, The University of Texas at Austin, 2000.

Index

'Abbasids, 15–16, 17, 19, 39, 43, 44,
  45, 74
'Abd al-Nasir, Jamal (Gamal Abdel
  Nasser), 28, 29
'Alawi, 5, 30, 46–47, 86
Al-Asad, Bashar, 34, 113
Al-Asad, Basil, 33–34
Al-Asad, Hafiz, 30, 32, 33, 34,
  47, 113
Al-'Asi (Orontes), 3
Al-Atrash, Farid, 141–42
Aleppo, 3; cultural influence, 64, 67,
  78, 137; *hammam* (bathhouse),
  82–83; history, 9, 15, 16, 17, 18,
  21, 32; *maristan* (hospital), 82; *suqs*
  (markets), 81–82, 90–92, 93
Alexander the Great, 11
Antioch, 11, 14, 19, 46, 64
Arabic: dialect, 2, 73; language, 73,
  80, 116
Arabs: Arab-Israeli conflict, 6, 28, 31,
  35; Arab Revolt, 22, 25–26, 45,
  147; ethnicity in Syria, 5–6, 39

Aramaic, 8–9
Arameans, 11
Architecture: Aleppo house, 85;
  Bedouin tent, 87–89; contemporary,
  89–90; Damascus house, 83–85;
  Islamic urban institutions, 77–83;
  village, 85–87
Armenians, 6, 7, 8, 54, 55, 148
Asmahan (Amal al-Atrash), 142
Ayyubids, 18–19, 44, 79

Ba'ath (Party), 29, 30, 31, 70, 113,
  122, 123, 127–30
Bani Ghassan, 14
Basketry, 97
Bedouin, 3–4, 5–6, 7, 64, 65, 86, 87,
  94, 97
Bilad al-Sham, 2
Birth, 116
Bisra Eski Sham, 78
Buwayhids, 16–17
Byzantines, 12, 14, 16, 20, 44, 46,
  64, 78

About the Author

JOHN A. SHOUP is Associate Professor of Anthropology at Al Akhawayn University in Ifrane, Morocco. He is also the author of *Culture and Customs of Jordan* (Greenwood, 2007).

Recent Titles in
Culture and Customs of the Middle East